T0340144

THE ROBERT K. GREENLEAF CENTER
FOR SERVANT-LEADERSHIP

THE ROBERT K. GREENLEAF Center for Servant-Leadership in Indianapolis, Indiana, is an international nonprofit educational organization that seeks to encourage the understanding and practice of servant-leadership. The center's mission is to improve the caring and quality of all institutions through a new approach to leadership, structure, and decision making.

The Greenleaf Center's programs include the worldwide sale of books, essays, and videotapes on servant-leadership and the preparation and presentation of workshops, seminars, institutes, an annual international conference, a sponsorship program, and the archive project that enabled production of this volume of Greenleaf essays.

Through dissemination of Robert Greenleaf's ideas about servant-leadership, a number of institutions and individuals have been changed. Servant-leadership is now used as an institutional model, as the basis for educating and training nonprofit trustees and community leaders, as the foundation of college and university courses and corporate training programs, and as a vehicle for personal growth and transformation.

For further information about the resources for study and programming available from the center, contact:

The Robert K. Greenleaf Center for Servant-Leadership
921 East Eighty-Sixth Street, Suite 200
Indianapolis, IN 46240
phone (317) 259–1241; fax (317) 259–0560

ON BECOMING
A SERVANT-LEADER

Robert K. Greenleaf

ON BECOMING
A SERVANT-LEADER

Don M. Frick   Larry C. Spears

editors

○

foreword by

Peter F. Drucker

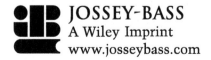

JOSSEY-BASS
A Wiley Imprint
www.josseybass.com

Published by Jossey-Bass
A Wiley Imprint
989 Market Street, San Francisco, CA 94103-1741   www.josseybass.com

Jossey-Bass books and products are available through most bookstores. To contact Jossey-Bass directly call our Customer Care Department within the U.S. at 800-956-7739, outside the U.S. at 317-572-3986 or fax 317-572-4002.

Jossey-Bass also publishes its books in a variety of electronic formats. Some content that appears in print may not be available in electronic books.

Credits are on page 392.

Interior design by Claudia Smelser.

Library of Congress Cataloging-in-Publication Data
Greenleaf, Robert K.
        On becoming a servant-leader : the private writings of Robert K. Greenleaf / editors, Don M. Frick, Larry C. Spears.—1st ed.
        p.   cm.
        Includes bibliographical references and index.
        ISBN 0–7879–0230–6
        ISBN 978–0–470-2200-7 (paperback)
        1. Leadership. 2. Associations, institutions, etc.
        3. Organizational effectiveness. 4. Management. I. Frick, Don M.,   date.
II. Spears, Larry, date. III. Title.
        HM141.G685   1996
        303.3′4—dc20   95–52069

CONTENTS

PART THREE
Leadership and the Individual:
The Dartmouth Lectures

PART FOUR
In Person with Robert K. Greenleaf

CONTENTS

FOREWORD

BOB GREENLEAF AND I worked together, and fairly closely, for fifteen years—beginning when I moved back to the New York area after seven years in New England (we moved to Montclair, New Jersey, close to the Greenleafs) until Bob left the Bell System and the New York area in 1964. When Bob started the Bell System Advanced Management School in Asbury Park, New Jersey, I was the first outside speaker he brought in, and I remained one of the key speakers—always taking the last day to discuss the Bell System's strategy—until the school was discontinued. Bob also introduced me to the chief executive of the Bell System, whose consultant I became, a relationship that continued well beyond Bob's leaving the Bell System himself and one that ended only when I moved to California in early 1971.

In turn, Bob was one of my key speakers at the President's Course of the American Management Association, which I helped organize and of which I was the cochairman for about ten years, from the mid 1950s to the mid 1960s. After I had moved out to California, in the early 1970s, I invited Bob to come out to join us in a conference of senior executives on the board of directors, which I organized and ran. Bob came and joined us for this seminar three years in a row.

Bob Greenleaf and I knew that we shared the same beliefs and values, but our relations were always professional, rather than personal or social. We also went about our work very differently. In fact, our aims were quite different. When I worked with him, Bob was always out to change the individual, to make him or her into a different person. I was interested in making people *do* the right things, in their actions and behavior. Bob was interested in motives; I was interested in consequences. This became very clear to both of us in the first session of the Asbury Park school when one of the senior participants asked, "What do I do?" and Bob said, "That comes later. First, what do you want to be?" The man then turned to me, and I said, "What do you think will work?" All three of us burst out laughing.

In addition—and I only became aware of this quite recently when I reread Bob's books after the news of his death a few years ago—Bob was very much concerned with what people should *not* do. My books, by contrast, are brimful of examples of successful or effective action.

In short, Bob was a moralist and I am a pragmatist. This divergence did not get in the way of my admiration for Bob Greenleaf and my tremendous respect, but we usually talked of quite different things when we talked about the same subject, even though we always agreed. I am not at all sure that Bob was aware of the difference between the two of us. I suspect that he was not always at ease with me. The world needs both types of people, of course. It needs a Socrates—and Bob was truly a wise man—and it needs Sophists like myself who are concerned with getting things done and with consequences. The funny thing is that I am probably as much a moralist as Bob was and he may have been as much a pragmatist as I am. I only know that I am not effective as a preacher. I am effective as a teacher, and the two are very different things.

Reflecting on Bob Greenleaf brings back very old and very fond memories of a truly remarkable man. I am delighted that the Robert K. Greenleaf Center for Servant-Leadership will ensure, through books like this one, that his memory and his lessons will not be forgotten.

Claremont, California   Peter F. Drucker
FEBRUARY 1996

PREFACE

ROBERT GREENLEAF is best known for his series of essays on
the servant theme. The first of these that was widely distributed, *The Servant as Leader,* was published in 1970. In quick
succession, he wrote and published *The Institution as Servant*
and *Trustees as Servants*. These seminal essays, plus a number
of others that relate the ideas of servant-leadership to businesses, education, foundations, churches, and the society at
large, were collected in the book *Servant Leadership: A Journey
into the Nature of Legitimate Power and Greatness* (Paulist
Press, 1977, 1991).

During the last fifteen years of his life, Greenleaf continued
to expand the implications of the servant-as-leader idea
through his writing, consulting, and lecturing. When he died in
1990, he left more than ninety unpublished essays, along with
diaries and personal papers. In these, we see not only the seeds
that germinated and flowered into his later mature thought but
also a glimpse into the deep curiosity and mysticism of the man.
This volume, along with its companion book, *Seeker and
Servant: Reflections on Religious Leadership* (Jossey-Bass,
1996), brings to the public for the first time essays that reveal
Greenleaf's evolution in thinking over a period of fifty years.

Many of the illustrations and themes that appear in this volume are also used in other published essays, and several appear
more than once here. Each is integral to the essay where it appears, however, and presents fresh insights on the subject at
hand.

Greenleaf worked on various writings in this book over a period of years. Sometimes an essay was begun, put aside, and

revised several years later. More often, he completed a first draft and added bits and pieces during the next few months, never fully revising the first draft to integrate his later thinking. In the process of preparing these essays, the editors have attempted to keep as much of the original drafts as possible, combining later additions only when Greenleaf clearly indicated their relevance to the original work. For all his methodical work habits, Greenleaf left openings for the inspiration of intuition, which seldom resulted in tidy papers for later editors!

This volume attempts to track, through his own writings, the evolution of Greenleaf's thinking on the key issues in his writing: power, ethics, management, organizations, and servant-hood. It contains biographical references that are more intimate than most of his published essays, and it therefore also serves as a sketch of his personal development as a servant-leader. Some parts are heavily theoretical, for Greenleaf believed in the efficacy of lessons that could be learned from the social sciences and other research sources. Other sections read like a hand-book for soul development. In the end, for all his rational skills, Greenleaf was content to "stand in awe before the mystery" that was spirit.

Part One, "The Ethic of Strength," was begun in 1959 and completed in 1965. It is a remarkable guide for one who longs for practical techniques to develop the inner life, a life of *strength*. For Greenleaf, living a useful life, in touch with inner and outer worlds, was an *ethical* choice. "The Ethic of Strength" was written as a short book but was never published. It was directed toward young people but is relevant for anyone who would eschew grandiosity and strive to become a leader who effects change by beginning with the self.

Part Two, "Essays on Power, Management, and Organizations," explores the quandary of how to use power without violating the principle that one uses to justify power in the first place. This theme is familiar to readers of *The Servant as Leader* and various other published essays by Greenleaf. Ever the practical idealist, Greenleaf gives dozens of examples of how power has been used and misused in the twentieth century. He also offers tools for exercising persuasive power, including listening skills. He articulates an answer to the old debate about ends justifying means, an idea that is astounding upon further reflection: *The means determine the ends.*

Greenleaf's writings on management could fill an entire book—and then some—but the essays presented here represent the evolution of his thinking from 1935 to the end of his life. The 1935 essay, "Industry's Means for Personality Adjustment," looks to the development of people as the key to effective management. This put him on the enlightened fringe of management thinkers for that day. Other essays on management suggest ways that people can be developed, including a fascinating team technique described in "Behavioral Research: A Factor in Tomorrow's Better Management." The management essays conclude with Greenleaf articulating a theory of "conceptualizers" versus "operationalizers." Near the end of his life, he began to suspect that people who were gifted operationalizers (managers) probably do not have the skills to be great conceptualizers (idea people). Greenleaf never considered himself a good manager, though he had a staff of nearly twenty toward the end of his career with AT&T. He saw himself as a thoroughgoing conceptualizer, and his ideas may give hope to both kinds of people who can discover the power of teaming with their opposites.

In the essays on organizations, Greenleaf explains the impact of the giant AT&T organization on his evolution in thinking about organizations. Typically, he does not call his career at AT&T a "job" but rather "an adventure in spirit." Readers involved in organizations, both large and small, will find lessons here for their own situations. In the essay "Manager, Administrator, Statesman," Greenleaf argues that for the good of the entire organization, able managers must be joined by leaders who care for the whole organization, who have the statesmanlike ability to see beyond the horizon and prepare for the future. When people with complementary skills are in place—managers, administrators, and statesmen—the way is clear to create a distinguished institution. In his advanced years, Greenleaf wrote an analysis of one institution he knew very well, where he spent the last years of his life. Those who care about our elderly will find wisdom here from a man in the full flower of maturity.

"Leadership and the Individual," presented in Part Three, was Greenleaf's last major essay before writing *The Servant as Leader*. It was delivered as five lectures at Dartmouth in 1969. For people who have not read *The Servant as Leader*, this section will serve as a solid introduction to ideas presented in Greenleaf's formal writings. In many ways, it is more readable than some of his later essays, more conversational and expansive, and less abrupt. It focuses on the radical, personal responsibility each person should claim for problems that are normally seen as "out there" but are ultimately "in here."

Finally, Part Four, "In Person with Robert K. Greenleaf," is a treat for all who wish they could sit down and chat with this remarkable man. Dr. Joseph DiStefano had the privilege of doing just that in December 1986. At the time, DiStefano had been a friend and protégé of Greenleaf's for over twenty years. During this conversation, Greenleaf describes some of the influences that prepared him to write about the servant theme, people he had known, and activities that had a powerful impact on his work. He also describes reactions to his essays, talks about his writing style, and speculates on what might prompt the servant motive in people.

Robert Greenleaf's evolution toward servant-leadership was a gradual coming to what he had always been, at the deepest level. He was neither perfect nor always right. He could be irascible and wry. He was probably a true introvert, in spite of his public exposure. But he was a brilliant synthesizer who progressively articulated a philosophy that was congruent both with rational thought and inner mystery and with his own life experience. In this volume, "Greenleaf the pamphleteer," as he once described himself, touches chords that continue to sound in the reader.

Indianapolis, Indiana   Don M. Frick
February 1996   Larry C. Spears

ACKNOWLEDGMENTS

THIS BOOK WAS MADE POSSIBLE through the support of two grants from the Lilly Endowment, Inc. We are particularly indebted to Craig Dykstra and Ed Queen for their belief in the Greenleaf Archives Project. During the first two years of this project, a special panel carefully reviewed nearly one hundred pieces of unpublished work by Robert Greenleaf, written over a period of fifty years. We are most grateful to the other members of that panel and wish to acknowledge their major contributions to this project: Dwight Burlingame, Joseph DiStefano, Anne Fraker, Newcomb Greenleaf, and Larry Lad.

We are particularly indebted to Anne Fraker, one of our colleagues at the Greenleaf Center, for her significant editorial contributions to this book and its companion work, *Seeker and Servant: Reflections on Religious Leadership* (Jossey-Bass, 1996). We also wish to express our appreciation to our other colleagues at the Greenleaf Center: Michele Lawrence, Geneva Loudd, James Robinson, Richard Smith, and Kelly Tobe. Our journey in servant-leadership has been enriched through our relationships with the following past and present Greenleaf Center trustees: Bill Bottum, Linda Chezem, Diane Cory, Sister Joyce De Shano, Joseph DiStefano, Harley Flack, Newcomb Greenleaf, Carole Hamm, Jack Lowe Jr., Jeff McCollum, Andy Morikawa, Jim Morris, Paul Olson, Bob Payton, Sister Joel Read, Sister Sharon Richardt, and Jim Tatum. Additional thanks go to Dick Broholm, Peter Drucker, Karen Farmer, Bob Lynn, Marcia Newman, and Parker Palmer.

Special thanks go to the Franklin Trask Library at Andover-Newton Theological Seminary, especially to Diana Yount, who helped organize Robert K. Greenleaf's archival material from which these essays were drawn.

We also wish to thank our editors at Jossey-Bass Publishers, Alan Shrader, Susan Williams, and Xenia Lisanevich, for their own work for, belief in, and support of these two books.

Don Frick would like to thank his family for listening to him quote Greenleaf essays at the oddest hours, especially his loving wife, Karin; bright sons, Dan and Matt; servant-leader sister, Linda Linn; brother-mentor, Jack Frick; and parents, Irene and the Reverend Jack Frick, both of whom shared with him a love of language. Don also owes a debt to Dr. Ann McGee-Cooper that can never be repaid: first, for modeling servant-leadership and, second, for giving him a copy of *The Servant as Leader*, which launched him on this decade-long journey.

Larry Spears would especially like to thank his family and friends for their love and encouragement along the way, especially his wife, Beth Lafferty; his sons, James and Matthew; and his mother and father, Bertha and L. C. Spears. He would also like to thank the following people and institutions for their support and inspiration: James Autry, Steve Brooks, John Burkhardt, Roberta and Robert DeHaan, Vinton Deming, De Pauw University, Max DePree, *Friends Journal*, Joseph Goss, the Great Lakes Colleges Associations' Philadelphia Center, John Gummere, John Haynes, Todd Howell, Frank Killian, Eva and Richard Krebs, Roger and Verona Lafferty, Michael Revnes, Karen Schultz, Peter Senge, Alice Simpson, Elissa Sklaroff, Debra Spears, and the W. K. Kellogg Foundation.

Finally, we wish to express our deep appreciation to the many women and men everywhere who strive to be servant-leaders. Your efforts at nurturing spirit in the workplace truly inspire others to servant-leadership.

—*D.M.F. and L.C.S.*

ON BECOMING
A SERVANT-LEADER

INTRODUCTION

ROBERT K. GREENLEAF CONSCIOUSLY CHOSE to have an impact on society but not become famous. He was an introvert who spent his life as a public teacher, a moralist, and a practical mystic, yet invested a career at AT&T training managers who, of necessity, concerned themselves with the day-to-day matters of getting things done. He was a person who cared deeply about our wider society and global culture, arguing that organizational structures should change, but who also believed that authentic change—at any level—happened only when it began in the inner solitude of single individuals. For all these seeming paradoxes, Greenleaf's life forms a pattern of the whole, under the unifying theme of the servant.

This volume presents previously unpublished essays by Robert Greenleaf that track his personal and professional development as a "servant-leader," a term he coined in the 1970 essay *The Servant as Leader*. The ideas presented in that small booklet, and writings that followed until his death in 1990, have influenced a whole generation of management and organizational thinkers. "Servant-leader" is not necessarily a term that Greenleaf would apply to himself, although others have done so. The idea of the servant, however, did suffuse his thinking over a lifetime, and it led to some radical conclusions about how organizations could work and be governed.

The Servant-Leader Idea

In *The Servant as Leader,* Greenleaf wrote:

> The servant-leader is servant first.... It begins with the natural feeling that one wants to serve, to serve *first*. Then

conscious choice brings one to aspire to lead. . . . The difference manifests itself in the care taken by the servant—first to make sure that other people's highest-priority needs are being served. The best test, and the most difficult to administer, is: Do those served grow as persons? Do they, *while being served,* become healthier, wiser, freer, more autonomous, more likely themselves to become servants? *And,* what is the effect on the least privileged in society; will they benefit or, at least, not be further deprived?[1]

Greenleaf goes on to say that authentic leaders are chosen by followers, that the ability to lead with integrity depends on the leader's skills for withdrawal and action, listening and persuasion, practical goal setting and intuitive prescience. Clearly, servant-leadership is a notion that begins with the self, with inner lights that illuminate outer outcomes. In many ways, it is a thoroughly American philosophy, based on a deep and high vision, tested by pragmatic results. Furthermore, for all of its seeming optimism, the body of servant-leadership writing reveals an American suspicion of unchecked power and an insistence on measurable performance. Yet at the same time, servant-leadership contains elements of Eastern thought, with an emphasis on reflection.

As Greenleaf refined his thinking on servant-leadership, he wrote about its implications for institutional structures, for trustees, foundations, churches, governments, educational institutions, and the human spirit. The evolution of his thought on these matters follows these general lines: Everything begins with conscious choice by an individual who wishes to serve first. In our century, however, *institutions* mediate much of the caring, and institutions can also function as servants. To do so, they may need to change some of their operating principles and structures. Tracing the lines of authority even further, we find that trustees control institutions. Trustees have unique roles that are different from those of operating managers, and they should find the courage to exercise leadership in those roles. Greenleaf believed that churches were still a dominant influence in society, so he wrote about the role of churches in influencing the people in their communities who were trustees and leaders. Continuing up the ladder of accountability, Greenleaf recognized that seminaries trained ministers who led churches. He urged schools of religion to begin developing a theology of institutions and to begin training people to chair the boards that control institutions. He felt that foundations had a role in getting this movement started within seminaries. Finally, Greenleaf spent his last years thinking and writing about how to "inspirit" people, organizations, and cultures. Through all this, he returned often to the importance of offering exceptional, able young people the support needed to develop into servant-leaders.

Following this logical but unusual line of reasoning, many of Greenleaf's friends and colleagues argued that he had got it all wrong, that seminaries would never take on the role he described, that institutions had no interest in the radical kinds of changes he prescribed, that he might have done well to stick to his original, lofty notions of the individual servant-leader. In response, Greenleaf never claimed he was totally right. He simply invited others to offer their own suggestions on how existing institutions, using available resources, could begin implementing the changes that he believed were necessary for the evolution—perhaps even the survival—of our best ideas and institutions.

The times are finally catching up with many of Greenleaf's ideas. Management and organizational thinkers like Max DePree, Peter Senge, Peter Block, and Stephen Covey, among many others, emphasize the importance of an ethical base for organizations, the power of trust and stewardship, and the personal depths that authentic leaders must honor as they empower and serve others. A number of organizations have restructured their operations based on the ideas of servant-leadership. No two resulting organizational charts look the same because each organization adapts ideas according to the experiences and insights of its own people.

One of the marvelous and frustrating things about servant-leadership is that it is not a tidy, "how-to" checklist. It is a philosophy that embraces certain principles but few prescriptions.

Larry Spears, executive director of the Greenleaf Center for Servant-Leadership in Indianapolis, has identified ten critical characteristics of the servant-leader: listening, empathy, healing, awareness, persuasion, conceptualization, foresight, stewardship, commitment to the growth of people, and building community. Others have generated additional lists, which all prove that servant-leadership is not a destination; it is a path.

Robert Greenleaf

Robert Kiefner Greenleaf was born in 1904 in Terre Haute, Indiana, and died in 1990. His "first career," with AT&T, spanned thirty-six years. While there, he worked in management research, development, and education. By his own admission, he turned down promotions that would have led to more money and responsibility but would have taken him further away from his primary mission at AT&T: to influence the institution from the inside, using his unique gifts. In one of the essays in this book, he reveals that an AT&T president once described him as a "kept revolutionary."

In 1964, Greenleaf retired from AT&T to pursue his "second career" as a writer, consultant, and teacher. He worked with a number of major institutions, including the Ford Foundation, the R. K. Mellon Foundation, the Rockefeller Institute, Lilly Endowment Inc., the Mead Foundation, the American Foundation for Management Research, the Massachusetts Institute of Technology, Dartmouth College, and Ohio University. In the year of his retirement, Greenleaf cofounded the Center for Applied Ethics, which evolved into the Center for Applied Studies and then, in 1985, into the Greenleaf Center for Servant-Leadership, which is headquartered in Indianapolis, Indiana.

Occasionally, Greenleaf privately published copies of his essays or speeches and distributed them to friends and colleagues around the country. A minor underground of influential leaders, educators, and management thinkers began following his work. In 1970, after reading Hermann Hesse's *Journey to the East,* Greenleaf wrote the essay that would change his life: *The Servant as Leader.* The response to this slim work was so overwhelming that it was reprinted in ever-larger press runs. More than half a million copies are now in print worldwide. Greenleaf continued writing and publishing until a few years before his death.

In *Spirituality as Leadership,* Greenleaf expressed a credo that summed up his life's work:

> I believe that caring for persons, the more able and the less able serving each other, is what makes a good society. Most caring was once person to person. Now much of it is mediated through institutions—often large, powerful, impersonal; not always competent; sometimes corrupt. If a better society is to be built, one more just and more caring and providing opportunity for people to grow, the most effective and economical way, while supportive of the social order, is to raise the performance as servant of as many institutions as possible by new voluntary regenerative forces initiated within them by committed individuals, *servants.* Such servants may never predominate or even be numerous; but their influence may form a leaven that makes possible a reasonably civilized society.[2]

Robert Greenleaf also wrote his own epitaph, one that shows his lifelong identification with average, working people:

Potentially a good plumber
Ruined by a sophisticated education.

PART ONE

THE ETHIC OF STRENGTH

MANUSCRIPT FOR A BOOK

The great opportunity is to discover in one's mature years an unrealized growth potential. Growth, not in terms of external achievement, but in the things that are important in the quiet hours when one is alone with oneself; growth in the capacity for serenity in a world of confusion and conflict, a new kind of inner stamina, a new kind of exportable resource as youthful prowess drops away.

The search is the thing.

The work exists for the person as much as the person exists for the work.

Robert K. Greenleaf

ALL HIS LIFE, Robert Greenleaf was a seeker, not of titles or awards or money, but of inner strength. His journey—and his curiosity—led him up and down a maze of pathways. Near the end of his "first career" with AT&T, Greenleaf, already nearing sixty years of age, pulled together his deepest wisdom about the process of developing personal *strength* and wrote *The Ethic of Strength*.

At various times, Greenleaf called *The Ethic of Strength* a book, a collection of essays, and a series of conversations. This short work, discovered among his papers after his death in 1990, was written for young people. In the end, however, it is a revelation of Greenleaf's own spiritual journey. Along the way, he met an impressive number of fellow travelers. Greenleaf counted among his friends such diverse thinkers and doers as Alfred Korzybski, the semanticist; Gerald Heard, a prominent writer on religious and spiritual issues; Aldous Huxley; top leaders in business, education, psychology, and organizational management; and dozens of impressive personal friends with whom he maintained a lively correspondence. In addition, he found in his wife, Esther, intellectual companionship and emotional balance.

In a way, *The Ethic of Strength* summarizes the belief Greenleaf had developed throughout his life that change in a culture, society, organization, family, or political system always begins with the individual. It is an idea that he stated more precisely in *The Servant as Leader,* published within a decade of writing this collection of essays. *The Ethic of Strength* serves as a guide to inner evolution that is both mystical and practical. It predates many of the so-called Third Wave human potential psychological theories that emerged in the late 1960s and early 1970s and presages many of the same insights.

The Ethic of Strength outlines the starting point for one who would become a servant-leader. One begins with oneself, with an attitude of awe for the mystery that underlies animating Spirit, with a decision to learn competencies, to continue learning, and to make a difference in the world as it is. One embraces the potential for personal greatness while rejecting grandiosity. Most of all, one becomes—and remains—a seeker.

TABLE OF CONTENTS

PREFACE TO THE ETHIC OF STRENGTH

by Robert K. Greenleaf

THIS COLLECTION OF ESSAYS is the fruit of many discussions over the past ten years with individuals and groups of persons interested in their own growth and development. The general plan of these chapters emerged from work in 1959 and 1960 on the subject of managerial ethics with the Program for Senior Executives, which meets twice a year at the School for Industrial Management at the Massachusetts Institute of Technology. It is augmented by materials from a lecture at the Harvard Business School on May 6, 1965, at the Musser Seminar on Ethics and Business.

In speaking to these young men and women about to enter business, I made two assumptions about them. I assumed first that they wanted to excel, to assume some important responsibility and carry it with distinction. Otherwise, why would they spend two years of hard work and a lot of money for a graduate business degree? They could achieve mediocrity without such an investment. I assumed further that they were especially concerned about their ability to be right and just and honorable in all of their dealings. I did not try to persuade the ones without such a concern that they ought to have it. I would not know how to do that. And in writing this version of the lectures, I do not conceive of this as a how-to-be-successful book for those who do not have the intelligence, the drives, or the sensitivity that augur for success. I do not know how to build these either.

Rather this is addressed to people well endowed in values and abilities who are determined to live optimally in terms of accomplishment and rightness.

A prominent old Quaker lawyer whom I knew many years

ago told me of being asked by a nephew who was coming of age, "Uncle, I am thinking of law as a career, but I am bothered about one thing: how does one keep one's Quaker conscience and be a lawyer, provided it is an educated conscience?" The story was offered as good advice, a generalization applicable to the whole of the world of affairs.

This really states the dilemma of the world: good people with educated consciences. If people can be classed as "good" or "evil," the troubles of the world are not so much the result of the acts of evil people as of the fact that good people do so poorly.

A tender, uneducated conscience is much easier to live with if one does not have the urge to achieve. If one has a sensitive conscience that one chooses to respect and not to educate, and if one is determined to achieve, to carry some important responsibility with distinction, then one has a special sort of problem. If one lives a normal life span, one must, near the end of one's life, make a retrospective judgment that it has been a good life, good for oneself and for other people. The world is a better place because of who one is and how one did one's work. And this reckoning can be a major issue in one's life. Erik Erikson calls it the crisis of ego integrity versus despair.[1] Gerald Heard speaks of the ordeal of second maturity.[2] This is the burden that all able men and women of conscience must bear. They have not only the necessity to make the effort to live by values that the game, as normally played, does not require, but they must ultimately ask the searching question, Did I do well enough? And they must ask this question even though the world is dazzled by the evidences of external accomplishment.

Wordsworth speaks of the Happy Warrior as one "who makes his moral being his prime care."[3] I am not advocating that every person make his moral being his prime care because I'm not sure I would want to live in a world where everybody did. All good people would make a pretty dull world. Also I believe, as Emerson apparently did, that some good is born of evil.[4] Without the presence of evil, good would have little meaning. Furthermore, if a young person arrives at maturity without a tender conscience, I have no formula for providing one. And if one lacks the intelligence, drives, and sensitivity necessary to be an achiever, I do not know how to build them. But if a young person has both, I am mightily concerned that he or she carry an active, aware conscience into the rough-and-tumble of the world of affairs and succeed at something of genuine importance. This is a problem I think I understand, and I have some experience to offer on how to deal with it.

The young men and women addressed in this book are very concrete people of the contemporary younger generation as I have known them intimately in business, in schools, and in my home over the past few years. I shall address them as "you" because I still think of this as a talk; and I shall talk as if you intend to respond—if not to me, then to someone with a sense of urgency about your problem as shared.

Contributors to my thinking have been so many and my indebtedness to them is so great that I can only make a general acknowledgment of their help.

This is written as a comment on personal experience and searching. I do not think of it as a contribution to new knowledge, and I did not have the structure of any established science or discipline in mind when I wrote it. It is simply a presentation of my own thinking and beliefs so that they can be shared with other interested seekers; it is a statement to which they can respond with their own thinking and experience. I hope to elicit a dialogue of sorts in which the reader will note his response, then reexamine what I have said and make his own responses anew, thus clarifying and solidifying his own position.

This book is the best effort I am capable of making at this time to enter into such a dialogue with responsible people in the hope that, in managing their end of the dialogue, *their* ethical strength will grow as I am sure mine, imperfect as it still is, has grown through struggling to sharpen my understanding of what makes people ethically strong.

SOMETHING TO HOPE FOR

MUCH OF THE BEST COMMUNICATION, especially to the young, is oblique. To hammer on a point and say, "This is it!" is often to lose it.

A professor of sociology in a class on labor problems made such an oblique remark that had a profound effect on me, although twenty years went by before I could accurately assess its full meaning. As a college senior, I was as open to vocational choice as one could be. The only thing I was sure of was that I didn't want to go to school anymore. My generation was not as biased in favor of continuous schooling as young people are today.

Quite casually one day, Professor Helming said, "There is a people problem in American business, and some of you folks ought to get in and work on it." He said it in no more words than these and passed on without further elaboration.

That settled it for me. Upon graduation, I set out to get a job with a business that employed a lot of people. The father of a classmate of mine offered me a job in his small thriving business. It was the kind of job an ambitious young man should reach out for. But it didn't have enough people. So he helped me find my way to the kind of business I was looking for.

It didn't take long to find that business and to be employed. I had never thought of working for this particular kind of business, but that didn't matter because it met my major requirement—it had a lot of people. When my first job turned out to be digging postholes in a fetid, mosquito-infested swamp, I had some qualms. But this didn't last long, and it was a good way to start. I have never regretted that then, and during my earlier years, I had learned something about hard, disagreeable, routine work and something about the people who spend their lives doing it.

One of my regrets about the intervening years, during which my work has been of a more sophisticated nature and my residence has been in the unreal suburbia of a great city, is that I have lost the close living contact with these people that I once had. My real affinity has always been with the people who do the routine work of the world. When they were my immediate associates, I found so much more of a kind of integrity, a precious humor, and a grace among these people than I have ever found anywhere else. This conclusion has always puzzled me. Have I lost something? Does naive simple directness have something that sophistication can never have? Or may I hope that the so-called intelligent, ambitious people might acquire in their mature years some of this kind of integrity, humor, and grace? Especially humor: Oh that we could all laugh more!

This is a disturbing legacy from my early years. Perhaps the root of this persistent feeling comes from an experience when I was twenty years old. I had dropped out of college to earn some money to continue. My work was with a large construction company on one of their big jobs: paymaster, surveyor, general adjutant for the company on this job. The company had overextended itself in taking on this job. In an emergency, I ran it by myself for a month with four hundred men. Because the community didn't support a workforce of the size needed, this job was manned largely by workers from distant places, the "floaters" of the then-chaotic construction industry. Many of them had served time in jail. They were patrons of brothels; they gambled away their wages and got drunk frequently; they carried guns and knives. Nobody got shot or badly cut during my tenure, but there were some pretty rough fights. They worked hard when they worked, and they built a good building.

I was the young college kid, and I should have been an outcast, but I wasn't. Never have I been in any group for any purpose where I felt so completely the supporting influence of my associates.

In making up my payroll one Saturday, I made a mistake and paid out about $100 that I shouldn't have. In a $20,000 payroll, this wasn't a big mistake percentagewise, but I felt pretty bad about it. I was sitting at my desk in the office shanty on the following Monday morning, feeling, and probably looking, pretty disconsolate when a big six-foot-four steelworker with an enormous chew of tobacco bulging in his cheek poked his head in the window and asked, "What's the matter with you?" I told him, and he said, "Any idea who's got it?" "No," I said, "not the slightest idea." "Too bad," he said, and walked on.

About ten o'clock he was back in the shanty with two fellows literally by the scruffs of their necks. "Cough up," he said. And they did.

When I left to go back to school, the fellows on this job gave me a nice gold watch.

Maybe they saw in me an image of some of their own unfulfilled aspirations. There could be a lot of things in an experience like this, but its impact was impressive, and I will never lose it. It has no doubt cast a haze in my mind over the distinction that is sometimes drawn between the good people and the bad people.

So I left something behind me when I turned in my tools on my last manual job. This was a long time ago, and though many years went by before I really missed the something that has been lost, I have not forgotten it, and I intend to recover it.

During most of the ensuing thirty-four years in the business of my choice, my work has been concerned with better understanding the art of management and helping people be more effective in the practice of that art. I have worked at it in many ways and from several different assignments. It was not by accident that twenty-nine out of those thirty-four years have been spent in jobs that didn't exist before I had them.

I haven't done much managing. My time has been spent more in watching, studying, brooding about management—trying to organize knowledge and communicate about it. But I have done enough managing to see it from the practitioner's point of view. A simple definition of the ability to manage with which I have initiated many discussions of the subject runs like this: it is the ability to state a goal and reach it, through the efforts of other people, and satisfy those whose judgment one respects, under conditions of stress. This definition ignores the personality qualifications so often associated with a stereotyped view of managing. It admits some who are normally barred because they don't meet some arbitrary but irrelevant requirement. And it bars some who create the illusion of having the ability because they are supported by somebody who knows how. This definition says, in effect, that anybody who can do it has the ability.

Over the past several years, I have discussed this definition with several thousand managers in many kinds of undertakings. The fact that the majority regard it as novel is one of the motivating factors that led me to write this collection of essays.

I have chosen to address this modest book to a general reader rather than explicitly to a management audience for another reason. Over the past two years, the character of the invitations I have received to speak on the subject of managing has changed. Whereas the usual opportunities would be with schools of management and with practicing managers in business, government, and military establishments, of late there has been a new variety, groups as diverse as an association of nurses, a conference of social workers, and one of public school administrators, the student body of a girls' college, a seminar of ministers convened on the theme of religious awareness in a secular culture, a school of doctors studying to be psychiatrists, the professional staff of a research institution, the faculty of a Protestant theological school, the faculty of a Catholic university, and an association of administrators of alcoholism programs.

This has involved me with a lot of people: with the young and the old, with big people and little people, with the very intelligent and the moderately intelligent, with sophisticates in the lore and jargon of managing and people thinking explicitly about it for the first time. Through all of these discussions runs a common thread: a need, a searching that will permit a person to achieve a measure of serenity in a tradition-poor society.

Most people are not trying to escape their obligations; they will accept stress, trouble, and confusion. But they have a sharp need to learn to cope better with their circumstances, to feel more adequate with their total obligations. I am not talking here about the sick, the incompetent, the morally depraved. It is our *best* people, the aspiring people, that have shown this need. And I feel it myself.

It is clear that whether the problem is what to do with a crying child or how to resolve a great issue in world affairs, we of our generation have a new kind of inadequacy. Tradition no longer supports us as it once did. Modern persons do not ask, "What would my mother or my predecessor have done about this?" Only the remaining primitive people respond this way anymore. Modern people, under the prod of conscience, are more likely to ask, "What is the best knowledge available to me, what is the *right* course of action?" To establish what is right, we do not rely nearly as much on tradition as we once did.

We are more on our own resources for our important ethical decisions. When we face a practical situation in which we feel obligated to act, each of us relies heavily on his own reasoning and intuitive powers. We view as weak and indecisive those who frequently have to ask someone else. On our own we draw on knowledge and experience sources of which we are aware, and we make a conscious choice, a decision, for which we are individually responsible. In some respects, it usually is a unique decision, not wholly like a decision ever made before. This, it seems to me, is the heart of the problem. There has always been some of this. Even in a primitive society there is a little of it. But in a relatively short period of time, the area of decision making in which tradition no longer serves us well has been enormously widened.

With this has come a loss of certainty. Primitive people might be "wrong" a good deal of the time. But they are certain, serene in their error. We who have moved with change and broken with tradition have more new knowledge and more knowledge about old things than people have ever had before. But with this we are aware, as humans have never been before, that today's truth may be tomorrow's error. There is also the vague, nagging suspicion that in the process of enlarging our storehouse of knowledge *about* the vast resources of wisdom of the race, we have lost direct contact with much of it as wisdom—wisdom to be used, not just to know about. Knowledge never learned in schools loses something when it is taught.

Too many illusions have been shattered to encourage the hope that the certainty of a tradition-bound society can ever be recovered or would be wanted even if it could be recovered. We have gone too far. The roads back do not look promising. Living as we do under the threat of instant and complete annihilation of all life on the face of the earth, thoughtful people no longer hope for certainty.

Of course, there is really nothing new in this state of affairs as far as individuals and small groups are concerned. People have always lived under this threat all of the time, and they have managed to be cheerful about it a good deal of the time. But the thought that *all* of life could go and that one human being could touch it off, this is new, and it has brought a new concern. Awful as it is to contemplate, the risk *may* be worth it if the concern is powerful enough. If this could somehow influence what people hope for; if this new concern could bring about a better investment of the self—that part of the self that people are yet free to invest; if more meaning could come to many where meaning is feeble—then this terrible period could be viewed as humankind's great opportunity. Great periods of the past have been ushered in by prophecy, by enlightenment, by many things. This one could be brought by the most powerful demonic force yet invented by humanity.

But there will need to be some new hopes. It will do no good to hope that this monster will go away. He is here to stay. He may get bigger rather than smaller. The clock cannot be turned back on this one. One hopes—if one learns to hope at all—with this thing looking over one's shoulder all of the time.

I have no new hopes to offer, only some old ones restated. People can hope that as they live from day to day, they will be able to see more clearly the infinite possibilities in each day, in such things as humor and dignity, courage and caution, heroic and commonplace, mind and heart. Men and women can hope that their bonds to the limitless cosmos will grow stronger; that their natural response to all creatures will be one of interest and affection; and that as they face opportunity or the necessity for decisions, they will do perhaps better than they know—the best they are humanly capable of at that moment, or come reasonably close to it. These are probably as much as mortals have ever been justified in hoping for realistically.

What follows in this book is the fruit of my own search—up to the moment of writing this—for a point of view, a way of working with my opportunities, the pursuit of which will build *strength:* strength to hope, strength to venture and create, strength to sustain my role as an active and effective person in contemporary life.

These chapters are written as conversations with seekers who have suffered enough of the frustrations of hoping, of choosing, of deciding to be ready, if what is offered seems reasonable, to try something—and work at it.

2

A CONCEPT OF STRENGTH

A WISE OLD LADY whom I knew many years ago ran a farm and loved horses. She once dropped the remark, "It is an art to drive hard with a light hand." Whenever I set out to do something where I have to drive a little and push a little to get it done (and what gets done without some of this?), I try to remember this bit of wisdom. It gets done better if I can do my driving, my pushing, with a light hand.

This saying also comes to mind when I see people (including myself) dealing with issues of conscience. Somehow concern with the good is so often found in company with the dour countenance, the long face, the blue nose, the evident tension of internal conflict. I have long resolved that if I cannot find the right path by means of good cheer and a light touch, I shall forget about being good and let the ends be what they will. These means I will not forsake. I am much surer about the verities of means and attitudes than I am about the rightness of *any* action or result.

One of the difficulties of using the word *strength* as the symbol for a primary object of ethical striving is that it has meanings and connotations that distract. Pictures of people who are represented as strong tend to show the set jaw and the unquiet eyes. Grim determination, the head bloodied but unbowed— these are the stereotyped attributes of strength in a person. They seem quite opposed to cheerfulness and a light touch. But *strength* is a good word. I want to give it a special meaning, and

I am going to stay with it in spite of the liabilities that some of its connotations impose.

We are concerned here with doing right, doing what is ethically sound. In my experience, nearly everybody who faces a choice or a decision wants to do right. One wants to do what is morally or ethically right, wants to deliver on obligations, and wants to act with competence. Not everybody has the same degree of this want to do right, and not everybody feels this want all of the time. But few who are judged to be in reasonable health are completely devoid of it.

We will not be concerned here with what is right or wrong in particular situations. This has been the subject of exhaustive studies by students of these matters over a long period of time. I have not made such a study. Besides, codes describing what is right and wrong differ among individuals, among families and neighborhoods, among cultures, religions, and vocational groups, and they change with the passage of time. I have assumed that you want to do right; that you have some code, some standards by which you hope to guide your actions; but that you have a problem of decision, of finding enough good choices, of making the best possible choice. Therefore, we will be concerned here with the problem of deciding or choosing. This is universal and timeless.

As I have observed it, the dilemma of the average person facing a practical problem is not so much that one doesn't know an adequate ethical code or doesn't want to practice what one knows to be right. Rather, when facing a decision in which ethical choices are involved, the ethical dilemma can be summed up as follows: (1) one doesn't *know* enough and doesn't see enough choices to make a good choice possible; (2) one doesn't see either the problem or one's choices *soon* enough to use one's initiative prudently; (3) one lacks the perspective on the future to see the long-run consequences of the available choices; (4) one cannot see how to make one's way or fulfill *other* obligations if one elects what one regards as the best choice; (5) therefore, if one is ethically sensitive, one cannot act with the assurance of rightness enough of the time to maintain a sufficient belief in one's own ethical adequacy. If one cannot act with rightness often enough to make it worthwhile to try, then there is little incentive to try. Rightness, therefore, is something we need to strive to be pretty good at, or the game won't be worth the candle.

I have chosen to view the ethical dilemma just outlined as the need for *strength*. *Strength* is defined as the ability to see enough choices of aims, to choose the *right* aim, and to pursue that aim responsibly over a long period of time. This calls for some elaboration.

First, *ability*. As used here, it embraces both the know-how and the disposition to do.

Then, *the right aim*. What is *right* for a particular individual in a particular situation? To some extent, it will be the fruit of a creative act. It is something that fits the occasion as nothing that has ever been codified would fit. In weighing rightness, we should bear in mind that all things change with time and that one's view is enlarged and enriched with experience. Furthermore, we are functioning in an unright world, so total rightness is seldom our choice. The big question, then, is how a person should judge whether the contemplated action is the closest to right that one is capable of getting.

One is really anticipating the future, because one's surest judgment about the rightness of many acts emerges only with the lapse of time. One begins by testing the available choices by traditional ethical and moral values. What does the code say? What light does historical, moral, and ethical thinking throw? What kind of guidance do the standards one embraces provide? Relatively few questions of choice are answered clearly and finally by these tests, but they take one a long way on some issues.

Then one judges one's choice within the frame of reference established by meaning in one's own life. Who am I, what kind of person am I, and what am I seeking to become? These are important questions because what I am and what I will become are molded largely by the opportunities I seek and the choices I make in the practical issues I face.

If one bears obligations for others (and who doesn't?), how will these be affected? One is not wholly free to make choices that may be ideally right by some standards but destroy opportunity for somebody else.

Further, one must ask, "Do I know and have I assessed the widest possible range of choices? My intentions may be the best, but when I choose, I can do no better than the alternatives of which I am aware."

In a few short paragraphs, I have disposed of questions to which students of ethics and morals devote lives of study and volumes of discourse. I hope I have said enough to raise a question, with those who have not reflected on it, about the assumption held by many that choosing the right aim is a simple matter. In a society in which traditional ways have been shattered by the explosion of knowledge, in which the end of the revolution in knowledge is not in sight, the choosing grows progressively more difficult.

Concern about what is right should be on the mind of every person every day of his or her life. Most of us in the Western world have been brought up to respect the Judeo-Christian ethic. But this is not a static concept anymore. It is being enlarged by new knowledge and, as the world becomes one, by ideas from other cultures.

The choosing is complicated further by the idea that the choice generally isn't made in the moment of decision as a highly rational view of things might pretend it is. If we could make a mechanical analogy of the human decision-making apparatus, we would say it was a sort of computer with memory banks, stored-away resources consisting of values, experience, emotions, knowledge, customary ways of working with the resources. On this machine are buttons representing possible events and conditions in the outside world. In the moment of decision, we simply push the buttons that tell the machine what the external situation is, and it makes a grand synthesis from the resources available to it. In mechanical terms, the choice is preset. Give the machine the right signal, and out it comes.

This sounds horribly deterministic, but it isn't. It only says that at the moment of decision, there is a heavy deterministic factor. Volitional choice is represented largely by what has been put into the machine up to that point. Even if the analogy held in every detail (which, of course, it doesn't—it is just a mind teaser), there remains a vital step. The final act in decision making is the decision to decide. One can always say to the machine, "No, I won't take that one. Reprocess it!" The only thing that saves the pitcher in the baseball game from being a complete robot is that he can, and occasionally does, shake his head at the catcher, saying, "I don't like that signal. Give me another one."

Here, again, in a few paragraphs, I have disposed of the question of decision making and deterministic moral philosophy. People devote their lives to these subjects too. I only touch on them here because they are part of the frame of reference within which any consideration of ethical choice must take place.

To follow our definition of *strength* another step, what of *responsible pursuit?* This term is used in the sense that the person who has chosen an aim *thinks, speaks, and acts as if personally accountable to all who may be affected by his or her thoughts, words, and deeds.* This is a large and seemingly impossible order. But nothing short of this as a goal will do.

Finally, to complete the elaboration of the definition of *strength,* what about that *long period of time?* How long is long? It is long enough for the consequences of error to emerge. And that can be a very long time.

To repeat the definition, because the remainder of this book will rest upon it, *strength* is the ability to see enough choices of aims, to choose the right aim, and to pursue that aim responsibly over a long period of time.

What follows is based on the thesis that the building of *strength* and everything that supports it is an ethical requirement.

In a tradition-poor society, I see no alternative but to enlarge the meaning of ethics to include the nurturing of *strength* and to judge as ethically deficient those who do not put adequate effort into the pursuit of *strength*. The contention throughout this book will be that the pursuit of *strength* is not an option but an ethical requirement, and *no one* will be judged ethically adequate unless his or her own personal *strength* is the prime concern, right to the end of life.

3

THE SEARCH

DURING WORLD WAR II, I became a beekeeper. This was partly out of patriotic motives, partly because sugar was scarce, and partly because something about bees interested me. I soon discovered, however, that I was not a natural beekeeper. I never gained the immunity that the books promised after many stings—and I got stung a lot. When I went out to work with my bees, I dressed like a knight in armor. But no matter how elaborate my protection of gloves, nets, and clothing, the bees always got to me.

My honey production was good, and I was grateful for that. But clearly, the bees and I didn't get along. They didn't like me, and I didn't like them. It was a bad deal. So after three years, I gave it up.

Fifteen years went by, and insofar as my conscious memory was concerned, my beekeeping dropped into place alongside many other experiences. Except as a social conversation piece, it seldom came to mind. Then one late-summer day, I was eating a picnic lunch out of doors, and the yellowjackets were out in force, being their natural annoying selves. My rational estimate of yellowjackets is that their sting is worse than bees'; they are irritable and aggressive and bees generally aren't, and aside from some slight pollinizing service, they don't produce anything for man. My rational estimate of yellowjackets would be definitely lower than bees, and bees and I didn't get along.

To my surprise, this day I felt no annoyance at the yellow-jackets, and I found my hand going out for them to crawl on if they wanted to—and some of them did. Later I found that this urge extended to all stinging insects, including bees. Over two or three years, I have held many stinging insects. I've been stung once or twice, but I didn't mind it. Now I find that something has been added to the interest I originally had in bees: I have an *affection* for them and their kind.

If, in the course of the fifteen years since I had failed as a bee-keeper, I had set down a list of the gifts I would like to receive, affection for the stinging insects would not have been one of them. But in that period, I had learned an important lesson: one does not ask for gifts. These natural gifts, these dispositions to hold attitudes that give largeness of self, come unannounced. They have a newness and a freshness about them, and some-times they go when they are most wanted. One cannot ask for them because until they have been given, one really doesn't know what they are. If such a gift has been enjoyed and then lost, it probably went for a reason, and it won't come back just by being wished for.

Strength, as I view it in all its aspects, is like that. It isn't like muscle, to be developed by exercise and flexing. It does not come as the direct result of conscious striving. It is not the end product of a series of logical steps. It does not emerge sponta-neously as the result of embracing a belief. Nor is it the product of "good works," useful and desirable as these are. And it is not likely to come from the routine practice of religious observance, granted that this, too, may have its virtues.

Strength is not manipulable. It is of a different order. Some hint of process is given in the following analogy, attributed to Herbert Spencer, in which he speaks of a mechanical procedure and draws a moral from it.[5] It concerns the process of rolling sheet steel. As Spencer relates it, occasionally a sheet of steel would come through the mill with a bulge in it. The uninitiated might say, "Run it through the mill again and straighten it out." But, Spencer points out, this would buckle the sheet at the point of the bulge and ruin it. The traditional method of removing the bulge was to lay the sheet on a large steel table and, with a smooth-headed hammer, start tapping it gently a few inches from the edge of the bulge and striking away from the bulge while going around and around. In this way, the surrounding metal is gradually stretched away from the bulge. With each trip around the bulge, the hammer is brought closer to the center. If the job has been done carefully, when the center is reached, the bulge has disappeared.

"The moral, applicable to many social processes," says Spencer: "avoid hammering on the bulge, but hammer diligently around it!"

Against the background of all the negatives, all of the ways that do not encourage strength, Spencer's analogy gives us a cue: *hammer diligently around it.*

What does this suggest to the pursuer of *strength?* What can one do and do diligently?

Here we come to a parting of the ways. Those who know what they want, or think they do, and intend to go after it go one way. Those who can't make up their minds sit at the crossroads hoping that someone will pick them up and take them somewhere. Those looking for an *answer* that will guide them will turn to the records of wise people who presumably know. Some will respond to the idea that there are gifts around, if one can dispose oneself to receive one. They will choose the faint, slightly trodden path, which is nevertheless a path—but it is marked "destination unknown."

This is the path of the search, the search about the seeker and his resources. Because the destination *is* unknown, one becomes interested in the search for the sake of the search, not with precise objects in mind that are expected to add up to something. *The search is the thing;* one becomes lost in it and accepts what comes.

All of this probably sounds mysterious and illogical to anyone disposed to rely mainly on formal logic and the highly rational. But since *strength* is a universal need, no one should despair that it may never be obtained. It is viewed as a gift that anyone willing to be receptive can receive. Like any other gift, some recipients will accept it more readily than others. And in the end, every person will have to find his or her own way to become accepting in order to receive it. All I can do now is share my own experience.

The search is concerned with self-knowledge. Since as far back as Socrates we have heard that "the unexamined life is not worth living." Most of the spiritual teachers I know about affirm that position.

What is meant by self-knowledge requires some reflection in our times because of the development of psychotherapy and the various analytical schools wherein, under professional guidance, the evidences and attributes of personality are systematically studied and interpreted. We are in the midst of a psychological revolution. It is difficult for any but the serious students to know where this field is and what it can contribute to the search for *strength*. The most one can say is that intensive work with a psychological guide may or may not be helpful to the individual search. The trouble is that professional opinions vary widely concerning the utility of any special approach to self-knowledge. Furthermore, psychological guidance is individual with the practitioner, regardless of the "school" to which he or she belongs. Here, as in so many areas of contemporary life, tradition does not help the individual make the decision, and the expert sources do not agree.

So the prudent course, unless one has some special, personal leadings, is to take into account only one important phenomenon of the human mind: the several levels of consciousness. About their existence there does not appear to be much question. But when one asks how they function, one is led into speculation on which there is wide disagreement.

As one layperson talking with others, I have found the iceberg analogy useful. The conscious mind, of whose functioning we have some direct awareness, is represented by the small amount protruding above the waterline, and the unconscious is represented by the vast mass below. There is a good deal of speculation about what is below the waterline. Some people hold that every experience, every sensation ever felt by a person, is recorded there. Some would include racial memories and aspects of the culture.

There is reason to suppose that the unconscious process has its own reasoning apparatus and that upon receiving the appropriate signals, it produces hunches, insights, and intuitive promptings.

When the unconscious storehouse of experience is sufficient on a certain question, it can exert a powerful enough influence to overrule the conclusions of the conscious mind and block visual perception, for instance, from actually communicating what the conscious mind clearly and logically knows is on the screen of vision. The demonstrations of this phenomenon as developed by Adelbert Ames have to be experienced to be believed, but they are very convincing.[6] There seems to be little question that by the time we reach maturity, we have a vast amount of experience stored away that effectively conditions perception and sometimes will not permit us to perceive correctly. When it can be clearly demonstrated that stored-away experience will not permit us to perceive what we clearly know is there, respect for these underwater resources is confirmed.

Awareness of the below-the-waterline resources and how they influence us comes in many ways. It comes through otherwise unexplained promptings of intuitive insight, through dream imagery, through the occasional free-flowing pen in writing, through unintended and unexplained slips in speech, through reverie and semisleep, and in other ways.

The *search* begins, then, with an awareness of one's vast mental resources beyond conscious memory and reasoning. One can expand one's theories about awareness to any extent one desires through the study of the writings of the serious students of this subject. However, my own intuition tells me that one does this at one's peril. It is not a preoccupation that is constructive for everybody, and I know of no evidence that would support the claim that the gift of *strength* would be favored by such a pursuit.

Simply practice being aware. Look, and be still. Feel, and be still. Listen, and be still. Give the practice of awareness time, time when you are alone.

Pay attention to what comes from below the waterline of consciousness. Write down dreams if you can—but don't analyze them. Pay attention to your thoughts upon waking, upon going to sleep, during reveries. Keep a daily journal—write freely what comes to mind in response to the events of the day (not a diary description of the events themselves). Write down a dream and then extend the dream in the journal. Look critically at what you've written, but don't change it or throw it away.

I have postulated that you are a seeker with the intelligence, the drives, the tenacity, and the sensitivity that augur for success. With these you must also constantly cultivate your awareness "above the waterline." Let me give you an illustration from my own experience.

One of the significant events of my life was a chance incident about fifteen years ago when I pulled the emergency cord on a New York subway train to save a man's life. The doors had closed on his arm as he was about to enter, and he could not get loose. The conductor failed to notice as the train took off, dragging the man down the platform to certain death if the train was not stopped before he reached the end of the platform. Fortunately, he was hooked to the middle of the train, and there were a few seconds for action.

He was caught in the rear door of the car in which I was seated in the middle. The car was comfortably filled, perhaps seventy-five people, some of them standing. I became aware of the emergency by the commotion at the end of the car. A crowd converged on the door, clawing at it and shouting, "Stop the train!" "Pull the emergency cord." "Open the doors!" An emergency cord hung overhead. No one pulled it. A similar cord was in the opposite end of the car. No one near it was going for it either. Two or three precious seconds went by before

I realized that it was up to me; so I ran for the cord at the opposite end, bowling over a few people as I went. And I made it just in time.

It was terribly important that a life was saved, although I never learned the man's name and he doesn't know mine. I am glad it is that way. But this wasn't what made it a significant experience. Its significance, for me, is what I learned about some of my contemporaries. Almost all of the seventy-five people in that car were closer to one of those emergency cords than I was. Why was I the one to pull the cord? This puzzled me. But I had a hunch about it, and over the next few months I conducted the following experiment.

At lunch or on other appropriate occasions with New Yorkers who ride the subways regularly, I described the situation to the point where I went for the cord. "What would you do?" I asked. Almost everyone said he would pull the emergency cord. "All right," I said, "there are three subway systems in New York, and the cord is in a different place on each system. This is the Independent line. Where is the cord? You have about five seconds to act: one, two, three, four, five." I tried this on about fifty people before I gave it up. No one I tried this on could tell me in five seconds where the cord was. Nor, in fact, did I find anyone who was sure where the cord was, given an unlimited amount of time to think about it. Yet they all rode the subways every day. It caused me to wonder what people think about as they ride along. They aren't always reading or sleeping. Where is their awareness?

The significance of this experiment is that if, as a regular subway rider, a person never thinks, as he rides along, about the possibility that some day he might have to pull the cord, and if he fails to fix in his mind where the cord is, under the stress of the emergency and the shortness of time he is not likely to be the one who pulls the cord. One responds, in an emergency, to what one has preset and firmly fixed in one's mind in calmer moments prior to the emergency, when the reasoning about an anticipated situation is done. In an emergency, one does not go through elaborate reasoning—there isn't time, and the stress is too great; one acts largely on one's preset reasoning.

What I learned from this is that very few people accept that this is a dangerous world—morally, physically, intellectually— and hence they do not choose to be aware of where they are, who they are, what kind of world they live in, or what its traps and hazards are. Consequently, they do not think much about what could happen and what they would do under certain anticipated conditions. For the prudent person, these must be preset in advance so that in the real-life emergency, all that one has to do is assess the exact circumstance; the rest has all been determined in advance. One has chosen to act responsibly, and one has prepared for it before the emergency arises.

What can we make of this? Awareness is a combination of a constant conscious scanning of the environment and the concurrent searching question, "What would I do if I were in the action spots within my view?" The scanning is done partly by reading and listening to language. But it is also direct and elemental looking, listening, smelling, feeling, and constant questioning; "What is going on here?" "What would I do in certain circumstances if action by me were appropriate?" The capacity for intuitive response is constantly exercised by questioning oneself: "What is likely to happen? How probable is such an occurrence? What would I do if such and such did happen?" *Constant* is the important word. Successful people must do this constantly. Unless one does this constantly, one's capacity to respond is not sharp. The tragedy at Pearl Harbor is a classic example of uncultivated awareness and a dulled capacity to respond. Even though there were repeated warnings, there was little awareness. Even when the radar watcher picked up the signal of the approaching plane, there could be no response. The routine patrol had been carried out. Routine had supplanted awareness.

The trap that sometimes brings failure to otherwise successful people is to substitute routine for awareness. Awareness is a constant reaching out and responding to everything in the environment: the people, the sunset, the sounds of the street, the smell of flowers, the clackity-clack of the subway wheels. It is not tiring or boring. In fact, it is quite the opposite: it is the essence of life. Be able to withdraw into the silence, but do not turn off the current to the antenna so that you miss the signal that will bring you back in a flash.

Awareness is awareness. It isn't something one ever turns off. This isn't an exercise, a "daily dozen" that one does for ten minutes each morning. The effort is always to be aware, always to know that something important is going on all of the time.

This is the beginning of the search, the effort toward the opening of awareness. Since what is there to be aware of is individual and personal, each search is a unique undertaking.

I can suggest five concerns that I have found helpful as a means for getting on with the search:

The concern for a sense of responsibility

The concern for openness to knowledge

The concern to live and act now as if the future is now

The concern for entheos and for personal growth

The concern for purpose and laughter

These are covered in succeeding chapters.

4

THE REQUIREMENTS OF RESPONSIBILITY

IN MY YOUTH, I watched the rise and fall of a public citizen in my town. He was a successful businessman, a local captain of industry, an important person in the town.

He rose in public influence because he was able and hard-working, showed interest in the community's welfare, and was honest in the conventional sense. In his later years, it became apparent that his concern for the wider community was more academic than deeply personal. His influence declined, leaving a wreckage of lives and institutions. He died a bitter and disillusioned man. As a public citizen, he was judged a complete and tragic failure.

As I see it now, he lacked something important. His contemporaries, who trusted him with power and respected his influence, were not aware of the deficiency. It was a lack that he could have corrected had he been aware and had he accepted the obligation to correct it. He lacked an adequate sense of *responsibility*.

Responsibility, as the word will be used here, requires that a person think, speak, and act as if personally accountable to all who may be affected by his or her thoughts, words, and deeds. People are affected by neglect as well as by assertive actions. Therefore, responsibility is affirmative and imposes obligations that one might not choose. It is also negative in that it restrains or modifies what one might choose to think, say, or do.

As stated, this is idealistic. In an imperfect world, it is a goal, something to work toward, even if never to accomplish fully. *Awareness* is important. The big question, Is the *trend* right? Am I moving? Am I moving in the right direction? Is my sense of responsibility growing, deepening, becoming sharper and more insistent?

The requirements of responsibility are internal rather than external. Responsibility is not seen as an act of conformity. Rather, it is the key to inner serenity. Responsibility is not tested by a formula, a code, or a set of rules. A sense of responsibility is an attitude, a feeling. It is an overriding point of view, the color of the glasses through which one sees the world, the frame of reference within which one's philosophy of life evolves.

The potentially strong person acquires, early in the mature years, the feeling of total responsibility for the wider community of which he or she is a part. This person doesn't necessarily *act* totally responsible—that might not always be appropriate for the novice—but *feels* responsible, totally responsible. The things that are good for the society please this person, and the things that harm it cause pain—deep down inside. Other things being equal, the young person who gets this attitude first will come out best, in terms of strength, over a lifetime. So many other things fall into place when this basic attitude is right.

Most of us develop this attitude of total responsibility toward our families; but it becomes qualified and attenuated as it radiates to the wider community. The wider community requires more of this familial feeling than it usually gets. If it is seriously lacking for long, there will be no community, no civilization, and in the end, no family. The relatively short life span of democracies in the history of the world might be explained by a decline in the range and intensity of familial feeling, a basic erosion in the sense of responsibility on the part of persons who are perfectly capable of being responsible and whose lives would have greater significance for them if they cultivated their sense of responsibility.

Like other attitudes, the feeling of total responsibility is born, not made. Everybody is born once. But like other creative persons, the responsible person is born twice. The second birth comes when he or she learns to ask the searching questions that bound the requirements of responsibility. Moreover, one learns to ask these questions reflectively.

To do anything reflectively demands that one be alone with one's thoughts and accept the presence of a deeper self with which one may have only tenuous communication. The turmoil and the fitfulness of the mind of the active person in the workaday world is quieted, and the question is asked, asked not of one's conscious awareness for a quick rational response, but asked simply in the stillness of the quiet—asked and asked and asked. One does not press for an answer, nor does one flagellate oneself if the answer to the question seems negative. The asking of the right question, reflectively, is the conscious means whereby a new internal climate is created, a climate in which a new constructive attitude might be born and grow. It *might* grow. And it will choose its own time and be what it is when it comes.

What are the right questions to ask reflectively? I do not know of a standard set of right questions. The development of the feeling of total responsibility is a search, an individual search. The questions will be peculiar to each searcher, and they will probably change as the search progresses. We can get suggestions from the records of other seekers; but in the end, we must each ask our own questions.

The following are the questions that seem important to me now in my own search.

1. *Am I contemporary?* Do I have a sense of history? Am I living in the current phase of developing history? Do I look with open wonder at contemporary politics, philosophy, religion, economics, art, music, literature, science (both natural and social), business development?

I am *not* asking myself, Am I in the avant garde? Am I pioneering the development of any of these fields? I am certainly not asking that I accept or approve of all that I hear. The question, rather, is, *Can I hear* the communication from the growing edge of my times? Am I able to hear what is being said to me before I judge it? Am I listening, really listening? Do the voices of my more creative contemporaries speak to me because I am living in the developing stream of history and because I am in tune with my times? One cannot deal responsibly with contemporaries if one can hear only the voices of those who are dead, either the really dead of the generations past or those who are yet alive in the flesh but dead in spirit because they have nothing constructive to say to the times in which they live.

2. *Am I connected?* Am I on the growing edge of the contemporary phase of history but still connected to the main body of people and events?

I might be a prophet, speaking to future generations but not to the present. Prophets are useful and necessary, but they are not necessarily strong people among their contemporaries. The future may hail a man of our times as a great prophet, but he may be disconnected as we see him today and, therefore, not in touch with enough of his contemporaries to wield the influence of *strength* in our times. One person might be connected in the early part of his or her life and a prophet in the later part. But one can't be both at once, not if the main focus of one's life is to embrace an active, responsible role in the larger society. It is said of Beethoven that when in his advanced years he began to compose his late quartets, he was asked by a friend, "What's happened to you? We don't understand you anymore." Legend has it that Beethoven replied, "I have said all that I have to say to my contemporaries. Now I am writing for the future." History proved him right. It took a long time for those later quartets to be understood and loved.

3. *Do I see evil as an aspect of good?* I am not viewing this theologically. Much as I would choose to embrace the good and

work to have it prevail, I would not want to live in a world in which there is no evil. Much as I would like to have good health, avoid illness, and help others do the same, I would not want to live in a world in which there is no illness, no suffering, no death. Medical researchers now point to the adverse consequences of the promiscuous use of antibiotics. They say we must not set out to destroy all of the so-called unfriendly bacteria. People cannot survive in a world in which the destruction of what we currently view as unfriendly is carried on with too much vigor.

Responsibility brings one face to face with the cold facts that progress does not flow from the simple choosing of the good and rejecting the evil. It comes when we accept that we have only good and some aspects of good that we do not understand. Progress in responsibility is hastened as we are moved, from the inside, to stand in awe and wonder in the face of the ineffable mystery and thus open ourselves to insights that only the responsible and the strong can receive.

4. *Do I accept that there is no virtue that, carried to the extreme, does not become a vice, no sound idea that, overworked, does not become absurd?* There may be absolute values in the world, but by the time mortals have filtered them through their biases, distorted them with imperfect reasoning, and warped them through inexact vocabulary, the values are only approximate.

A good example of a virtue that, carried too far, becomes a vice is *integrity*. In most ways, there would be no practical limits on the goodness of integrity. But take the example of the person whose integrity compels him always and in every situation to say exactly and completely what he thinks. This might be an absolute form of integrity. It would also be irresponsible.

In the realm of sound ideas is the idea of *freedom*, external freedom, one of our most precious concepts. Such as we have of it has been achieved and defended at the cost of great struggle and vigilance. Yet this idea can be carried to the point where every form of external restraint on a person is rejected. We end

45

with no law, no government, no roads, no schools—an absurd end for a basically sound idea.

5. *Am I sure that in choosing a right aim, I have not become self-righteous?* The dictionary definition of *righteous* puts it as "free from wrong, guilt, or sin," a state no person ever achieves. Pride in the illusion that one has achieved it is disastrous. The pretense that one has made it by going through the motions, keeping the law, is equally damaging.

The trap in pursuing the good is that one may be overtaken by the feeling that one is wholly good and therefore not like other people. There is no surer way to become disconnected and lose the sense of responsibility than to become self-righteous.

6. *Am I prepared to accept that I will never have the comfort of being "ideologically" right?* This is a tough question for the brittle, the fearful, the dogmatic, the "allness" people. To such persons, the persistent asking of this question—reflectively and in the quiet hours—may be devastating. But it may be the only way that the sense of responsibility can be opened.

The rightness of my aim will not be justified by conclusive evidence, airtight reasoning, or immutable law. It will have its own validation.

Whenever a person says to himself or herself, "Now I fully understand this," or "This is the final or complete truth," the chances are that he or she has blocked the possibility for further growth in knowledge or insight in that area. In fact, by taking these positions in only a small area of knowledge, one may limit one's capacity for comprehension in general.

It is probably equally limiting to pursue the absolute since it is unattainable. Human growth in understanding is not a movement toward certainty; it is best described by words like *perspective, enlargement, insight.* One comprehends, one feels a part of knowledge, one becomes mobile in one's feeling and ventures with greater assurance. But there is no certainty. And in the world of practical affairs, this constitutes an aspect of stress. Stress can only be balanced by serenity, which has its roots in the vagueness and tentativeness of all with which we work.

7. *Am I willing to cultivate the "growing-edge" people among my contemporaries and, by so doing, accept the censure of those who are far from the growing edge and don't want to look at it?* The growing-edge people are those who are pushing the frontiers of knowledge and experience. They are the connecting links with the future. They are the ones who best understand the flow of history from the past through the present and into the future.

Not all that is odd and strange is on the growing edge, and it takes some discernment to know. But one must take the risks that go with probing the growing edge. If one waits until it is perfectly respectable, life will have passed one by. This is like any research: one must follow several false leads for every good one found.

The growing-edge people are those who are most open to knowledge and who are living as if the future is now. They are not necessarily the intellectual giants of our time. They are often lonely people and not difficult to know.

Those who shun the growing edge can be counted on to censure any interest in it. They don't want to look at it, and they don't want anybody else to look at it either. This has always been true. It must be expected and accepted (but not praised).

8. *Am I sensitive to the needs and aspirations of all who may be affected by what I think, say, and do? And being sensitive, am I willing to say the words and take the actions that build constructive tension?* I must know something about who the people are who may be affected and what their needs, feelings, interests, and aspirations are. Since I can have only approximate knowledge, I must work at it to know as much as I can know.

The best assurance of knowing is to be interested, to take the time to listen, and to have a developed skill for doing so. So much of the desire to be sensitive and know is thwarted because the doors of perception are closed; and they generally don't open by wishing.

But when I know something about the people who may be affected by what I think, say, and do, I have a further problem. I also know that the well-being of the other person may depend on a constructive tension that I may be able to create; therefore, I must weigh my responsibility for saying the words or taking the actions that will bring this tension about.

Am I willing, for instance, to say a firm "No!" to my child and thwart his desire, thus bringing on bad feeling?

If I am in a leadership position, am I willing to say, "Do it now!" when it would be more pleasant all around if I said, "Tomorrow is OK"?

Am I willing to rise in my group and jar the prevailing harmony by saying, "I oppose this action, and I will use every strategy at my command to block it"? Or will I say, when the occasion demands, what Voltaire once reportedly said: "I disapprove of what you say, but I will defend to the death your right to say it"?

Gentleness, in itself, is not always kindness. The act may seem hard and unreasonable to the recipient at the time, but it may be the most constructive kindness. Many a person has been fired from a job with immediate devastating effects only to say later that it turned out to be an enormous favor. This is not cited to justify indiscriminate firing. The point is that seemingly harsh actions like this do produce a level of constructive tension in some cases without which it is unlikely that the individuals involved will surmount their own life problems.

The trouble with passive gentleness is that it may be the cloak behind which hides the unwillingness to develop the concern, the real affection, and the *skill* required to be kind. For instance, the child who knows that there is an abundance of concern and affection is more likely to respond constructively to a firm "no" than if there is doubt on these points.

But one walks a dangerous razor's edge in these matters. The tension-producing action can have its origin in a senseless compulsion rather than in a sane and informed sense of responsibility that grows out of concern and affection. One can never be absolutely sure that one is operating from a sane and informed sense of responsibility, but one can be surer if the development of *strength* in all its aspects is a prime obligation.

9. *Can I accept that the best possible compromise is right?* The needs and interests of those who may be affected by my thoughts, words, and deeds are rarely identical. Sometimes they vary widely. What is a right action for me is therefore the best fit for the disparate situations—a compromise. It is probably not ideally right for any one of those who are affected.

Great idealists capture the popular imagination more readily than the great compromisers, but this may be because so many who make up the popular voice have never lived close to the resolution of important conflict. To the informed person, the inspired mosaic of compromise can have heroic qualities that no idealistic conception can ever achieve. Compromise makes life on this earth possible, with normal human beings living in relative freedom. Gerald Heard called compromise the art of the probable.

10. *Do I have a view of myself on which progressively greater strength can be built?* Everyone who would grow in strength needs a self-view that will sustain the search. This is the most difficult of perspectives to get: to see oneself and to know who one really is, to judge the attitudes and direction sets that one sees, to know that one is husbanding one's resources— mental, emotional, physical—as the most precious of assets. So many people I see about me think they are prudent when they are conserving their property but wasting their lives.

When I look at myself, above all things I want to see a being who is serious and yet not serious, someone in whom cheerfulness and lightness of step are at all times dominant. I want to see myself at once at the center of the universe—influencing its course with every word, thought, and deed—and at the same time a minute instrument of the cosmos acting in harmony with the others.

11. *Am I striving to make a creative act out of conformity?*
This sounds like a contradiction, but every necessary circumstance that is essential to an orderly, productive society can
be made creative, meaning that something new and important
can be brought into being in the process. There are plenty of
circumstances in which no creativity arises, but that is because
the person involved doesn't want to be creative, doesn't try, or
isn't strong enough.

Some conformity is a necessary circumstance of *organized*
constructive action. It can be overdone, and often is, but all organized effort requires that the participants conform to a procedure, a way of thinking, a way of acting.

Being creative, bringing something important into existence
that wasn't there before, can be done under *any* circumstance
by a strong person. It can be done while somebody is using his
power to grind an operation down. It can even be done under
conditions of ruthless suppression. Creativity is favored by less
harsh circumstances, but its optimum functioning in practical
affairs would not be under conditions of complete encouragement and permissiveness, with no requirement for conformity
(if these conditions can even be imagined).

Bringing something new into being is seen as a significant
pursuit only when it is hard to do, when there are real obsta-
cles. I realize that there may be fields of creative work in which
this generalization would not hold. But if one is to act responsibly, as an aspect of strength, I submit this as an important question: can one make a creative act out of conformity?

Strength, which includes responsible pursuit, is not seen as a
necessary goal only because the conditions of life are difficult,
although it would be judged partly this way. Rather, the world
is seen as presenting conditions that are "good" for people because it lays down the challenge to aspire to strength. "Grow or
perish," it seems to say.

What about the weak, those incapable of *strength;* are they
simply to be run over by these circumstances? One must say

that this question is really not addressed to the pursuers of *strength*. They didn't make the circumstances. They are simply trying to respond creatively to what they find.

I would rather view *strength* as something that anybody could get more of, if the desire is there. The people with the greater capacity and the greater want have the obligation to develop superior *strength* and use it for the general good. This has been the rule of social survival as long as we have any record. Many valuable gifts to society are made by persons who are not strong and who need the shelter of the strength of others. The ethical obligation is on those who have the capacity for *strength* to develop it and to use it to create the shelter for those who need that shelter to make their contribution.

In summary, these are one man's views of questions to be reflected on, not rules of conduct. These are not given as a checklist on which to build a personal program of self-improvement. Dr. Karl Menninger coined a term that he applies to newly trained psychiatrists who, he says, tend to see in their first patient all of the symptoms they ever heard about and set out to cure them all at once. He calls this *furor therapeuticus*.[7] In our context, we would call it *furor responsibilitas*.

I suggested earlier that all who would be strong become journal writers. As the questions are asked and allowed to sink into the inner mental apparatus, *write*. Write what comes to mind. Ask the questions, reflect on them, and write something every day. Occasionally, reread what you have written and extend it. Cultivate spontaneity. Let the pen capture the fleeting insight.

All people who are capable of it need to pursue some discipline that will develop their sense of responsibility and keep it sharp. They need it so that they can do their best with their own capacities and obligations. They also need it so that, in the heat of action, they can distinguish the responsible from the less responsible among their contemporaries. This is terribly

important because no society or organized segment thereof—
whatever its purpose—can long survive and serve a purpose unless it has the collective capacity to put its trust in those whose
sense of responsibility sings!

5

OPENNESS TO KNOWLEDGE

JOSH BILLINGS ONCE SAID, "It is better to know nothing than to know what ain't so."[8]

For building strength, there is a large difference between "knowing" a lot and being "open" to knowledge. Openness to knowledge helps one achieve the state in which one sees a wide enough range of choices in a practical situation and is able to choose the best one. Many so-called knowledgeable people are no better at seeing a wide range of choices and choosing a good one than people who don't know so much. The mere memory of data and the capacity to refine it with elaborate reasoning processes does not take one very far in the pursuit of *strength*.

To be *open,* one is aware of and has accepted the risks—to one's own inner personal apparatus as well as in the judgment of the outside world—that go with disposing oneself to receive the communications, from any source, that add to *strength*.

One of the difficulties in making too much of one's adherence to the standard virtues is that it may dull one's receptivity to creative inspiration in the moment of decision. It is well to know as much as one can about traditional views of right and wrong, but one must not expect that the right choice for very many occasions will emerge directly from this storehouse.

When one is responding to knowledge in an open way, one may seem to be lacking in consistency, the "foolish" kind of consistency that Ralph Waldo Emerson called the "hobgoblin of little minds."[9] Unfortunately, this kind of consistency is sometimes seen as a virtue even though the results are disastrous. The hard choice may fall between being weak and consistent and being strong and inconsistent. The important thing is to be as right as we can.

We live with a veritable surfeit of knowledge. The libraries are bulging; they can't even store the books. A scholar in English literature recently said that so much criticism of the works of Shakespeare has been written that a fast-reading Shakespearean scholar couldn't read it all if he did nothing but read this particular material from age eighteen to age seventy. This is becoming true of many fields.

This raises a question. With this abundance of knowledge, what is profitable for a person to try to know? In the moment of a practical decision, most of us don't go to the library. We don't even consult our friends. We act on what we know. And most of us want to do better. Out of my own observation and experience I have gathered a few ideas that may be helpful to the person who would make some effort to be better served by what knowledge can perform.

But first there are some problems about knowing for those who want to be open to knowledge so they can be strong. Knowledge is not like money in the bank. One cannot simply reach into the account and draw an amount equal to the need. Sometimes those who seem to have the most in the bank find that the teller won't pay when they hand over their draft. Others who seem to have little on account sometimes come up with a gem of wisdom that would do credit to Solomon. Let us look at a few problems that might help explain this anomaly.

1. *We don't really know a lot that we think we know.* The vast storehouse of knowledge in the unconscious mind is not the same stuff that is in libraries. For each of us, it is possibly the complete record of our particular experience. Much collective wisdom may also be deposited there. Each of us apparently has a center that will process this knowledge, deal with a complexity of issues, and deliver a conclusion at a speed that makes

the most elaborate electronic computer a child's toy. The electronic computer has the advantage, in a world that pretends that conscious rationality is all, of evident predictability on performance. The operator knows pretty well the data the computer has, can check the accuracy of the result, and can schedule its operation. But compared to what the unconscious processes of an ordinary person can do, it is a relatively feeble (though nevertheless important) instrument.

Many years ago, I attended a class in the mathematics of sampling taught by a famous mathematician. I was not enough of a mathematician to take in much of it, but my teacher was a philosopher who knew something of the problems of dealing with the real world.

One day, while discussing the limits of statistical prediction, he made the point that no mathematical calculation ever takes one all of the way to a practical decision. There is always a gap, usually an important gap. The object of mathematical research is to reduce this gap, but it will always be there and it will always be an important discrepancy. The problem is how to fill the knowledge gap and get the best possible assurance of a good decision.

He used this illustration. "If you were the head of a business in which the purchase of coal was important, such as a railroad (then rather than now) or a steel mill, and if for some reason your customary source of coal was no longer available, you would have to find a new source of coal. Since the quality of coal varies from one location to another, you would face a decision as to what coal to buy. You canvass the market, and you are offered coal from here and there. Which is the best coal for your purpose? Remember, you're going to buy a lot of it, and the wrong choice could be costly just to try it out.

"If you are a modern manager, you will get samples of these available coals and send them to a laboratory to be tested. Pretty soon you will receive a report in which the various coals are compared as to BTU content, rate of combustion, kinds of gas, kinds of ash, and so forth. Now you are sitting at your desk preparing to make your decision. You note, however, that one coal is preferable in one attribute and another in some other quality. How are you going to decide? If you're smart," he said, "you will get the advice of a man who *knows* coal. He will be a man who has seen a lot of coal, worked with a lot of coal, made a lot of decisions about coal. He *knows* something that will help fill in the gap. Your decision will have a better chance of being right than if you did not have the benefit of this *knowledge*."

This is a simple illustration, but it makes a point. The gap is filled by a *person* who can bring a decision out of his experience. "But isn't this a conscious rational decision? Can't the gap be explained in logical terms?" one might ask.

Perhaps it can, but this is probably not the way the coal expert arrived at his decision, not wholly. The chances are that he made his decision first and developed his conscious reasoning afterward. He developed the conscious reasoning partly to check his intuitive judgment, partly because a world that makes a fetish of conscious rationality requires it.

Some light is thrown on this subject in a little book by the late U.S. Supreme Court Justice Benjamin Cardozo called *Nature of the Judicial Process*. It has a chapter on the subconscious processes of a judge. Cardozo says:

> As the years have gone by, and I have reflected more and more upon the nature of the judicial process, I have become reconciled to the uncertainty. . . . I have grown to see that the process in its highest reaches is not discovery, but creation.
>
> We like to figure to ourselves the process as coldly objective and impersonal. The law, conceived of as a real existence, dwelling apart and alone, speaks through the voices of priests and ministers, the words which they have no choice except to utter. . . . "The judges of the nation," said Montesquieu, "are only the mouths that pronounce the words of the law, inanimate beings, who can moderate neither its force nor its rigor."

At the opposite extreme are the words of the French jurist Saleilles, in his treatise *De la personnalité juridique:* "One wills at the beginning the result; one finds the principle afterwards; such is the genesis of all juridical construction.". . . I would not put the case this broadly. So sweeping a statement exaggerates the element of free volition. . . . None the less, by its very excess of emphasis, it supplies the needed corrective of an ideal of impossible objectivity.[10]

2. *Knowledge gets lost and has to be rediscovered.* How often do we make a mistake and reprove ourselves by saying, "I once knew better. How did it get away from me?"

Stefansson, the anthropologist and arctic explorer, who should know something about cold and frostbite, once told the following story.[11] Primitive people who live in the cold areas have always known, Stefansson said, that if a person gets too cold, he should take himself as quickly as he can to where it is warm. And conversely, if a person is very warm to start with, he can endure cold longer than if he was cold to start with. They "knew" this because it checked with common sense and people living in cold countries tested it with centuries of experience.

Then about 1800 a German doctor named Hahnemann invented a new medical science called homeopathy. He revived an old theory, *similia similibus curentur*—"like should be cured by like." Hippocrates and, two thousand years later, Paracelsus had both used the term. The essential tenets of homeopathy are that the cure of a disease is effected by drugs that are capable of producing in a healthy individual symptoms similar to those of the disease and that to ascertain the curative virtues of any drug, it must be "proved" on healthy persons. This medical principle flourished in a dissenting medical sect and was taught and is still being practiced to some extent. But it made few inroads on the thinking of orthodox medical people.

One place where the idea spilled over and produced a standard remedy was in the treatment of frostbite. Because snow takes on the temperature of the surrounding air, in subfreezing weather, snow is below freezing. If the temperature is low enough and if enough snow is rubbed on the cheek of a perfectly warm person, it will produce frostbite. This, said Stefansson, met the test of a homeopathic treatment, and the rubbing on of snow became the standard frostbite remedy and was widely adopted. The advocacy of this remedy stood up against the second law of thermodynamics for nearly one hundred years; that law, simply stated, holds that if two bodies of different temperatures are brought together, heat will flow from the warmer to the colder but not the other way. It is interesting to go through the file of Red Cross handbooks beginning in the 1930s when the recommendation for treating frostbite read something like this: "The frozen part should gradually be restored to its normal temperature. This should be done by vigorous and continued rubbing of the frozen part with snow or very cold water. As circulation is restored, *gradually* [italics theirs] change from ice water to cold water and finally to water at room temperature. . . . Do not use warm water until circulation is restored, as it may kill the tissues." Gradually this was modified until the present recommendation: "Firm pressure against the part by the warm hand is helpful, but rubbing with the hand or snow is definitely harmful. . . . Rubbing the injured tissue increases the risk of gangrene. . . . Bring [the person] indoors as soon as possible, give him a warm drink and quickly rewarm the part . . . that is still cold and numb by immersing it in water at body temperature (90°–100°F)." This is an interesting illustration because this particular corruption of sound knowledge by a false theory happened in one of the oldest of the professions. But it serves to remind us of the relatively recent date at which science entered the field of medicine and systematic ways of separating the more from the less true began to be used.

But Hahnemann made a contribution: he experimented with drugs and raised an effective challenge to conventional medicine. Dr. C. F. Menninger, father of our contemporaries Drs. Karl and William Menninger, received his initial medical training in a homeopathic college. His biography makes an interesting comment on the contribution of homeopathy: "Homeopathy gained in popularity because it worked, patients treated by homeopaths got well where patients treated by all alleopaths often did not. Perhaps Hahnemann was an intuitive genius who was cursed by one of the worst systems of rationalization in medical history. Without wishing to be, he was an iconoclast; he destroyed the conventional use of the *materia medica*. In doing this he did mankind a great service. People no longer died of the cure; if they died, they died of the disease."[12] In other words, conventional medical practice was so harsh and destructive that even a system based on a wild hypothesis would do better if, by chance (and this one did do it), the new treatment was gentler and interfered less with natural processes. But if Stefansson is right in his conjecture that Hahnemann's theory caused a harsh destructive method to be substituted for an effective one, in the case of the treatment of frostbite it caused sound knowledge to be lost. It took one hundred years to recover the loss, and the needless suffering in the interim cannot be calculated.

I have not used this incident of lost knowledge to disparage the medical profession. It is simply the best account I know of to illustrate a universal phenomenon—a process of "losing knowledge" that happens to all knowledge and each of us, a process that complicates the problem of knowing.

"Remember, ever remember," said Rousseau, "that ignorance has never been productive of evil, but that error alone is dangerous; and that we do not lose our way through what we do not know but through what we falsely think we know."[13]

3. *New conscious knowledge disturbs our feeling of certainty about what we know.* If we accept the premise that most of us operate from day to day with a heavy dependence on intuitive decisions, then the intrusion of new conscious knowledge may confuse us, especially if it suggests a radical change of direction.

One day, the head of a small but very successful manufacturing company came to see me on the recommendation of a mutual friend. His was a family business, in existence for about fifty years, and my caller was the grandson of the founder. At the time of his visit, about a dozen members of the family worked for the company. They all owned an interest, and they constituted the board of directors—his boss.

They were having trouble with their internal relations, and he was finding his chief executive role pretty stressful. The company had grown slowly and now employed about a thousand people. It was highly unsystematic in the way it was organized and managed. In fact, as he described it, I pictured unbelievable confusion that had become quite painful to the owners. But they were *very* successful. They made a good product, they were highly thought of, and they made a lot of money.

My caller's problem was that he had been to a business "doctor" who had made a diagnosis and had written a prescription—a "specific." The prescription was for the imposition of a conventional system of management: organizational charts, position descriptions, operating procedures, and so forth. The company didn't have any of these. But these things, the patient was assured, would reduce the pain and confusion and would make a better business.

After a brief conversation about the nature of the problem and the prescription that had been given, my caller seemed to forget about me and began a soliloquy. It was as if he held the pill in one hand and the glass of water in the other as he talked about the possible consequences of taking or not taking the pill. The dilemma was fairly simple: the pill would probably ease the pain, and that was worth something, but what about the business? There were many well-organized businesses that could not match the performance or the earnings of his company. Would this painkiller take the edge off the secret of this company's success, which my caller confessed he did not understand? This company was one of a few survivors out of hundreds in its particular field that had made a start and had failed in the course of fifty years. What did this company have that the others didn't have? How could he be sure that this secret of success was not so inextricably interwoven with the pain and confusion that the specific remedy could not discriminate? He even quoted Hamlet to the effect that he might do better to bear the ills he had than to fly to others that he knew not of.

This was an interesting look into a torturous confrontation between the urge to innovate and the secret of success.

4. *Anti-intellectualism.* The set of anti-intellectualism is the tendency to disparage people who know, to hurl epithets like "infertile egghead," and to deny that some people are better thinkers about practical problems than others. The opposite extreme, too much reliance on the expert, which is present in more authoritarian cultures, is just as damaging. But anti-intellectualism seems to be a phenomenon peculiar to mid-twentieth-century American culture. Even the so-called intellectuals sometimes appear to be anti-intellectual when dealing with questions outside their own special fields.

The pursuit of openness to knowledge and the development of the capacity for better intuitive insights is viewed as a distraction and a delay. There is the temptation to say, in effect, "I am successful; therefore, I know." Intuitive insights cannot be better than relevant stored-away knowledge and experience. Our knowledge sources and the meaning of our experience are changing constantly. Older people may be responding intuitively to knowledge and experience stored away when they were young. It may no longer be relevant. Yet there is stubborn resistance to the idea that we can all know more and learn to think better about our problems. When pressed, a characteristic response of the anti-intellectual is, "I don't want to *know* any more about the problem. I only want to know what to *do* about it."

5. *Scholastic rigidity and exclusiveness.* One of the factors complicating the problem of knowing for pursuers of strength is the restrictive bias among scientists and scholars. It shows up in the tendency, the attitude set, to reject out-of-hand knowledge that does not emerge through ways of discovering knowledge in which they are trained and with which they feel comfortable. It is, of course, asking a lot of a person to be ready

to examine knowledge from any source (especially if it raises a question about what one, in one's expertness, thinks one knows). After all, how do we really know a heresy except that the wrong person expounds it?

This is a particular problem in the social sciences. Here the knowledge sources span the gamut from rigorous quantitative research that produces little new knowledge but a lot of proof about what it does produce to history, literature, and philosophy, which are loaded with knowledge but not much proof. When one has a problem to which social science knowledge would apply, one has a real dilemma. Where does one turn? Alcoholics Anonymous is an outstanding example of an alternative (and now we have a group working with drug addicts on the same basis). Here we have a devoted group of amateurs accomplishing something significant with one of the most vexing problems of our time. Perhaps someday, trained people using the tools and knowledge of science will do as well, but at this writing, they have a way to go.

The ordinary unspecialized person who is seeking to be strong and open to helpful knowledge often finds an exasperating dilemma: scholastic rigidity among those devoted to the pursuit of knowledge, presumably his or her servants. Each specialized branch of science and knowledge (and there seem to be new ones added almost every day) is tending more and more to focus its communication and its listening on those who approach knowledge in a particular way. One of the most discouraging moments I've had in recent years was when a professor in a field of knowledge of immense importance to ordinary living, a man whose scholarly life is devoted to questions in which all pursuers of strength are keenly interested, told me that his forthcoming book, which he explained to me most lucidly, would be written in a professional jargon so that it would be understood only by highly specialized scholars like himself. He is a man who is perfectly capable of stating his ideas with sufficient precision to meet the requirements of scholarly rigor and still be understood by the general reader. But he chose not to do so.

Who is to speak to general readers so that they can know what they need to know to be strong?

The foregoing is not intended as a diatribe against scholarship. The point is that restrictive biases are everywhere, and scholars are no exception. Biases block openness to knowledge in the scholar as well as in the man in the street, and they have a common denominator, a block that limits the development of the man and his effectiveness. I know that elaborate defenses can be made for these restrictive biases. Whether it is the manager who says, "I don't want to understand more about the problem, I only want to know what to do about it," or whether it is the scholar who says, "I have some important new knowledge for humankind, but I will communicate it only to scholars like myself," I have listened to the defenses of these positions (and a lot of others), and they are all spurious.

My own private amateur diagnosis is that some aspects of these defenses may be traced to arrogance or conformity, which are deep in human nature and are not unique to our time; but the major justification for these defenses seems to be something new. I believe it is a reaction to a pervasive frustration to which few people reading this book are immune.

We in mid-twentieth-century America have achieved the highest level of material existence we know anything about. We have more knowledge and more facilities for producing and testing new knowledge than people have ever had before. We operate economic and social units that are larger and more complicated than anything of which we have a record. In short, we live in an amazing period of historical development. Yet on all sides we are threatened by evidences of moral decay, by the depletion of natural resources, by the contamination of the air we breathe and the food we eat, and by threats to all existence of a magnitude never before faced by people on this earth.

Thoughtful people, good people with a spontaneous urge to be constructive do not see sufficient meaning in their existence to move with assurance, so they hide behind some self-justifying position that protects them. This is frustrating, and should be.

Fortunately, there is no panacea, no easy way out. The frustration must be resolved, and doing so is not easy.

If my amateur diagnosis is correct, if anti-intellectualism and scholastic rigidity and exclusiveness are reactions to frustration, what is the motive that is being blocked, and what is blocking it? I believe that the motive is that every man and woman has a destiny, a purpose. The block is that he or she has lost contact with it, and pride in material and intellectual achievements stands in the way of recovering contact.

Many have tried and are still trying to state this goal, to define our destiny. Emerson in his grand style came about as close as anybody to putting it in words in the closing lines of his essay "The Uses of Great Men." "The destiny of organized nature is amelioration," he said, "and who can tell its limits? It is for man to tame the chaos; on every side, whilst he lives, to scatter the seeds of science and of song, that climate, corn, animals, men may be milder, and the germs of love and benefit may be multiplied."[14]

Poets, philosophers, and prophets have been stating and restating the big dream, the overriding purpose, the destiny of humans since our earliest records. But the explosion of knowledge in this century has overwhelmed us. We know so much and are so busy developing new knowledge and discrediting old knowledge that we have lost sight of our goal, so we won't get hold of what we need to be reasonably right on the ordinary problems of everyday living. With all of our knowledge and all of our learned people, closedness to knowledge is the common malady of us all.

6

THE PRACTICE OF OPENNESS

AT THE OUTSET OF CHAPTER 5, I made a distinction between knowing a lot and being open to knowledge. It is important to know some things that one can get by reading, listening, reasoning, and remembering. But these won't take one all the way when the next occasion for a decision presents itself. They may not, in fact, take one very far. Soaking up a lot of knowledge to be remembered is not the best preparation for wide-ranging decision making.

I realize that by taking this position I am laying myself open to the question, "Then why are you writing this book?"

I was once asked a similar question when I was addressing an assembly of managers on the subject of communication in business. I was developing with some emphasis the point that a person really cannot "tell" another person anything important when a gruff voice spoke up from the deep recesses of the auditorium: "Then what are you doing up there talking?" he boomed.

When the laughter subsided, I conceded that the man had a point. But then I gave this explanation of my position: "What I am saying now is said with the intent that it will not mean much to you unless you respond with your own thinking as if this were a dialogue in which you have a responsibility at least equal to mine. Your *response* is what is important to you, not what I say."

I feel that way about this book. I have tried to say some things about my own experience, observations, and beliefs that will stimulate you to reexamine your own experiences and beliefs. Furthermore, I have a few suggestions of things to try that even if tried and rejected as not useful may add some perspective on your own experience. As an aspect of *strength*, only your knowledge of your own experience will be of much help.

Here are a few things to try that may help the opening process.

Think of your unconscious mind as a well. Let the communication to which you are exposed drop into the well, uncensored by logic or criticism. Listen to the splash, the intuitive response; let it happen, let the response form itself, don't labor it. Judge it afterward.

Listen to what is really said; look at what is really there. If you don't, you can't properly conceptualize what must be dealt with. We don't see or hear or conceptualize adequately until we let the signal speak directly to the below-the-waterline knowledge.

Learn to let the sense of the total situation speak first; set the critical-analytical apparatus in operation later. Dr. Karl Stern, in his biography, *The Pillar of Fire,* tells of his greatest teacher in Germany, Dr. Volhard, who "claimed to be able to diagnose any, even the most complicated type of valvular lesion of the heart, without even touching the patient. . . . This was no idle boast. He trained us systematically to observe. He never gave any form of didactic lectures (you can learn all this from books) but confronted us with the patient at the beginning of the hour. It was amazing how much one could see without examining the patient, or without knowing anything about the history. . . . When I think of such teachers as Volhard, I seem to know the answer to the problems of academic education."[15] The theory of this kind of teaching is that if the student becomes preoccupied with the mechanical and analytical procedures before learning to *see*, he will never learn to see. The analytical wheels spinning will get in the way.

One must learn to shut the noise off the circuit so the *total* knowledge available can be seen and heard. My father was a very intelligent man but with little formal education or status ambition. He was apprenticed as a machinist at an early age and worked at that vocation most of his life. By the time I was old enough to be interested in his work, he had developed the reputation in my hometown as the local expert on stationary steam engines. This was before individual electric motor drives were common on factory machines. All local factories had steam engines, usually large ones that drove a number of machines through overhead shafts and belts.

The custom was for the custodian of an ailing engine to seek out my father on a Sunday when he was free from his regular work and persuade him to come and look at the ailing engine. Frequently, I went along.

Two of these visits I recall vividly. One was to a factory that had bought a new steam pump, a rather small, simple engine that had been installed without the benefit of expert help. The complaint was that it wouldn't run at all, a rather uncommon condition for a steam engine. Usually, a steam engine that is not a total wreck will make some sort of gesture when the steam is turned on. But not this engine; it made no response at all.

I have a clear recollection of my father walking up to the engine and standing there looking. Several of the men from this factory were there chattering away about all of the things they had done to try to make this engine run. I don't think father was listening; at least he didn't respond. He had cleared the noise off the circuit. The problem was in the engine, not in all of this talk. He was attending to the engine with great concentration. I believe this was what was going on: the "problem" of the sick engine was communicating directly with his considerable experience with steam engines. The communication was going through, uncensored by logic—pure basic communication.

After what seemed to me a long time of silent looking, probably three or four minutes, and without making a move—he seemed almost to be in a trance—he said, "You know, unless somebody has invented a revolutionary new kind of engine the like of which I have never seen, this is the first engine I ever saw that had a bigger intake pipe than its exhaust pipe." The fellows who set up this engine had simply put the live steam into the wrong end of the engine.

The second experience of this kind that I recall clearly was quite different. This was at a paper mill that made wide, heavy, brown wrapping paper. It was a huge long mill driven by a big engine with a prodigious flywheel. This engine performed satisfactorily when running at normal speed driving the mill, but whenever the mill was being closed down or started up, the engine developed a terrific vibration and gave some signs of shaking itself loose from its moorings.

Again, Father just walked in and looked at the engine and didn't seem to listen to all of the talk about its bad behavior and all that had been done to try to correct it. Pretty soon he said, "Start her up." Then, "Close her down." Both times there was a frightful racket. Then he asked, "Have you got a sledge?" A sledgehammer was produced, and he crawled in beside the big flywheel and gave the keys that locked the flywheel to its shaft a few sharp raps with the sledge.

He crawled out and said, "Start her up," and she purred. No vibration. This huge flywheel had worked itself loose from its shaft after long use. In starting and stopping, it would slip on the shaft—ever so little, but enough to give the place a good shaking up.

It could be said that my father had the advantage that all consultants have. He wasn't trapped by the previous errors or the blind spots that had developed in the people who worked intimately with these engines. Nor did he have such problems with the engines he managed personally. He had wide knowledge about and real empathy with steam engines. I cannot, of course, say with certainty what kind of mental process was operating while he stood silently looking at a sick engine. There may have been a precise checklist in his mind that he was running through consciously. But I doubt that this was the case. It seems more likely that he had developed the habit of looking at what was really there in a way that permitted the total situation to speak directly to his unconscious fund of knowledge while he kept the circuit clear for an intuitive response.

I have had the experience of walking across a large factory floor with a perceptive manager. Hundreds of people were performing many complicated tasks. There were no signals perceptible to me that all was not well. After a five-minute quick tour with no stops for the detailed examination of anything, the manager went to his office, summoned an aide, and gave directions that revealed that in those five minutes, he had made a large synthesis of the current state of affairs on that factory floor that the careful examination of a sheaf of statistical reports would not have revealed. Against his extensive background of experience, buttressed with a good sharp mind, he was able quickly and accurately to perceive and conceptualize the total situation.

I believe that this quality can be developed by most intelligent persons. Just practice looking, listening, smelling, feeling while keeping the analytical apparatus quiet—keeping the noise off the circuit. When one reaches the profound conclusion that much intellection is just noise and practices dispensing with it at appropriate times, one is well on the way to sharpening perception. This may call for an occasional venture as a researcher in which a person makes a special mission to find out about something that is important to him—not from libraries but from prime sources.

That great line from the prayer of Saint Francis, "Grant that I may seek not so much to be understood as to understand," suggests something. It suggests that deep in the set of the normal human temperament is the tendency to broadcast rather than to receive. We would rather talk than listen, rather put out than take in. This gets in the way of openness to knowledge. To be open, one needs first to accept that unless one has made a conscious effort to learn to listen, one probably isn't a good listener. Also, unless someone else has observed and reported on our communication habits, we probably don't know whether we listen or not.

Listening might be defined as an attitude toward other people and what they are attempting to express. It begins with attention, both the outward manifestation and the inward alertness. It includes constructive responses that help the other person express both thoughts and feelings. The good listener has trained his or her memory to retain what is expressed and to refrain from piecemeal value judgments. The good listener remains in a position to assess the relationship among facts, opinions, attitudes, and feelings being expressed and is therefore able to respond to the total expression of the other person. The good listener tries to hear everything that is said, not just what the listener expects or wants to hear. Listening, so defined, is a discipline that improves face-to-face relations; it saves time in the process of communicating, and it gives the listener a better grasp of what other people have to tell him and how they feel about what they are saying. And good listening communicates something that is universally good: attentiveness.

Everyone who aspires to *strength* should consciously practice listening, regularly. Every week, set aside an hour to listen to somebody who might have something to say that will be of interest. It should be conscious practice in which all of the impulses to argue, inform, judge, and "straighten out" the other person are denied. Every response should be calculated to reflect interest, understanding, seeking for more knowledge. Practice listening for brief periods, too. Just thirty seconds of concentrated listening may make the difference between understanding and not understanding something important.

One day about a year ago, a doctor, a professor from one of our medical schools, came to my office with a most interesting problem. His school had made a study of doctors in action. Researchers in white coats had posed as assistants to practicing doctors while carefully observing what went on. One of the conclusions in the study was that an important lack in many doctors impaired their diagnoses and harmed their relations with their patients: they didn't listen to the patient, didn't listen to what they had to say about their symptoms. This lack was judged important enough that the decision had been made to incorporate formal training in listening into the medical school curriculum. Some of the researchers had heard that I had some interest in teaching people to listen, and they wanted to know what my experience could contribute to their effort. Their study of doctors in action gives the best evidence I have seen of what a critical skill listening is in all human relations. And no one can assume that he or she has the listening skill unless a competent judge has watched that person in action and has said so. Listening skill is not a sequitur to any other skill I know about. One may be superb in every other aspect of one's operation but this one and not know about it. And the inability to listen may be the most costly of the human relations skills to be without.

Teach. Every pursuer of openness should regularly prepare to teach something to somebody. Willing students aren't hard to find if one is prepared to teach something of interest.

Act on insights. Unless one trusts intuitive insights, one doesn't get them. Unless insights are acted on, they don't speak with assurance. This may give one the reputation of being impulsive. But all creative people are impulsive. Only highly rational people are not impulsive. One can't be everything; if openness as a path to *strength* is an important goal, then one had better regard the highly rational with a jaundiced eye.

However, since rational people are numerous and need to be taken into account, open, creative people need to learn to rationalize. Intuitive insights need to be supported, after the fact, with sound reasoning. This not only tests the validity of the insight but also helps give credence to intuitive insight in a world that likes to think it is wholly rational.

Develop respect for thinkers. Try to know at least one. This doesn't have to be an Einstein or a person of great repute. But it should be someone who has practiced openness for a long enough time that the acquaintanceship will be a source of stimulation.

Learn to withdraw and return. One of the great stories from the New Testament gives the account of the mob bringing the woman taken in adultery and saying to Jesus that the law says she should be stoned and asking, what does *he* say? He doesn't say anything for a while. He sits writing in the sand. I like to think of this as a *withdrawal* from the stress of the incident while he listens to the inner voice of inspiration. Then he *returns* to make that tremendous response: "Let him who is without sin among you cast the first stone." Could any decision, any response, have been more right than that?

Finally, the pursuit of openness requires that one be alert to relevance. The cultivation of the intuitive, which is what openness is about, leads one close to the line that separates reality from unreality. If one is too cautious about approaching this line, one cuts short the possibility of optimum use of available resources. If one ventures over the line often or for long, the search is nullified.

Just as the navigator keeps a sharp eye on the signs that mark the navigable channel, so the pursuer of *strength* through openness keeps a sharp eye on the markers that establish relevance in the real world.

7

THE FUTURE IS NOW

A RECENT HEADLINE STORY was the admission by a prominent citizen that a public action of his was a serious error. This action had been widely reported and condemned. The man, his associates, and his work were hurt. "I did not foresee the consequences of my involvement," he said.

So often life is like that. The act is judged wrong by the course of subsequent events. The wrong was apparent at the time of the action; it was spelled out in the act itself. But perhaps it was only a feeble signal at that time. However, when the chain reaction of consequences had run its course, the signal was deafening. In practical affairs, where few actions are wholly right, the test of the consequences, through foresight, is crucially important.

Speaking of the job of a prince, Niccolò Machiavelli had this to say about the importance of foresight: "Thus it happens in matters of state; for knowing afar off (which it is only given a prudent man to do) the evils that are brewing, they are easily cured. But when, for want of such knowledge, they are allowed to grow so that everyone can recognize them, there is no longer any remedy to be found."

The "lead" that a leader has—and I mean the true leader, whose strength is in his personal capacity and not in his power—is probably what Machiavelli was talking about. Because this "is only given a prudent man to do," other things are likely to be equal.

One would not give much to the legendary French revolutionary who was attending a soirée when he heard a commotion in the street. With a quick glance out the window, he grabbed his cane and his beret and rushed for the door, shouting, "The mob is in the street. I must find out where it is going because I am its leader!"

We live under the notion that *now* is an infinitesimally small fragment of time by the clock, that what has gone before is history about which we may have some memory, and that the future is an indefinite space out ahead about which we know nothing. We can project certain trends—but beyond this we know nothing.

This view may be all right for the makers of clocks and other literal-minded people, but for those who seek to build strength, it is not enough.

Now, for some people, may be a fairly wide span of clock time. It may include some of yesterday and some of tomorrow. This idea may be disconcerting to people who have a heavy investment in certain kinds of order. But so far as the human mind is concerned, our prevailing concept of time is a *convention,* not an immutable law, and we are entitled to make any other assumptions if they will serve us better. We know that in dreams, elaborate events are consummated in a short period of clock time and that under the influence of certain drugs, the human mind, without hallucinating, will in some cases stretch the instant of present time to a phenomenal extent.

So for the pursuers of strength, we will choose the assumption that it is possible for *now* to encompass much of what is conventionally called the future. Perception of the future will depend on awareness just as perceiving *now,* as conventionally viewed, also depends on awareness. Awareness varies among individuals and is developable.

Dr. Paul W. Pruyser, writing in the *Hibbert Journal* on the idea of destiny, has this to say about what goals do for us:

> [A] characteristic of goals is that they seem stretched out in
> time before the person and are also experienced as here and

74

now due to the effort with which they are approached. Tasks and goals are not in the past; their present being is in the mode of potentiality and their actualization is eagerly awaited. Faced with a goal, the person brings as it were the future into the present by formulating the goal in terms of a task which is with him here and now, and which demands his concentrated attention. One "meets" a task by searching for a solution, which means that one is confronted with it and contemporaneous with it.[16]

As with knowledge, one carries the systematic handling of objective data as far as it will go. Weather, temperature, sea level, in fact all natural phenomena that are cyclical or where experience suggests certain sequences provide the conscious rational mind with a basis for prediction. But other events, some human events, are not so predictable by our present statistical methods. Our methods will no doubt improve. But at best they will give us only a limited probability, and we may need more than that to be strong. So, as with knowledge, we fill in the gap between what conscious rational knowledge gives us and what we need to know.

Foresight, filling in the gaps, could probably be explained by natural law if we knew enough about it. Certain people have a gift of prescience, but we are not concerned here with gifts of this sort; rather we are concerned with what anybody who is disposed to make the effort can do to improve his grasp of the future.

A suggested hypothesis is that the computer that is part of the unconscious mind can do some fantastic things in the way of constructing a concept of the future. It can do a trend prediction job, too, except that as contrasted with the statistician, this computer can conjure with the subjective and the imponderable as well as with the objective and the quantitative.

Probably we don't *foresee* events; by our efforts, we bring the future into the present. This is partly a result of an attitude; we see it that way, we are overtaken by the feeling that present time is a wider span than the click of the camera shutter.

75

How wide? I see this as a matter of cultivation. What kind of cultivation?

One can build one's awareness of the connecting links that bind a wide span of clock time together. These are the progressing events that are moving from the past into present time and going on into the future. One *must* have a sense of history to see this movement. This is one of the anti-intellectual's big blind spots: *he doesn't want to look at history.* In his view, to look at history is to look back. "We believe in progress; we only look forward." This is a serious block, to reject what is behind the present moment because it is gone.

Awareness that comprehends the future views time as a process. We are involved in a large matrix of events. A friend once said of his four-year-old son's egocentricity, "His world is a six-foot sphere. He's in the center of it, and he moves it around with him." We tend to think of maturation as the shedding of the youthful egocentricity. A better view would be to think of growth as a process of mutation in which one's view of the world changes from the simple childhood world of things and immediate persons to a vast complex of events, a limitless sphere of actions, ideas, feelings. But each one of us can still see ourself at the center of our own unique world. Our awareness spans all directions all of the time.

This gives us a cue: to bring the future (and the past) into the present and live as if all is *now* requires for most of us convention-bound people some sort of disorientation process to break us away from the rigidity of the clock time convention.

There is a way to work at this. When one has learned by practice to clear the noise off the circuit, to suspend intellection *and* imagination and attend only to sensory impressions, one can allow a new view to intrude into this field of awareness. This is the view of the self as a unique, precious, sentient being, located at the center of this limitless sphere of actions, ideas, feelings, influencing and being influenced by it in a very special way, unlike that of any other being that ever lived. The most wonderful society I can imagine would be one with the infinite variety of human nature we now have but leavened by a few who have substantially achieved this view of themselves and who are effective in leading the rest of us to achieve as much of it as we can.

As a help in the *disorientation* process, one might practice thinking regardless of the consequences. One must be willing to confront and reflect on the full range of thought that the mind can produce. Constricted thinking can only *answer* questions; the comprehensive view of life as process can only be within the framework of questions *asked*. If I have a problem, if I've reached a block, my first stance should be, What questions can I ask about it? Instead of getting into a state of tension trying to get the answer from what I already "know" (which is probably insufficient, or I wouldn't be blocked), it seems a better course to ask questions. Questions define what is not known. This opens up the search.

To bring both past and future into the present, one should have a hypothesis about the stages of one's own development. Old age, death, the loss of those near and dear should be encompassed in this view of the self, at least by the time one has reached the middle years.

Truth there may be, but we mortals, at best, perceive it dimly, as through a glass darkly. The tenuousness of our knowledge about what we call the future does not stand in such contrast when we accept that all we perceive is tenuous. Dogmatic people, in the present, are usually dogmatic about the future—and wrong.

It has been said that if the means are right, the ends will also be right. The future is being made by the means being used today. If one will study the means being used by oneself and one's contemporaries, the shape of the future will be more apparent.

Meditative time is important, time when the intellectual sound track is clear and the visual screen is blank. Then sensory perception is sharp and the image of the self is paramount. This need not be a large block of time in which one is withdrawn from the world. The real art of meditation is to learn to manage it amid the tumult. Some of the most valuable creative insights come when, in the heat of the contention of the work of the world, one can mange to withdraw (and not get caught napping) so that the total resources of the mind can function. One must learn to receive inspiration under stress because the circumstances of most important decisions that require a view of the future are stressful for everybody, regardless of status or intellect.

The life of Thomas Jefferson is as good an example as one could want of foresight in action. The young Jefferson had drafted the Declaration of Independence, the war was on, and he was world-famous. The obvious commonsense course for him was to assume a vital role to help win the war. He could have had any spot he wanted in the military, in diplomacy, or in the central government. He was importuned on all sides to take some responsible post. But he rejected them all. He went back to Virginia to undertake work of vastly greater importance than anything he could have contributed to the war. Except for the defense of Virginia, he had no further part in the war.

His position, which he kept to himself because he could not show his hand, was that the war would ultimately be won; there would be a new nation with a new government, and that nation would need new law; he would develop that law by getting it enacted, statute by statute, in the state of Virginia while the war was being fought. The government of Virginia was in a state of flux, and it offered an ideal laboratory for developing a new system of law. This became Jefferson's mission until 1784. In terms of his contribution to the new nation, this period may have been his greatest. Its significance far outranks the earlier period when the Declaration was written or the later period when he reentered politics and became president. Furthermore, this was his great creative period and the period of his greatest personal effectiveness. It was at this time that his whole life was in the best balance—he was following the leadings of his own foresight.

In this period, he wrote an impressive array of new statutes and proceeded with great vigor to get them enacted into law. Five major areas concerned him: the holding and disposition of land, religious freedom and the separation of church and state, a humane criminal code, slavery, and education. He was not successful in getting all of his more than one hundred statutes enacted during this period, but for the next hundred years, this file of Jefferson's statutes was a rich source of new legislation. When the new nation was born, here awaiting it was a tested and thoroughly debated framework of new law. It is one of the really remarkable examples of bringing the future into the present by an individual setting a goal and working with great vigor to bring it into being.

But the greatest foresight, the most difficult and most exciting, is the influence one wields on the future by helping the growth of people who will be in commanding positions in the next generation. One cannot bind the future to one's own wisdom. By the time any one of us has crystallized his or her wisdom so that something could be bound to it, it is out of date. Crystallized wisdom is not the essence anyhow. The character of our society and the institutions in it cannot with safety be bound to any currently held ideas, nor can they be altered radically to conform to any fixed idea of what they ought to be in the future. But the future *can* be radically altered by the kinds of people now being prepared for the future.

Let us return for a moment to Jefferson and a story of my own. When my son was about fifteen, the family was touring historical Virginia. In Williamsburg, as we were walking into a particular house, one of those that had survived from colonial times, I said, "This is where Thomas Jefferson was born." My son, who knew his history, promptly challenged me: "Dad, what's the matter with you? Jefferson was born on the other side of the state at Monticello. We're going to visit there later."

"Yes," I conceded, "that is where the baby Thomas Jefferson was brought into the world. But here is where the Jefferson of history was born. Here George Wythe lived. As a young man,

Jefferson studied law with Wythe and lived with him in this house. Wythe was a fellow legislator during Jefferson's most creative period—when he was writing the new law of Virginia. The influence of George Wythe in maturing the Jefferson of history was incalculable, much greater than that of his parents. Without this timely influence, Thomas Jefferson might have been Virginia scholar and country gentleman and no more. Everything we know about him suggests that this was his natural bent. His public conscience came from George Wythe. That's why I say that Jefferson was born here, in George Wythe's house."

Somebody needs to do for young people today what George Wythe did for Thomas Jefferson. Our very best influence needs to be brought to bear on our potentially best young people in the formative years from sixteen to twenty-five when the crisis of identity is being met, when the big questions—Who am I? What am I? What is my destiny?—are being confronted.

Somebody needs to paint the big dream, to give our age a goal that will lift the eyes of young people off the ground and make them want to stretch their horizons.

The future is being made now. The future *is* now!

8

ENTHEOS AND GROWTH

THE WORD *entheos* and its companion *enthusiasm* have had an interesting history in English. Making their appearance in literature at about the same time, the late sixteenth century, they come from the same roots—*en,* "possessed of," and *theos,* "spirit." But their meanings have been quite different. *Entheos* means possessed by the spirit in a positive constructive sense. *Enthusiasm* until quite recent times meant the corruption or perversion of entheos. Entheos was the real thing; enthusiasm, its imitator or destroyer. Enthusiasm today is the less profound, the more superficial. Entheos is the essence, the power actuating the person who is inspired.

I choose the word *entheos* with this connotation because to be strong in the times we live in—to choose the right aim and to pursue that aim responsibly over a long period of time—one must have inspiration backed by power.

Inspiration and *power* are emotionally charged words. But *strength* is not passive; it needs an emotional charge! That is why I believe we must recapture *entheos* as an important word in the common vocabulary.

Entheos is an imperative if the ethical obligation to develop *strength* is accepted—if it is accepted as a prime concern over the adult life span. To accept this as a binding ethic when society at large does not accept it calls for a sustained inner prompting—entheos. New ethics evolve not from idealistic pronouncements but because determined individuals practice them, in opposition to the prevailing sentiments of society if necessary, and demonstrate their validity.

But there are other reasons why the sustaining power of entheos is important to all who will keep their heads above water in the times we live in. First, the rewards and satisfactions for those who seek to wield any kind of influence are cyclical. Everybody who is enterprising, who is pursuing some sort of goal, has ups and downs. When one is down, in the doghouse, as we all are once in a while, one needs sustenance, something to help muster one's own resources. This calls for entheos.

Then there is the uncertainty of decision making—seldom enough data or enough time. Yet a decision must be made, the possibility of error must be faced, one must suffer the consequences of error if one is wrong and bounce back prepared to do it all over again under the same conditions. This also calls for entheos.

Further, everyone is faced with the conflict between the necessity to conform and the imperative to maintain one's own unique individuality and integrity of personality. The forces that would destroy the integrity of personality are sometimes powerful and pervasive. With skillful use of modern psychological knowledge, the pressure to break a person can be extreme. When trapped, people usually stand without the aid and comfort of their fellows. If they are to survive, they too must have entheos.

Entheos is seen as a basic spiritual essence. It is the sustaining force that holds one together under stress. It is the support to venturesome risk-taking action. It provides the prod of conscience that keeps one open to knowledge when the urge to be comfortable would close the door. It provides a linking concept by which whatever religious beliefs one has are kept in contact with one's attitudes and actions in the world of practical affairs. It nurtures a powerful concept of the self.

Entheos does not emerge in response to external incentives. In fact, it may persist where incentives operate to destroy it. The individual cannot will it. All that can be willed is the search, and there is no pattern for the search. But some tests are suggested, some indicators that may be misleading and some that may point to the sound growth of entheos.

First, some misleading indicators:

Status or material success. One may be conspicuously successful and at the same time may be destroying oneself and everything that is personally important. One might achieve the status of material success and entheos would flourish too. But the former would not be a valid indicator that the latter was present.

Social success. It may be more comfortable to be with the nongrowth people. They may be disposed to like each other's company better. One may bubble with enthusiasm in the less profound sense, one may be bound with great loyalty to a closely knit group in a worthy cause, and still entheos may not be an important factor in one's life.

Family success. One may enjoy the finest of family relationships and be cited as a model, yet nothing deep may be stirring that would suggest entheos.

Busyness. Of the possible misleading indicators, this is one of the most difficult to penetrate. It is illustrated in a few sentences in a story from the New Testament:

> Now as they went on their way, he entered a village; and a woman named Martha received him into her house. And she had a sister called Mary, who sat at the Lord's feet and listened to his teaching. But Martha was distracted with much serving; and she went to him and said, "Lord, do you not care that my sister has left me to serve alone? Tell her then to help me."
>
> But the Lord answered her, "Martha, Martha, you are anxious and troubled about many things; one thing is needful. Mary has chosen the good portion, which shall not be taken away from her."[17]

Viewing this story as mythical symbolism, a great deal of wisdom is communicated about the common human problem among people of good motives—compulsive busyness. Superficially viewed, Jesus' rebuke of Martha is an unkind cut at one who is doing the work of preparing a meal. Carefully examined, it is *much* serving—*unnecessary* busyness—that is being criticized. Mary has *chosen* the better part. By implication, Martha has chosen to be busy so as to avoid involvement in spiritual teaching. Also, by implication, Martha resents Mary's interest in matters of the spirit.

This story is relevant to much of the busyness that we see around us every day—compulsive busyness. Somebody is avoiding something. Beneath the surface, there is a drive to avoid the implications of growth. Busyness is often like a siren, beckoning to distract one from pursuits that would take one to greater depths of experience. It can involve us in the most worthy of good works only to distract us from entheos and deny us the privilege of being really useful.

These four—status and material success, social success, family success, and busyness—are common misleading indicators of the growth of entheos. Each can be a worthy state of achievement. In combination, they can be impressive. But an abundance of all four can cause entheos to be stifled.

I was going over this ground with a group of businessmen one day when I noticed that the status man in the group had dropped his head and tears had come into his eyes. I had spoken to his condition.

Now, what of some valid tests of growth of entheos?

First, two paradoxes. The first is concurrent satisfaction and dissatisfaction with the status quo. One is effective in what one is involved in and feels constructive in it and at the same time has an urge to be on with the search that will lead to new levels—and is working at that. The second is a concurrent feeling of broadening responsibilities and centering down. One's outlook and undertakings are expanding while at the same time one is more clearly formulating "this one thing will I do."

There is a growing sense of overriding purpose in all that is undertaken. Purpose becomes pervasive in all thinking. It is not an obsession. It quiets and enriches all of thought.

Interests are changing, both in pattern and in depth. Older, shallower ones drop away; new, deeper ones replace them.

The difference between the outside and the inside images of the self shrinks. One becomes willing to be seen more as one is.

One becomes more conscious of the good use of time and more bothered by the waste of time and is better able to put first things first.

Whatever one's work is, one has a growing sense of achieving basic personal goals through it. Those greener pastures on the other side of the fence are not so attractive.

All of life becomes more unified. All aspects of it seem more to reinforce one another.

There is a developing view of people. All people are seen more worthy of being trusted and believed in and are seen less as beings to be used, competed with, or judged.

The growth search for entheos is probably not to be expected among persons who still see themselves as "on the make" in our kind of striving, and the striver will have difficulty keeping these two pursuits separate. One's sun does not need to have set before the growth search begins, but status and material striving needs must definitely have taken a permanent secondary place.

But neither can the growth search be left for old age and retirement. In fact, one defers it beyond age forty at one's peril. Erik Erikson has called our attention to the generativity versus stagnation crisis that comes in this age range. One cannot make the wrong choice at this point and hope to recover growth initiative with ease.

The great opportunity, though, is to discover in one's mature years an unrealized growth potential: growth *not* in terms of external achievement but in terms of the things that are important in the quiet hours when one is alone with oneself; growth in terms of the capacity for serenity in a world of confusion and conflict, a new kind of inner stamina, a new kind of exportable resource as youthful prowess drops away.

But in this search, one does not—one cannot—stand alone. A positive step that every pursuer of *strength* should take is to have the humility (and the good sense) to seek a confidant, someone with whom one shares the problems of the search. I have come to feel that this is a most urgent necessity among my contemporaries. I also believe that until one takes this step, the urge to develop *strength* has not taken hold—not in a fundamental way.

This is not the usual kind of personal relationship. But then, *strength* as discussed in these pages is not the usual kind of human attribute. What is suggested here is that the seeker after *strength* should reach for an unusual level of relationship with at least one person. It would mean the kind of friendship that few people have; it would be deep, and it would be durable. Out of this relationship would come a kind of perspective on oneself, without which *no one* can know that his development is sound. It would mean a dependable resource to check knowledge, to stimulate foresight, and to nourish entheos.

What kind of person should a confidant be? He or she needn't (probably shouldn't in most cases) be a professional counselor. The confidant should be a mature, sensible, congenial person (not a perfect person—there aren't any of these). Some of the tests I would apply would be these:

> Does the confidant have an unconditional positive regard for me?
>
> Does the confidant have an empathic understanding of my feelings, frustrations, aspirations, and so on?
>
> Does the confidant have the experience to comprehend the complexities of the situations in which I am involved, and is he intellectually sharp enough and responsible enough to require that I make my very best representation of my situation as I see it?

> Can the confidant communicate his understanding of
> my situation to me in such a way that I can understand it
> better myself?

One should not look to the confidant for answers to any of the basic questions that one might ask about oneself. The confidant will help in the opening of awareness. The relationship will also serve to check the rightness of one's thinking. Much of the benefit will come from requiring a person to organize his or her own thinking from time to time in order to present it to an informed listener. The wisdom supplied by the confidant ought not to be the main purpose of the relationship.

The confidant relationship is a difficult idea for people who are attracted by the idea that they should grow in *strength*. Part of the resistance stems from the belief that if a person is to be strong, he or she must be self-reliant and self-sufficient. One should make it on one's own or not at all. This is a sound view about the action phases of *strength*. But in the preparation phases, this is not so. There are things that the detached and interested person can see about my ways of thinking and working that I sometimes cannot see.

A classical example of what the detached and interested person can see is in the eighteenth chapter of the book of Exodus. Jethro, father-in-law of Moses, had come to visit.

> On the morrow Moses sat to judge the people, and the people stood about Moses from morning till evening. When Jethro saw all that Moses was doing for the people, he said, "What is this that you are doing for the people? Why do you sit alone, and all the people stand about you from morning till evening?" And Moses said to Jethro, "Because the people come to me to inquire of God; when they have a dispute they come to me and I decide between a man and his neighbor and I make them know the statutes of God and his decision."

Jethro said to him, "What you are doing is not good. You and the people with you will wear yourselves out, for the thing is too heavy for you; you are not able to perform it alone. Listen now to my voice and I will give you counsel, and God be with you.

"You, Moses, shall represent the people before God, and bring their case to God; and you shall teach them the statutes and the decisions, and make them know the way they must walk and what they must do. Moreover, choose able people from all the people, such as fear God, men who are trustworthy and who hate a bribe; and place such men over the people as rulers of thousands, of hundreds, of fifties, of tens. And let them judge the people at all times; every great matter they shall bring to you, and any small matter they shall decide themselves so it will be easier for you, and they will bear the burden with you."[18]

The account says that Moses acted on the advice and that Jethro "went his way into his own land."

This is an interesting account. Jethro is the first management consultant on record and made the first formal statement of organization theory. Incidentally, not much basic organization theory has been added to this statement.

From this account we do not see Jethro functioning as a confidant in the full sense described here. But we do see his perceptiveness in noting an important weakness and making a suggestion as to how Moses could better organize to do his work. Moses, buried in detail, apparently could not see this for himself.

I give this example mainly to illustrate what the detached but interested person can do for a friend who is involved in important affairs. I also give it to show how far back in our heritage this idea goes.

As I have discussed this idea with contemporaries who also carry heavy burdens, I encounter another objection: Where, they ask, is the person who is capable of doing this for me, whom I would trust and who would *want* to do this on a non-professional (and hence unpaid) basis?

My answer has been, if this is a relationship you would really like to have, for your own benefit, then your best first step is to prepare yourself to perform this service well for somebody else. An effective confidant role is not a natural gift for many people. But it can be learned, and the learning itself may be a rewarding experience. Again I quote Saint Francis: "It is in giving that we receive."

9

PURPOSE AND LAUGHTER

WHAT ARE YOU TRYING TO DO? Of all the questions one mortal might ask another, this one is the most difficult to answer. This is the one question that is equally difficult for the humble peasant and the greatest mind that ever lived. The energetic doer of good works, the person of high principles, has just as much trouble with it as the indolent, the slothful, and the unprincipled. One person may be more articulate in answering it than another. One answer may resonate better with the current conventional view of how the question ought to be answered. But the second question, "What does your answer mean?" would likely leave the articulate person in greater trouble than the one who simply said, "I don't know" in the first place.

Walt Whitman had a few words to say about this:

> All parts away for the progress of souls;
> Of the progress of souls of men and women
> along the grand roads of the universe, all other
> progress is the needed emblem and sustenance.
> They go! They go! I know that they go,
> but I know not where they go;
> But I know that they go toward the best—
> toward something great.[19]

I think that he is saying that we cannot apprehend the ultimate, not with the knowledge that can be brought within any rational focus. But we "know" that it is the best, the great, the good, and by this we mean a perfection beyond our comprehension or attainment. We "know" it because we have postulated it and embraced it as faith; faith, as Dean Inge defined it—the choice of the nobler hypothesis.[20]

What *we* deal with is the needed emblem and sustenance, the symbol and the essence. These we can comprehend in an interior way; but even these lose much of their meaning when we tempt to bring them within the arbitrary structure of language so that we can talk about them. Only the poets seem able to deal with them, and they do it well only when they move at a level that is as abstract as music.

This suggests that in the area of ultimate purpose and its meaning, each person stands alone. Comradeship, fellowship, the confidant with whom one communicates only through language—these go with one to a point. But beyond that point, when one reaches for some contact with ultimate awareness—the source of ultimate strength—one stands alone.

The death and resurrection story suggests this to me, when viewed symbolically. I will try, at the risk of losing much of its significance, to express my feeling about it in words, in the hope that if it suggests a better view to you than you now have, you will be able to find a personal way back to that level of inexpressible awareness, the point at which it becomes an intimate treasure.

If one will take death symbolically, as transformation rather than as literal abandonment of the physical body, *this* death is of that part of existence that is concerned with effect, haunted by danger and worry, and the emerging transcendent personality is one of pure essence, purposefulness without regard to effect and with an immunity from hurt. I view this as a state that is possible of attainment in some measure by any person who accepts the requirement to live so as to dispose himself to the transformation.

But to the extent that one reaches this new level of awareness, the rational is transcended in two important respects. First, at this level of awareness, one no longer deals with one's intimates in terms of articles of faith that are clearly express-ible; this relationship is *denied*. And second, one no longer re-lates oneself to the cosmos as one would to a being with whom one communicates with words; this relationship forsakes one, and in its place comes the ineffable mystery that one regards with awe and wonder and stops there. This is the aloneness that goes with any contact with the ultimate consummation of the search. But those who achieve some contact with this state take on aspects of ethereal lightness, and in proportion, as they re-ceive this gift, they feel a special closeness with others who are at comparable stages in their own interior journeys.

This, it seems to me, is the end of the search—purpose at depth. But, some ask, does this not take one into remoteness from the world of practical choice, compromise, stress? How can one live in the real world and deal with concepts like these?

There is only one answer to these questions: almost everyone with intellect enough to know that one is alive *does* deal with purpose at some depth. One may not consciously do it often. In fact, one may deal with thoughts of this kind only in moments of anguish or in the face of death. But it is the common lot of men and women to speculate about the ultimate even though they may rarely converse about it.

Now, if the question were put "How can one sustain this kind of speculation as a part of conscious search for strength *in the face of* practical choice, compromise, and stress?" it is a dif-ferent question. Obviously, some discipline is required to deal with the distractions.

One way to view the question of purpose is to see it in as-cending levels from depth to surface. Beginning with the great-est depth, where all rationality is stilled, the next level—symbol and essence—is one which a person can contemplate and, with the resources of the deep mind, can ponder; but when one at-tempts to bring it within the scope of language, it loses much of its essence. Then we come to the surface level of purpose at which people speak of aims, goals, and objectives and lay them out for common discourse.

I am not suggesting that such a systematic ladder of levels exists in which there are discrete categories. Rather, when a person speaks of aims or goals, something of his contact (or lack of it) with the ultimate shows through, as does the relative depth and intensity of his experience in grappling with symbol and essence. Sensitive people do not need much contact with another person in order to arrive at a dependable estimate of where this person stands at the several levels of purpose. When a critic says of a verbal presentation of aim or goal, "This is just talk," he may be saying, "Not much from the deeper levels shows through."

There is no level outside of the purely mechanical in which the prudent person does not assess the person as inseparable from the aim he or she professes and from the deeper resources that mark the person who states the aim. Those who bear the responsibility for dispensing money or authority must constantly ask the question, "What will the *person* do with the aim I am about to empower him to pursue?"

I submit, with respect to purpose, that no person is to be trusted with any aim unless he or she has some contact, however tenuous, with ultimate purpose and unless his or her involvement is substantial at the level of symbol and essence. The person may not fit any established classification and may not identify with the language other people use to talk about such things. Consequently, the dependable judgment that others make before they trust is almost entirely subjective. Nevertheless, what is assessed is real, and if one is sensitive, it is just as substantial as the most literal material commodity. This kind of sensitivity is an important element in strength because no worthwhile aim can be carried out alone; one must decide with whom one will collaborate, with whom one will keep one's distance, and whom one will oppose.

Then the question is sometimes raised, "This makes a pretty grim and serious world; is it really worth living in?"

The few people I have known who were in the best contact with the deeper levels have been buoyant, fun-loving people

94

with a light touch. The lady farmer in Chapter 2 who spoke of driving hard with a light hand was one of these. She not only had the gift; she knew what it was and could talk about it. Great as was her concern for the problems of the world and serious as was her intent in grappling with them, she had a light, fun-loving approach to everything. Her house rang with laughter. It was a happy, healthy, constructive place.

If I had the chance to rub Aladdin's lamp—one rub, one wish—I would wish for a world in which people laugh more. One can cultivate purpose to the point of having a glimpse of the ultimate and still remain connected with people and events, *if* one has humor, if one can laugh with all people at all stages of their journeys.

I am not speaking of the coarse laugh at the crude joke.

One needs to be susceptible to spontaneous laughter, about everything and everybody, especially oneself. Even in the depths of sorrow, one must laugh. Joy and sorrow are not antithetical; they are complementary. All of life is at once essentially tragic and essentially humorous.

One of the really precious stories I treasure is about a friend of mine who in the prime of life was struck down by cancer and knew that his end was very near. In the city where he lived, he was a person of consequence and was a close friend of the mayor. But it was a large city, and the mayor did not hear of his friend's plight until a few days before his death. The mayor was an impulsive man with a large warm heart, and he immediately summoned his car to go to see his friend. He appeared bearing a gift, a bottle of whiskey—the best thing he could think of for a man in any kind of trouble. The beautiful part of this story is the dying man's response. With such energy as he could summon, he *laughed* with thorough enjoyment of the humor in this situation.

Purpose and laughter are the twins that must not separate. Each is empty without the other. Together they are the impregnable fortress of *strength* as that word is used here: the ability, in the face of the practical issues of life, to choose the right aim and to pursue that aim responsibly over a long period of time.

95

This is the point at which all speculation about purpose must arrive, whether the path is philosophy, theology, ethics, or the plain curbstone variety of reasoning with which the untutored are accustomed to dealing. The critical issues of life are intensely practical: confrontation, choosing, pursuing, and facing the ultimate judgment when the votes are all cast. And any speculation about purpose that does not lead the person who is capable of *strength* to pursue it with vigor over his life span had better be left in the library unopened.

We must develop *strength* in proportion to our personal capacity for it. We will all be judged by how well we achieve the *strength* possible within. Each of us must husband our own talent. We must each make the development of the attributes that go to make up *strength* our prime concern throughout our adult life. The judgment of ethical deficiency will be leveled at us if we fail to make the effort our individual capacity calls for.

My concern for the world is not that there are so many poorly equipped people in it but that the well-equipped people do so poorly. Something needs to be added to the current matrix of moral fiber. I see no alternative but to lay the burden on those who are already carrying more than their share. Those who think of themselves as *good* must become *better;* they must become *strong.*

"What is it like to be strong?" I have been asked. My answer has been that I am not strong enough myself to know with certainty. I am but a seeker along the way. I suspect, though, that *strength* will manifest itself in different persons in different ways. But I've had some intimations of what to expect.

> You will be free—on the inside. You may be in jail, but you will *feel* free. The freedom that is most important cannot be imprisoned. And you will have a better chance of helping to maintain a society in which external freedom is a right if you feel free—on the inside. The *search* will make you free.

You will be able to let all achievement come when it will and be what it will. You will not press.

You will be able to ask yourself such a basic question as "What is love?" and accept that the great ethical law of the Judeo-Christian tradition in which you live rests on this word *love* and yet not be disturbed that you do not know what it means and probably never will know.

You will be able to judge the erring action and not judge the essential person.

You will be able to listen, really listen.

You will be able to forgive. Failure to forgive rankles, distracts, reduces energy, stifles entheos.

You will put the steadying hand on the shoulder of the person in trouble and communicate something that words can't tell.

You will convince by your presence. Wherever you are, it will make a difference just because you are there.

This, I believe, is what strong people are like. But *strength* comes only in large measures—particular kinds of measures. The measures are graduated according to individual capacity.

Strength, then, is something that no person can have a little bit of. One must fill one's entire measure. In the long run, one is either strong or weak. The middle ground is not worth cultivating.

Walt Whitman said it well:

Allons, the road is before us.
It is safe, I have tried it, my own feet have tried it well.
Be not detained![21]

97

10

A DREAM

ALONG THE WAY I had a dream.

I am riding on a bicycle through a beautiful level woods in which there is a labyrinth of paths. In my left hand I carry a map of these paths. I am riding rapidly and buoyantly following my map.

The map blows out of my hand. As I come to a stop, I look back and see my map flutter to the ground. It is picked up by an old man who stands there holding it for me. I walk back to get the map.

When I arrive at the old man, he hands me, not my map, but a small round tray of earth in which are growing fresh grass seedlings.

ESSAYS ON POWER, MANAGEMENT, AND ORGANIZATIONS

One accepts, first, that means determine ends.

A search for the capabilities and possibilities in people is gradually supplanting the search for the liabilities. It is a more optimistic philosophy.

An important weakness in the concept of the single chief at the top of a managerial hierarchy is that such a person is apt to be a manager and to assume, by virtue of having the position, that he or she has all of the talents it requires.

Robert K. Greenleaf

ESSAYS ON POWER, MANAGEMENT, AND ORGANIZATIONS

WHEN ROBERT GREENLEAF SPOKE about any one of the issues of power, management, or organizations, he naturally began speaking about the other two. For Greenleaf, power was a good thing as long as it was exercised in a way that would enable the growth of people and institutions. Organizations provide the context for power, and managers are its primary conduit. Greenleaf completed the circuit of power. He showed that it not only went from the top down but also from the bottom up, from person to person, and from the inside out.

Greenleaf believed that the use of power was one of the most important defining characteristics of a servant-leader. Noble motives do not automatically result in the beneficial use of power; noble means must also be employed, and *persuasion* is the approach of choice for a servant-leader. The 1984 essay "Coercion, Manipulation, and Persuasion: Reflections on a Strategy for Change" makes a case for persuasion as a reasonable and realistic tool for institutional and social change.

That theme is more temperate in "Power in the Executive Office," a speech that Greenleaf ghost-wrote in the 1960s for the CEO of a major corporation. Another ghost-written speech from the same period, delivered by a university president, "Lessons on Power," is typical of Greenleaf's approach of addressing issues by stating deep principles, posing questions, and inviting readers or listeners to reflect on answers.

An earlier essay, "Building the Ethic of Strength in Business," is extracted from a talk Greenleaf gave to the Personnel Managers Club of Boston in the mid 1950s. In it, he puts forth an early version of his thinking on the attitudes and skills needed to become an effective persuader.

One irony about Robert Greenleaf is that he did not believe he was a natural manager, even though he spent years thinking, writing, and teaching about management. The fact that he was, to use his own terms, more of a "conceptualizer" than an "operationalizer" is probably the reason he could speak to managers and bring a fresh perspective.

"Industry's Means for Personality Adjustment," his first public talk in New York, brings great freshness for its time (1935). The real theme of the talk is the development of people. He would later use expressions other than *personality adjustment* to describe the development process, but this piece shows that he was already challenging traditional business attitudes toward employees from the very start.

Twenty years later, Greenleaf was advocating using the tools of behavioral research to develop people in business. In "Behavioral Research: A Factor in Tomorrow's Better Management" (1955), he explains a research model that would help develop qualities important for servant-leaders, especially the skill of listening.

Every organization has people who are natural operationalizers and conceptualizers. Greenleaf explains their characteristics in "The Operator Versus the Conceptualizer: An Issue of Management Talents" (1970) and goes on to explain in "The Managerial Mind" and other papers how important both are to the building of a great organization. Another important element is an environment favoring human growth and moral development. "Growing Greatness in Managers" (1962) offers suggestions for nurturing both.

The context for Greenleaf's notions about power, management, and organizations becomes clearer when reading "My Work at AT&T: An Adventure in Spirit" (1984). The glories and failures of AT&T led to mature thought on three critical roles in an organization, discussed in "Manager, Administrator, Statesman" (1986). For organizations that would aspire to greatness, Greenleaf offers practical suggestions for novel staff roles in "The Making of a Distinguished Institution."

A retirement community was the final institution with which Greenleaf was associated. Four years before his death, Greenleaf turned his discerning eye on that community and recognized organizational aspects that could enhance or interfere with the mission of the churches and other organizations that managed such institutions.

Greenleaf's theories are sometimes regarded as impractical. Such is often the case with prophets. His own assessment of his life's work combines vision and practicality: "As a theorist, I am an idealist," he observed. "As a practitioner, I am a pragmatist."

POWER

BUSINESS, ETHICS, AND MANIPULATION

RECENTLY, a bright young woman graduate student, who knew that I had just turned sixty-five, said to me, "One difference between your generation and mine is that many of us don't believe we are going to live to be sixty-five."

A study in one of our best liberal arts colleges showed that 40 percent of the students do not want to enter this society in any existing occupation and practically none want to enter business.

Attitudes like these are widely and deeply held among our ablest young people, and they are, in part, a response to what is seen as extensive manipulation. I believe that, if sustained, these attitudes will become a major force that brings about new ethics and new institutions and, in the United States at least, new business ethics and a new type of business institution.

Where do these attitudes come from? Where are they leading us?

In the frame of reference of the United States, it is clear enough why such attitudes exist. We live in the shadow of a nuclear holocaust, and some fool could pull the trigger any day and wipe most of us off this planet. And we seem to be on a collision course to destroy the environment by a combination of population growth, affluence, and careless exploitation of natural resources and disposal of waste. Then, long-standing indifference to and acceptance of injustice and poverty have brought us to a crisis of violence and distrust. Furthermore, the "business-military complex" has come to symbolize an evil force that manipulates us all. When linked with what is widely held to be a senseless and immoral war, in the eyes of many it has cast a shadow over perhaps three-fourths of the vocational opportunities available to young people. One can easily read the signs that we are on an irreversible path to destruction. It is no wonder that the outlook for so many young people is grim.

I am as aware of all of this as the next man; yet I am hopeful because another set of assumptions is possible.

The trigger may not be pulled, and we may muddle along as we are, with the nuclear threat hanging over our heads, for hundreds of years. A massive assault using all of our organizational and inventive powers to save the environment may, in fact, save it by at least halting the deterioration at this point. The present revolt against injustice and poverty could turn us about and set us an another path. And our military adventures in East Asia may come to be unbearable to enough people to get us out of there and transform our military strength into something more acceptable for the 1970s. Belief in these as possibilities gives hope a realistic base. But hope must also have a dynamic aspect that mere realistic grounds do not supply.

The dynamics of my hope rest on the widespread disenchantment with this society among contemporary young people and their determination to do something about its failures. There is a new revolutionary force abroad in the world—all over the world. Large numbers of able and perceptive people are challenging both the pervasive acceptance of injustice and the sharp disparity between, on the one hand, the quality of society they know is reasonable and possible with our available resources and, on the other hand, the actual performance of the whole range of institutions that exist to serve society. This revolutionary challenge is pressed with the greatest vigor in the universities, where the concern is most intensely felt for justice (rather than order), for the performance (rather than the form) of our institutions, and for the appropriateness (rather than the result) of power and authority. What I will call the *freedom revolution* will probably move inexorably, as most revolutions do, in ways that are puzzling, painful, and disruptive—and with some disastrous consequences.

I do not say this to condemn the revolution. Neither do I justify it. I simply want to acknowledge that I see in this sometimes frightening ferment the major thrust for integrity in the world today. It upsets and threatens me, as it does many others. But it also supplies the dynamic element in the hope I firmly hold to. Whereas I am hopeful, the young people who are generating the dynamism, the drive for integrity that nourishes my hope—they tend to be grim and despairing because they lack the experience with modern institutions that would give hope a realistic base. It is easier for me to listen to them and have my hope bolstered than it is for them to listen to me. And that is as it should be. But I regret the general hopeless feeling, because hope is essential if one is to face the imperfections and deal with them.

I come now to a further element of realism in my basis for hope—and this is the hardest for young people to accept. It is my belief, based on my own experience with the phenomenon of American business, that the decisive creative response to the challenge of the freedom revolution, the response that is more likely to turn things around than any other I know of, will come from the large business firm. The rest of this essay is largely an explanation of this position.

Part of the problem of dealing with our subject, business, ethics, and manipulation, is that the words *manipulation* and *management* (which is mostly a business term) have a common root in *manus*, "hand," and both words imply shaping other people's destinies. Whereas *manipulation* of men has long been taken as bad because it implies moving people without their knowing fully what is going on, until recently *management* has been accepted as legitimate. Now, as I read the signs, we are in a period of radical transition regarding power, authority, and decision making everywhere, and a cloud has settled over all leadership and management in any form. All institutions are affected by these trends, and institutional leadership is now quite different from what it was a few years ago. I suspect that it will be even more radically different in the future.

From this ferment has emerged the expectation, held by many people, that a manipulation-free society is a possibility— a "leaderless" society that is governed by a continuing consensus with full participation and with every motive behind every action fully exposed. I respect the motives of those who advocate this ideal state and admit to occasional utopian dreams of life in an influence-free society. But realistically, I do not see such a society in prospect, and I will deal here with the institution of American business as I know it in my own experience— a state of affairs in which strong, able people must lead, and therefore manipulate, if the goods and services expected are to emerge. In the United States, many of us would do better with less in the way of goods, though we need more services—health care, for instance. But whatever the level of goods and services, institutions will be required to deliver them. These institutions, if they are to rise above mediocrity, will have their ablest people as leaders, and those leaders will manipulate.

The issue, then, as I see it, is not whether all manipulation can be banished as evil but rather whether some manipulation can be made legitimate and if so, by what standards and how. What ethic should govern these times? I will speculate about what one new business ethic might be.

I cannot visualize a world without leaders, without people who clearly see the path ahead and take the risks of going out ahead to show the way. What reason is there for accepting the constraints of a society except that in it, the more able serve the less able? One way that some people serve is to lead. And anyone who does this *manipulates* others because he literally helps shape their destinies without fully revealing either his motives or the direction in which he is leading them. A leader may be completely honest about his *conscious* intent. But the essential artistry in his leadership, what makes him more dependable and trustworthy than most, is his intuitive insight, which cannot be fully explained. We have it from the great French jurist Saleilles that a judge makes his decisions intuitively and then devises the fine legal reasoning to justify them—after the fact.[1] So it is with the scientist on the growing edge of discovery. And so it is with the leader—whether he is businessman, administrator, politician, clergyman, or teacher. I cannot conceive of a duller, less creative world than one in which everything can be fully and rationally explained.

My search, therefore, day by day, is for a path through the maze along which people are accepted as they are and which leads to a world that is more benign. As I look out through my particular window on the world, I realize that I do not see all. Rather, I see only what the filter of my biases and attitudes of the moment permits me to see. Therefore, if in the course of this essay, I make a declaration without appending "it seems to me," please assume such a qualification on everything I say.

Traveling this path, I see the field of American business as almost without professional standards, it is not much supported by sentiment, there is no aura of professional sanctity to mask its shortcomings, and, because it is one of the least restrained of all fields of practice, at the low end of the scale there is much that is corrupt and very bad, while at the high end there is much at a level of excellence that is truly distinguished. The spread between the two extremes is wide.

Performance in any field or calling should be judged in reference to the obligations assumed for society, which differ from field to field. I know something of what goes on in the fields of education, government, religion, philanthropy, and health services. In my judgment, the businessman does as well by his obligations as do the others. None does very well.

The world of practice in all fields, as I see it through my particular window, is, on the average, mediocre. No field does very well when judged by what is reasonable and possible with available resources. This is what makes the subject of manipulation, or almost any other dimension of modern Western society, so interesting. How can we do better? We have the resources to do so much better, far better than the mediocre level that now prevails because so much leadership is poor.

The problem of doing better in the modern world, as I see it, is how people can perform better in, and be better served by, *institutions*—especially large ones.

In the United States at least, where business practice is shaped more by the influence of large institutions and where there is a wide range of choice as to what a business may be like, as a sub-culture, there is much to be found that is relevant to our theme, the manipulation of man, by exploring briefly how our big businesses came to be what they are—and how they may be different in the future.

Let me use the three largest American businesses in their fields as examples. Each of these is what it is today because each, at a critical period in its history, was headed by a building genius (not in either case the founding owner) who gave the institution the stamp of his personal values. Each of these building geniuses was an adequate leader and manager for his day, but each brought unusual conceptual powers—in defining the institution and establishing his values as its values.

At General Motors, our largest manufacturing concern, Alfred Sloan's unique gift was remarkable organizational insight and the growing of managers; at Sears, Roebuck, our largest merchandising company, Julius Rosenwald brought unusual humanness and trust; and at American Telephone and Telegraph Company, our largest public utility (and my old employer), Theodore N. Vail bestowed dedication to service supported by relentless technical innovation. Although Vail has been gone fifty years (he was the earliest of the three), AT&T is still his business—his personal values still dominate it. They have eroded some, of course, but fifty years is a long time for one man's recognizable influence to last beyond the man in something as transient as a business or in an institution as large as this one. It is the same with Sloan and Rosenwald, who came later. General Motors and Sears are still "their" companies.

These three companies rose above the level of mediocrity because three great leader-builders brought them there.

I do not cite these companies as paragons or models for the future. They have the same faults and frailties common to all human institutions at this stage of their development. But each of these, at a critical period in its growth, made a lunge forward and contributed something to the art of institution building. Whether they can do it again depends on the quality of people who emerge, inside, to serve and lead.

The test of leadership has not changed: what does the scorekeeper (or the several scorekeepers) say? The scorekeeper's rules have changed a bit, and they will change even more. There are more "publics" demanding satisfaction, and the "searchingness" of their scrutiny has increased. Business institutions have grown larger and much more complex, and the pace of innovation is sometimes breathtaking. Dealing with these conditions, large-business leadership has become a sophisticated calling, and the leader is much more concerned with building strength and bringing sharpness of focus to many people rather than with deciding everything himself. The contemporary business leader is just as much a determined institution builder as his predecessors, but he works differently, and his role is more difficult to understand from the outside.

The role of top leadership in large American business is shifting away from that of the dominant decision maker to that of manager of the information system. Leadership depends more on the pull of the overarching goals and building the competence and sustaining the autonomy of many decision makers. This, in turn, is supported by wide access to reliable and comprehensive information. The sanctions pressing on the individual for good performance are, first, his own pride and conscience framed within adequate information that guides him and tells him how he is doing; second, the social pressure of peers whose own performance is interlinked with his and who have access to the common pool of information so that they know how their colleagues are doing; and finally, the last-resort authority of the superior officer, which, in a good institution, is rarely used. The value of coercive power is inverse to its use—more so every day.

This is a hopeful and encouraging trend. It is made possible by a wide scope of freedom for quite autonomous institutions under the shelter of political democracy. But in the United States, the model for it has not been set by the government; neither is it the product of democratization within the firm. Rather it is the result of the growth of knowledge, relentless market pressures, and the emergence of some unusual business builders. Political democracy is a necessary condition, but it does not guarantee anything. The only assurance of a good result is the encouragement of the culture for incremental thrusts by large numbers of strong, free, able people as they serve and lead. Individual people doing the right things give a society its moral stature. This does not make a perfect society, but this is how such goodness as it has is built.

Earlier I said that I believed that the decisive creative response to the challenge of the freedom revolution, the response that is more likely to turn things around than any other I know about, will come from the business firm. I see the tentative first steps already being made. These will be accelerated as the freedom revolution brings more pressure to bear.

Business in the United States has not yet been as much affected by the freedom revolution as have, for instance, the universities or the church or government. Part of the reason, I believe, is that business has long been on the receiving end of advice in these matters and has moved along with advancing knowledge, whereas the universities and the church and government have freely advised but have not necessarily practiced. Consequently, the freedom revolution has first attacked the institutions that are the most vulnerable because their internal practices are most in need of renovation. Business is next on the list, I am sure. But I predict that the business firm will respond more creatively to the revolution of freedom than the church or the university or the government has—because businesses are relatively free from the "professional hang-up," because people in business live by fewer illusions about what the world is really like, and because the typical business as I know it is more humanly responsive than the others.

How, then, will businesses respond to the new conditions? How can they perform their expected functions in a way that the charge of manipulation recedes as a serious issue?

I have confidence that, after a bit of confusion, a new business ethic will emerge. And the best I can do at this point is speculate on what that ethic might be. I will confine my speculation to only one facet of the total problem of business ethics: the people who work in business. Many parts of the total business ethic need attention, but the one I will deal with seems the most basic.

What might the new ethic be (not a new idea but new as a firmly held business ethic)?

Looking at the two major elements, the work and the person, the new ethic, simply but completely stated, will be this: *the work exists for the person as much as the person exists for the work.* Put another way, the business exists as much to provide meaningful work to the person as it exists to provide a product or service to the customer.

The business then becomes a serving institution—serving both producers and users. At first, the new ethic may put these two on a par. But as the economy becomes even more productive and people get more sensible and settle for fewer "things," in the new ethic, service to producers may rise in priority above service to users, and the significance of work will be more the joy of the doing rather than the goods and services produced. There must, of course, be goods and services at some level, but in an era of abundance, they need not be the top priority. Not only will this view make a better society, but in the future, this may be the only way the user or customer can be well served— by accepting that serving is more important than being served and that the mere possession of money does not give one person an unqualified right to command the service of another. (We are partly there already.) Furthermore, the user or customer will be better served if he finds a way to communicate this belief to those who serve. A new consumer ethic will need to evolve alongside the new business ethic. I am close enough to this restless generation of young people in the United States to believe that the more able and discerning among them will not enforce their view simply by too many of the abler ones refusing to work on any other terms.

I have said that the idea is not new but that its adoption as a firmly held business ethic will be new in our time. In fact, as an idea, it is very old—at least 2,500 years. Its first formulation, to my knowledge, is in the Buddhist ethic, as one step in the noble Eightfold Path—right vocation, or right livelihood—as given in the Buddha's famous sermon at Benares.

Speaking to those in business who presume to manage, it is important that this principle be embraced as an ethic and not simply as a "device" to achieve harmony or increase productivity or reduce turnover. Some popular procedures, such as participation or work enlargement or profit sharing, may be manipulative devices if they do not flow naturally out of a comprehensive ethic. "Participative democracy" in industry, as it is now advocated in Europe, may, in practice, be another such device, especially in a large industry. I do not think it will flourish in the United States. Our unions are too astute to permit it, and involvement with it will divert attention from more basic matters.

Superficially, the freedom revolution is an attack on manipulative devices. But basically, this is not what the revolution is about. It is at heart a struggle for meaning and significance in individual lives. Manipulative devices, and manipulation as a concept, are attacked because they are visible targets. Just removing the evidences of manipulation (assuming it can be done) will not produce meaning and significance in individual lives. In an overcrowded industrial society, this can be done only by the institutions we now have, where most people spend their working lives, adopting an ethic in which meaning and significance are the goal—at least on a parity with other goals. And to bring it to parity, it must, for a while at least, be the primary goal. In the United States, this means that business institutions must adopt this goal. And its accomplishment rests on the ability of builders, leaders, to move these institutions (while keeping them intact and functioning) from where they are, with the heavy emphasis on production, to where they need to be, with the heavy emphasis on growing people. And they will do this while meeting all of the other performance criteria that society imposes for institutional survival.

When George Fox gave the seventeenth-century English Quakers a new business ethic (truthfulness, dependability, fixed prices, no haggling), he did it because his view of right conduct demanded it, not because it would be more profitable. It did, in fact, become more profitable because those early Quaker businessmen quickly emerged out of the seamy morass of that day as people who could be trusted. But the new ethic was a radical demand on those people, and they must have had apprehensions about it when it was urged on them.

The ethic suggested here is a radical one, too, and businesspeople will probably be apprehensive about it. Those who are moved to act on it are not likely to move so much in response to the moral imperative simply because the moral leader with sufficient stature to persuade them (as George Fox did with his followers) doesn't seem to be around. The new ethic will come, if it comes, as an acknowledgment (or anticipation) of the relentless pressure of the freedom revolution.

Very soon, across the whole gamut of our institutions, we may know how many determined builders there are who can move creatively with these times, in which powerful new forces for integrity are operating. I wager that in American business, we have a few leaders who will rise to the challenge. But they will not choose to announce, with great fanfare, a new ethic to deal with the new conditions. If they are wise, they will not announce *anything*. An ancient moral injunction tells us to "practice what we preach." A few businesspeople in the United States have learned the hard way to follow the modern version of that advice: "Don't practice what you preach; just practice!" Consequently, the wise businessperson will simply start the slow process of converting the large numbers of people within the institution who must share this view if it is to be viable. It will be noticed only in practice, and that gradually.

It will take some courage for a large business to make the ethical shift I have suggested. But only one such business need make this shift initially. When Henry Ford set up his assembly line to manufacture automobiles, ultimately everybody in that kind of business had to convert. So it may be with the new business ethic.

The process has already started in some businesses with the effort to accommodate the very able young people who have a clear individualistic style that they are determined to preserve and who need the excitement of a dynamic purpose. Such very able individuals are quickly given a track of their own to run on so that they can have the satisfaction of personal achievement. This is easier to do in a small business, but larger firms are learning to decentralize in a way that creates a variety of environments in which different styles of able people will flourish and be themselves. The corporate leader and his staff provide a context for all of this so that individuals have a clear focus of purpose, so that they can be supported when they need it and feel a part of a larger purpose without losing their individuality, and so that all the parts contribute to the total strength of the enterprise. (If a person wants to make his career with a large business and keep his individuality, he should choose a strong business.) This is the first step—to accommodate the wide differences and needs of the very able. A few strong businesses are well along with this step. The test? They have many able young people, but it is difficult to "raid" the businesses and lure the young employees away.

The second step, and the more difficult, is to exert a strong pull for growth on *all* in the enterprise who have unrealized potential and who want to grow. More people will want to grow when the climate is encouraging. Most large businesses have the staff resources to redesign the work so as to capitalize on individual strengths. Sometimes it means taking on a product or service that is not particularly profitable just because someone needs it. The specific imperative that brings this about will probably be the pressure from the *able* young people within the firm who are recruited under arrangements mentioned in the preceding paragraph.

The aim of all of this is *not* to motivate people. Motivation ceases to be what is done to people. Motivation becomes what people generate for themselves when they experience growth. Whereas the usual assumption about the firm is that it is in business to make a profit and serve its customers and that it does things for and to employees to get them to be productive, the new ethic requires that *growth* of those who do the work is the primary aim and the worker then sees to it that the customer is served and that the ink on the bottom line is black. It is one's own game. The art, of course, is how to do this in a firm that employs many thousands.

It won't be easy. But neither will it be any harder than other difficult things that large businesses have to do. And this time, ultimately, they will accept that they *have* to do. With that acceptance will come the belief that it is right, which makes it an ethic.

If done well, the change will come slowly, and those who demand instant perfection will probably say that nothing at all is happening. To stay alive and meet all of the other criteria that must be met, a business will probably continue to operate the old way while moving toward the new. There will be inevitable confusion. But this is what makes business leadership interesting.

In the United States, we are well on the way to accepting that the world owes every person a living. Now the next step may be to acknowledge that every person is entitled to work that is meaningful in individual terms and that it is the obligation of employers, in toto, to provide it. Whereas "a living" can be dispensed via money through a relief agency, "meaningful work" is likely to be delivered only within an employing institution that is living by a new ethic. And the practice of this ethic is a positive move toward a holistic society. Except among a few esoteric scholars, the case for the university as a place set apart from the world of work rests on tenuous grounds. Perhaps, experimentally at least, we should move toward a new institution that embraces both work and learning—learning in a deep and formal sense and all of the learning influence most people need. This requires a new type of leader, one who can conceptualize such an institution, generate enthusiasm so that many good, able people want to be a part of it, and provide the strong focus of purpose that builds dynamic strength in many. Great things happen when able leaders create these conditions. There are some able leaders in American business who can rise to the challenge to create these conditions. All that is needed is enough incentive to make them want to do it. Our young people are busy building that incentive.

People who do not know intimately the inner workings of large American businesses may find it difficult to appreciate what a profound effect on the business culture a new ethic like this will have. When the business manager who is fully committed to this ethic is asked, "What are you in business for?" his answer may be something like this:

> *I am in the business of growing people*—people who are stronger, healthier, more autonomous, more self-reliant, more competent. Incidentally, we also make and sell at a profit things that people want to buy so we can pay for all this. We play that game hard and well, and we are successful by the usual standards; but it is really incidental. I recall a time when there was a complaint about manipulation. We don't hear it anymore. We manage the business about as we always did. We simply changed our aim. Strong, healthy,

autonomous, self-reliant, competent men and women don't mind being manipulated. In fact, they take it as a game and do a little of it themselves. Consequently, as an institution, we are terribly strong. In fact, we are distinguished. How do I know we are distinguished? Because the best young people want to work for us. We select the best of the best, and once inside, they never want to leave. Any business that can do that is a winner.

Utopian? I don't think so. Most of our large American businesses have the capability and the resources to embrace a new ethic like this and act resolutely on its implications. And I believe that among them are several that have sufficient foresight and creative drive that they will prefer to run ahead of the freedom revolution rather than be run over by it. Such is the way that new ethics are made.

In the long perspective of history, this period of the 1970s may be seen as one in which, in the course of coming to grips with the moral issues of power, authority, *and* manipulation, a new view of how people are best served by institutions may emerge. Institutions are not necessarily more benign when they protest their idealistic motives, nor are they necessarily less benign when they admit to crass commercialism. One should not be surprised that a Ralph Waldo Emerson, who could see "the good of evil born," would observe, weighing his words carefully, that "the greatest meliorator of the world is selfish, huckstering trade."[2]

I predict that under the pressures of the times, the typical American business—because it is more flexible, more adaptive, more human, and more openly responsive to market forces and because in business, integrity of service (or lack of it) is more vividly and concretely demonstrated than in other types of institutions—will more quickly resolve the issues of manipulation in all of their manifestations. And it will accomplish this not by banishing manipulation but by sublimating it, and out of the alchemy, it may contribute something significantly new to the evolving knowledge of how people can better live and work together in societies.

If this proves in practice to be generally recognized, then there may be a radical realignment of expectations from institutions, and what society has traditionally expected from businesses, churches, schools, governments, and philanthropic foundations may be considerably scrambled. And if this happens, I wager that out of this scrambling, the business type of institution will emerge with a considerably larger role than heretofore. Witness the agitation in the United States to take the postal service out of the civil service and into a public corporation and the vigorous entry of a few of our aggressive private business firms into the "learning" field. This is happening, not because of any inherent virtue in business, but simply because, the way institutions have evolved, businesses are more adaptive and more responsive to opportunity.

Despite the ideological tensions in the world today, when any society really wants to accomplish something, it tends to draw on whatever works best. The builders find the useful pieces wherever they are and invent new ones when needed—all without regard to ideological coloration. "How do you get the right things done?" comes to be the watchword of the day, every day. In the United States, this is essentially the business way, the way to lift the sights of a mediocre society.

I suppose all of this reveals a bias. I admit a bias. If I were young again, I would again cast my lot with a large American business. I would do it because the United States is a business-dominated society (not in a formal power sense but simply by the sheer mass of the business presence), and any social advance will move, in part, from forces generated inside business. My own experience tells me that there is enough integrity in the typical business that I would be more useful and my personal growth would be better nourished by working inside rather than by trying to influence it from the outside. I would choose to join a large business firm because there would be more satisfaction in being where the action is (the action, not just the excitement)—

at the point where some of the critical issues of society must be resolved if the work of the world is to get done. And I would do it because I believe that if I accept the challenge to cope with the inevitable manipulation within an institution that is responding sensibly and creatively to issues and situations that require new ethics, I will emerge at the end of my career with a better personal value system than I would have if I had chosen a job in which I was more on my own and therefore freer from being manipulated.

This is the ultimate test: what values govern one's life—at the end of it?

Manipulation, as I see it, is one of the imperfections of an imperfect world. It is a social problem, but it is not first priority, and the reformer's zeal will blunt its point by attacking it as primary. *Mediocrity* (including self-serving behavior) in positions of influence is primary; and it cannot be dealt with by eliminating influence, as in the "leaderless society"—mediocrity will still be there.

Reducing mediocrity is a slow, difficult, person-by-person process in which the less able learn to identify and trust the more able who will diligently and honestly serve them. It is also a process in which able, honest, serving people prepare themselves to lead and accept the opportunity to lead when offered.

Reducing mediocrity in positions of influence by replacing the less qualified with more able, honest, serving people is a manageable task with our available resources. It can be done. And I am confident that it will be done on a substantial scale when the people and institutions that have the good of society at heart bring a clearer focus to their efforts and concentrate on the one thing that will turn us about the quickest: reducing the influence of mediocrity.

COERCION, MANIPULATION, AND PERSUASION

Reflections on a Strategy for Change

IDEAS ARE BORN in the minds of men and women, not in test tubes. Ideas exist in the imagination first; then venturesome persons take the risk of acting on them and may, in the process, verify, refine, or refute them. But they exist in the imagination first. People who require tested and proven models in order to act rarely originate anything. Originators, those who imagine and who take the risks of acting on an imagined idea, are the ones who move the world along.

The making of the blend of actions and resistances to actions that move a society forward or backward is one of the great mysteries that may never be resolved. The opportunity for one who wants to be a constructive building influence, to leave the world a little better than if one had not tried, is to make one's contribution to the blend, the meld.

No one wills to change the world. Change, if it comes, emerges out of the mystery.

My dictionary defines *civilization* as "a state of social culture characterized by relative progress in the arts, science, and statecraft; . . . and of the means of expressing the aspirations of the human spirit." Civilization advances or regresses as the meld of the building and destroying forces dictates. The most successful civilization-building effort (if one knew what it was) may find, at its close, that civilization has slipped back. The constructive effort, if it was truly constructive, may have had only the effect of causing the loss to be a little less than it might have been. Therefore, it was worth doing.

If one wants to be a civilization-building rather than a neutral or destroying influence, how does one know what to do, and how does one know, after the fact, that one has done it?

One accepts, first, that *means determine ends.* Then one is skeptical about striving directly for idealistic ends (somewhat regardless of means) and hopes, rather, to be a part of an evolving situation to which one makes one's contribution with right actions.

There is nothing new about this. It is part of the Eightfold Path proclaimed by the Buddha in his famous sermon at Benares 2,500 years ago. One takes the right actions in an evolving situation. Does one have purpose? Yes, another part of the Eightfold Path. But not an idealistic dream to be accomplished now as a result of one's effort.

How does one know what are right actions, for oneself, in the situation? One prepares! One gathers a sense of history, which gives some perspective on right actions. Then one cultivates the serenity that will provide some detachment from the fray so that one does not get caught up in frenzied effort. One becomes involved in, or initiates, something that is moving in an evolutionary way and studies how best to apply one's effort in the evolutionary process. One respects one's intuitive resources, which generally supply the last link between where conscious logic leaves off and the formulation of a decision for right action begins.

Then, and perhaps most crucially, one cultivates the acceptance that whatever course one chooses, one may be wrong. The result may be retrogression, damage, or no effect. The ultimate test will be the test of history, which the initiator of the action will never know. How can one accept that one may be wrong and keep it in the forefront of one's thinking all of the time and not suffer a paralysis of action? How? One never acts alone. One becomes a member of what is, in effect, a disciplined order of equals who share the concern and who are dedicated to work at it. Then remain open as a seeker. If one cannot manage either the relationship with colleagues or the sustained attitude of seeking, one is advised either not to initiate action on one's own or to follow the leadership of someone whose assurance of rightness of action is greater. There have been far too many disastrous consequences of actions by well-meaning but self-righteous people for one not to take this precaution. It might be called the ethic of restraint.

Finally, one chooses a means about which one will engage in a never-ending search for depth of understanding and by which one will constantly practice to improve one's skill. I will describe three that suggest a range of choice.

Coercion is pressure. "Do as I say, think as I do, speak as I wish—or else!"

Manipulation is the process of guiding people into beliefs or actions that they do not fully understand and that may or may not be good for them.

Persuasion involves arriving at a feeling of rightness about a belief or action through one's own intuitive sense. One takes an intuitive step, from the closest approximation to certainty that can be reached by conscious logic (which is sometimes not very close) to the state in which one may say with conviction, "This is where I stand!" The act of persuasion, thus defined, would help order the logic and favor the intuitive step. But the person being persuaded must take that intuitive step alone, untrammeled by coercive or manipulative stratagems of any kind. Persuasion, on a critical issue, is a difficult, time-consuming process. It demands one of the most exacting of human skills.

In "The Uses of Great Men," Ralph Waldo Emerson explains: "Great men exist that there may be greater men. The destiny of organized nature is amelioration, and who can tell its limits. It is for man to tame the chaos; on every side, whilst he lives, to scatter the seeds of science and of song, that climate, corn, animals, men, may be milder, and that the germs of love and benefit may be multiplied."[3]

Coercion

Coercion is pressure: "Do as I say, think like I do, speak as I wish—or else!"

Coercion may be overt and brutal, with obvious penalties if one does not comply. Or it may be covert and subtle, as when needs or desires are exploited. Or, in the name of justice of some other obvious good, a nonviolent but coercive pressure tactic is used to repress a malignant force.

Overt coercion has long been associated with violence. Evidence is accumulating that covert and nonviolent tactics may be a prime cause of violence. If so-called civilized people employ covert or nonviolent tactics to achieve their ends, when the conditions are right, the use of that coercive power may cause violence to be unleashed in the less civilized. Let's look at an example.

In the current contention over legalized abortion, both sides are stridently coercive in their pressure tactics. One of the conspicuous consequences of this has been the firebombing of abortion clinics. The antiabortion forces disavow responsibility for this. What they mean is that they did not authorize or instigate the firebombing. But are they not responsible? If both sides of this controversy would use only persuasive (noncoercive) tactics, would the less civilized be likely to be incited to violence? The thin web of civilized behavior that makes an orderly society possible is easily fractured. Those who regard themselves as civilized must not fracture that web. Coercive pressure, to achieve what each side in this controversy regards as just and moral, has a fracturing effect on civilization. Whoever commits the fracture must bear some responsibility for the violence that is unleashed.

This is not an argument for a coercion-free society in which there are no coercive pressures, even though idealists contemplate such a society. What we call civilization has not advanced to the point where enough people have confidence that a utopian, coercion-free society is viable. What we have is a wide range. At one extreme is a highly civilized segment that, if segregated and protected from intrusions, probably could operate a coercion-free society. At the other extreme are the violence-prone, who, by our present lights, must be restrained by force—coercion. In between are all shades and blends, many of whom can be led and influenced by the more civilized so that an orderly society is possible. When one realizes the diversity, it is a tribute to something that we do as well as we do.

But when the more civilized use coercive pressure on an issue like abortion, where the ultimate resolution is best in terms of the values of individuals, the civilized web is broken. We should have learned that from our ill-fated experience with the prohibition of alcohol. Enough people were convinced of the evils of alcohol in 1919 that the Constitution was amended. In 1933, we went through the elaborate process of repealing the amendment. This was not done because of a great change of sentiment about the evils of alcohol. The substantial majority that wrote temperance into law became convinced that we would destroy the country trying to enforce Prohibition. Temperance by persuasion was greatly set back by the resort to coercion. Much of the violence that plagues us today may have its roots in that dark era of the 1920s in which good people coerced when they should have persuaded.

The most civilized among us are the most capable of being persuasive. People who see themselves as civilized should resort to coercion as little as possible because the road to a higher quality of civilization is through less coercion and more persuasion.

A second example of the consequences when good people coerce is the universities. Universities hold great coercive power in their credentialing role. Thomas Jefferson, founder and first rector of the University of Virginia, would not allow degrees to be granted on the ground that degrees were pretentious. He wanted only students whose sole motivation was the desire to learn. He would be deeply troubled by our present condition, in which the degree has become a measure of social status, the ticket of admission to the better jobs, and a means of advancing oneself professionally and financially. And he could not have foreseen the problem created when twice as many of those tickets are issued as there are vocational opportunities where those credentials are helpful. The point is that the control of those tickets gives the universities great coercive power, a power that renders them vulnerable to the same corrupting influences that are inherent in holding any power.

Have there been violent consequences of using this power in the universities? The answer, admittedly speculative, is yes! While the Vietnam War and the civil rights crisis stirred the air as obvious proximate causes (aided by some astute fomenting), it is a reasonable surmise that the universities were vulnerable as a target of that violence because of their long-standing use of coercive power. Their vulnerability may have been sharpened because in the rapid expansion of universities after World War II, for which a good justification has yet to emerge, faculties used their improved bargaining power to reduce their teaching loads and accessibility to students. By the 1960s, students began to perceive the universities as being run too much for the benefit of faculties and too little for the service to students. One may accept some coercion if one perceives that is one of the conditions for being well served. But if the quality of the service is questioned, as it was in the universities in the late 1960s, the coercion is apt to be seen as arbitrary and pointless, something to rebel against and even, in the less civilized, something to attack with violence.

To close observers of universities in the late 1960s, some of the manifestations resembled massive mental illness. But a close examination revealed a logic. In retrospect, it can be seen as a rebellion against unjustified coercion. There is a warning in this to those who would be seen as civilized and who wish to render a service in which those being served are coerced: the institution and the individuals who staff it must be seen as dedicated servants. When there is discontent in the air, the servant image must be exceptional. A more civilized role would be to perform the service without coercing the persons being served.

We have just cited two contemporary examples of what most people would consider highly civilized institutions, the church (on abortion) and the universities. Both have used coercion with a high probability of violence as a consequence.

In the case of the universities, they became the target of the violence. In the case of the church, so far the violence has been targeted at what is opposed. But if the church persists in imposing its will coercively on others, it is a reasonable conjecture that when the conditions are right, the church will become the target of violence. That will be a sad day.

A third example is the current popularity of nonviolent resistance and protest, again by "good" people who feel they are advancing civilization, as the church and the universities surely feel they are doing. The great exemplar for these tactics is Mohandas Gandhi.

Gandhi was probably the greatest leader of the common people the world has ever known. He brought freedom from colonialism to India, he hastened the end of that uncivilized practice everywhere, and he left a concept of a good society that will keep us stretched for centuries. But there was a negative side. Gandhi was coercive, and the consequence of his coercion was violence, awful violence.

Gandhi as a person was peaceful and gentle, and he had a great dream for the future of India. But his tactics in wielding his influence were coercive, particularly his ultimate tactic, the "fast unto death." In this he was saying, without equivocation, "If you don't do as I say, I will commit suicide." Ultimately, he got his way; he was a primary force in bringing independence to India. But in three important particulars, he may be judged a failure.

First, British India was predominantly Hindu, but it had a substantial Muslim minority. As the independence movement progressed, there emerged a leader, Jira, who was as influential with Muslims as Gandhi was with Hindus, and he led the Muslims to demand a separate state. There were large concentrations of Muslims in the East and the West, and these ultimately became the core of a separate nation, Pakistan. But before independence, there were large numbers of Muslims in what ultimately became India and large numbers of Hindus in what became Pakistan. When the British withdrew and the new national governments took over, communal strife broke out between the two sects. It was a terrible, brutal struggle in which death and maiming ran rampant. Estimates of the casualties on both sides run as high as a million. In addition, to escape persecution by the Hindus, about one million Muslims emigrated en masse from the Eastern Indian state of Bihar to East Pakistan, where they suffered in the direst poverty as outcasts for thirty years beyond independence because their language and ethnic origins were not accepted by the East Pakistani Muslims, who are Bengalis. As of 1984, four hundred thousand Biharis were still there, living in misery.

A good deal of India's western boundary with Pakistan is still a cease-fire line and has been the scene of occasional fighting since independence. East Pakistan broke away as Bangladesh in a bloody war, with the support of India. In sum, the violence and suffering that ensued from independence has been enormous, and the end is not yet in sight.

The second failure that might be attributed to Gandhi is that at a time when sovereign national states were coming into question as the basis for a viable world society, Gandhi led India and the rest of the colonial world into a chaotic quarreling. National states, whose survival as autonomous entities is questionable, have been left as victims of military juntas and pawns in the power struggle among the stronger nations. There has already been much violence and suffering, and more is in prospect.

The third failure was Gandhi's great dream of a good society, which he dangled before the Indians. At the same time, he supported the political movement that formed the government after independence, for whom Gandhi's idealistic dream meant little. His great dream for India, his spiritual goal, envisioned a simple village handicraft society, the kind of society I now realize I would like to live in. It was not achieved. The dream is still alive, and someday a great persuasive leader may bring it to reality. But Gandhi did not, and could not, achieve it because of the flaw of coercion in his tactics. He was so obsessed with achieving independence quickly that he allied himself politically with other strong leaders who shared that goal but did not accept his great dream for a good society in India. Nehru, his younger colleague who became the first prime minister, was Western in outlook. He denigrated traditional Indian culture and religion and immediately set out on a fast course to industrialize the country (in which I, unfortunately, was an accomplice). Nehru revealed a great deal when he wrote in his autobiography, "In spite of my closest association with him for many years, I am not clear in my own mind about his objective. I doubt if he is clear himself."[4]

Gandhi must have been aware of much of this adverse judgment near the end of his life (he was assassinated by a Hindu fanatic shortly after independence) because he was reported to be a very sad man by those close to him.

If he failed in the three ways I cited, to what extent might his coercive strategy have been the cause? Let us examine how he might have proceeded when he returned to India in 1915, after his work with the Indian ministry in Africa, if his strategy had been to persuade the British to take gradual steps to give the Indian people autonomy rather than embrace a strategy that had the effect of compelling their colonial masters to grant total independence.

Gandhi partisans assert that he did continue to try to persuade the British. But can one persuade if one's basic strategy is to coerce? Persuasion begins with an attitude toward the persons or groupings toward which the persuasive argument is directed. That attitude accepts that one is persuaded only when one arrives at a belief or action through one's own intuitive sense of the rightness of that action untrammeled by coercive pressure of any kind. One cannot embrace that attitude and employ the strategy of nonviolent coercion to which Gandhi, by 1915, was deeply committed.

Let us suppose, though, that in 1915, Gandhi was deeply committed to persuasion. What corollary attitudes would that commitment embrace? One would be the acceptance that the British would retain their power as colonial masters until they were convinced that they should use that power to bring greater autonomy to the Indian peoples. The British knew about the Hindu-Muslim tension. In fact, there is some suspicion that they fueled that tension as a strategy for maintaining their own control. But with that knowledge, while they continued to hold the power, if they became convinced that they should bring the Indian people to greater autonomy, they could take the time that would be required to bring about a transition that would not provoke the disastrous communal strife that independence did bring. A first step away from colonial domination might have been better than a host of violent national states. As it was, Gandhi's coercive strategy had the effect of reducing British power. When the British were seriously weakened in the aftermath of World War II, they had no alternative but to grant total independence quickly before they had a national explosion on their hands. It has been argued that the British were not coerced, that the Atlee government, in 1947, voluntarily granted independence. That argument is a technicality. The British knew they were powerless to continue as colonial masters, and as the sensible people they are, they quickly granted independence. They were precipitous about it.

Gandhi may have had the skills and temperament to be a great persuader, and we cannot know, of course, had he adopted persuasion as his sole strategy in 1915, how it would all have come out. India and much of the rest of the colonial world might never have achieved sovereign independence. But it might have been better for them, and for the world, if they had not achieved it. Under the guidance of a more enlightened Britain, achieved partly by the influence of the great persuader that Gandhi might have been, the colonial peoples might have found a design for local autonomy in a stable world order. The older sovereign national states might have adapted. One thing seems almost certain: the precipitous granting of sovereign independence to India and Pakistan in 1947 was certain to result in monstrous violence and human suffering—as it did. Almost any other gradual transition would have had a chance of avoiding it.

It is not the purpose here to analyze all aspects of this vast and complex question. But it does seem clear that Gandhi's coercive strategy, able and powerful and visionary man that he was, was doomed to result in violence.

These three examples (church, university, political revolutionary) of the role of coercion in provoking violence do not provide a close and clear causal link between coercion and violence. One must examine the attitudes of the people using coercive power. Do they respect the autonomy of the people in whom change or support is expected, and are they willing to wait for the unpressured interior conviction, the intuitive feeling of rightness, to emerge in its own good time? If it is clear that they will not wait for that (and it is clear that neither the church nor Gandhi was willing to wait), and they create evident pressure to conform to their wills now, the tactic must be judged coercive.

Coercion is principally useful to destroy or impede something. Not much of value to humankind can be built with it. The pyramids stand as mute testimony to the sweat and pain of slave labor that built them. Gandhi could bring down the British Empire, but he could not build his good society—or even start it on its way. Coercive acts seem to disqualify persons from constructive roles, great as their idealism may be.

Manipulation

Manipulation is not sharply distinct from coercion, but it does rest more on plausible rationalizations than on the threats of sanctions or pressure. People are manipulated when they are guided into beliefs or actions by plausible rationalizations that they do not fully understand.

Leaders, those who have the talents that enable them to go out ahead to show the way—and who are recognized as being better than most at doing it—are particularly tempted to use manipulation as a means for keeping their followers with them. Because they are recognized as being better than most at leading, showing the way, they are apt to be highly intuitive. Thus leaders themselves, in their conscious rationalities, may not fully understand why they choose a given path. Yet our culture requires that leaders produce plausible, convincing explanations for the directions they take. Once in a while, they can simply say, "I have a hunch that this is what we ought to do." However, most of the time, rational justifications are demanded, and part of the successful leader's skill is inventing these rationalizations. They are necessary, but they are also useful because they permit, after the fact, the test of conscious logic that "makes sense" to both leader and follower. But the understanding by the follower, if he or she is not to be manipulated, is not necessarily contained in this rationalization that makes sense. Because we live in a world that pretends a higher validity to conscious rational thinking in human affairs than is warranted by the facts of our existence, and because many sensitive people "know" this, manipulation hangs as a cloud over the relationship between leader and led almost everywhere. It is the subject of much pejorative comment and a cause of distrust and resentment. Some manipulation is unavoidable because the leader is unable to give an explanation that brings understanding. There is no time for it, or those to whom an explanation is directed either cannot or will not take the time to understand.

Leaders are many kinds of people: not only those explicitly designated for or asserting leadership but also doctors, nurses, lawyers, teachers, pastors, parents, police officers, salespeople, automotive mechanics—any one who works through, serves, has some responsibility for, or seeks the consent of others. All may, and most do at some time, either coerce or manipulate.

Can this cloud that hangs over so many human relationships and is the cause of so much distrust and resentment be dispelled? Not easily. If a leader with a lofty purpose eschews both coercion and manipulation and if one with a base purpose embraces them, is not the latter apt to carry the day? Let us hold this question until persuasion has been discussed.

Persuasion

The dictionaries are of little help on the meaning of *persuasion*. In one, after three definitions that do not imply coercion, a fourth suggests coercion, and the fifth flatly states, "to bring to a desired action or condition by force." Thus *persuasion*, in its benign and helpful meaning, needs a new definition. Let me repeat the one I suggested earlier: that one is persuaded upon arriving at a feeling of rightness about a belief or action through one's own intuitive sense. Persuasion is usually a slow, deliberate, and painstaking process. And sometimes, in the process of persuading, one must endure a wrong or an injustice longer than one thinks one should.

Some who coerce also presume to persuade. But can they? It's unlikely. The persuader, in my view, approaches the relationship with clean hands, just as the man of peace does not bear arms when confronting one who is armed. The test, under the definitions used here, of whether one has been coerced or persuaded to a new belief or practice is that if one has the power, or would find it tenable, to continue the belief or practice, one has probably been persuaded. If, however, one has been reduced to powerlessness, or if one feels that the belief or practice is no longer tenable, one may have been coerced. The prime test of persuasion is that the change is truly voluntary. The powerless, in coercive terms, have the best opportunity to persuade. When they are effective, they become powerful as persuaders.

An act of coercion described in the Book of Matthew in the New Testament has had unintended consequences for followers of the Christian faith. When Jesus drove the moneychangers out of the temple, he provided, for people who want or need it, theological sanction for coercion. But he did more than that. By that act, in his terms, he quickly purified the temple. But in doing so, he affirmed the stigma of profaneness on money, which persists to this day in such epithets as "filthy lucre" and "money is the root of all evil." What if he had chosen instead to leave the moneychangers in the temple and had undertaken to persuade them to bring their practices within the embrace of the sacred? It might not have had much effect on the simple economy of his day, but in our times, enmeshed as we are in a vast, complex, money-dominated culture, it could make the difference between survival and disaster. If he had had only limited success, the world might now be different—and better—if he had chosen, in that one single instance, to persuade rather than to coerce. But if he had chosen persuasion, the account of it might not be in the record. Persuasion is usually too undramatic to be newsworthy, and Jesus did not live long enough for the persuasive approach to have a noticeable effect. So much of history deals with coercion because it is rapid, conspicuous, and dramatic and its consequences are so often horrendous. Significant instances of persuasion may be known to only one or a few, and they are rarely noted in history.

Consensus

Consensus is a method of using persuasion in groups. *Consensus* is used in its commonly understood meaning of unanimity or general agreement in matters of opinion, as opposed to taking a vote when differences exist. It is a meeting of minds that is achieved by individuals' being persuaded to accept a common point of view. They either accept the decision as the right or best one, or they agree to support it as a feasible resolution of the issue, being aware of the limited time for deliberation that may be allocated to any one issue. Whether they accept the decision as the right one or whether they merely agree to go along, the individual's position is intuitively derived in the absence of any coercive pressure to conform.

Almost always, a chairperson or leader guides the deliberation leading to consensus. The aim of the chair, who is a peer of the group's members, is to achieve consensus, a genuine meeting of minds, rather than to impose, or manipulate toward his or her own point of view. The art of chairing, in this sense, rests on four prime skills.

First, the chairperson has a deep understanding of the problem or issue under consideration and is able to articulate clearly and succinctly so that all will grasp it quickly. Patience is required to help those who are slow to understand or who have mental blocks or biases that hinder their understanding. If a few have unusual difficulty (or are resisting) understanding, a separate meeting between them and the chair is advisable. Time will be saved in the end by taking pains to make sure that the issue is understood before proceeding with discussion.

Second is listening. The chairperson is obviously intent on understanding the several points of view and states and restates the various positions until proponents are satisfied that the chair understands. The chairperson sets the model for listening in the hope that all will listen intently and seek to understand all points of view. Listening thus gives a temperate quality to the discussion that is conducive to reaching consensus.

Third, the chairperson will be sensitive to assess the course of the discussion and decide when it is feasible to begin to search for consensus. This may be early or late in the discussion, and it is possible that a group member has already proposed a basis for discussion. In one way or another, the chair states a consensus idea tentatively, asking, "Is this a possible solution?"

The chairperson will accept that finding a basis for consensus is as much a matter of language as concept. Therefore, chairing toward consensus calls for sustained inventiveness in searching for both language and concept that will make a consensus idea. In the event that the issue brings a contentious debate, the chairperson may need great tenacity in staying with the search for the resolving idea.

The fourth skill is needed when the issue is nearly, but not quite, resolved. One individual or a small number is holding out after the debate, in the minds of the majority, has adequately explored the subject and has used as much time as the press of other business will allow. At this point, the chairperson, with consensus still the aim, may ask to adjourn the discussion so as to talk privately with the holdouts. This is a critical stage in the process; the lone individual or the little group may be right and the great majority wrong. But the problem may be a matter of understanding, or there may be an emotional block, a personal animosity, an entrenched negative or perverse personality, or an impervious dogmatic position. The chairperson, in a private conversation, should undertake to determine what it is. If it is a matter of understanding the issue, an effort will be made to clear it up. If it is established that it is in one of the other three conditions, the chairperson will undertake to persuade the holdouts to change their position. Failing in this, there are some alternatives. Depending on the importance of the issue and the need for action, the chairperson might decide one of three things: initiate no further action, defer further consideration of the issue, or ask other members to try to understand or persuade the holdouts. If, after several have reasoned with the holdouts without persuading, the need for action is urgent, the chair might, after consultation, report to the group that an impasse has been reached that can only be resolved by eliminating the holdouts from the consensus.

This last step would be an admission of failure in the process of consensus. The test of the leadership of the chairperson in this regard, as in other aspects of leadership, is that failure is rare. In the infinite variety of human traits, some seem to constrain the individual from participation in consensus procedures. But it is better to set consensus as a goal, wherever this is feasible, and use the occasional impasse to eliminate those who cannot participate constructively in this process. Such persons may be of great value, but they may function best as lone workers or in groups that operate by majority rule.

A Strategy for Change

How might one view one's opportunities and obligations if one is able and is dedicated to the exclusive use of persuasion as a means for social change? Following are some suggestions.

○ Create and maintain a clear space between oneself and those who advocate, or inadvertently use, coercion, even in its mildest forms.

○ Do not reject the coercers as persons, even the most unsavory of them. Labor with them lovingly and persuasively, person by person, first to restrain their coercive tendencies and then, if possible, to move them across the gap that separates those who use coercion in any form from those who use only persuasion. But do not blur the gap; keep it wide and clear. If necessary, stand alone as a persuader, but find close colleagues, if possible, who will help make persuasion a disciplined approach and provide the constant checking of one another that such discipline requires.

○ Accept that "It's me, O Lord, standing in the need of prayer," and ceaselessly search for depth of meaning about persuasion and greater understanding of the intricate web of institutions in which most of us are enmeshed and in which coercion is rampant.

○ Learn to respect the integrity and autonomy of those whom one would persuade. Approach the relationship with the attitude of acceptance that oneself, the persuader, may change.

If one has prepared oneself to learn to persuade by positioning oneself and acquiring attitudes like those suggested here, how does one develop one's skills as a persuader and have a chance to be effective anywhere but on the fringes of this coercion-ridden world? What counsel could be given to young people, whose lifestyles may yet be shaped by conscious choices, on how a life can be lived as a persuader and stay afloat in these uncertain times? What is a tenable view of contemporary society that will help one orient oneself as a seeker so that one can answer these questions for oneself? A vignette of such a view is offered as a context for judging where and how a new persuasive influence may be most useful in our time.

We live amid a pervasive leadership crisis. It is a crisis without precedent, and it affects all dimensions of life. There have always been and probably always will be leaders, persons who are most able to foresee where to go, who are willing to take the risks of going out ahead to show the way, and who are trusted by those who follow them. People have been poorly served before, as many are now, by those whose leadership they choose to follow. What is different in our times is that, in the past hundred years, we have moved from a society of artisans, farmers, merchants, and professionals, with small government and military, to widespread involvement with a vast array of institutions—often large, complex, powerful, impersonal, not always competent, and sometimes corrupt. There is nothing like it in our history. Recent experience with these institutions has brought a new awareness of serious deficiencies in our common life that are clearly traceable to leadership inadequacies that result in these institutions' both serving poorly and hurting people. Part of this leadership failure can be attributed to the predominance of coercion within our institutions, and this may in turn be due to the failure of so many who could persuade, and who might lead more fulfilled lives as persuaders, to make their influence felt in the leadership of institutions. Some resources have long been, and may always be, devoted to rescuing people from the hurt of "the system," whatever it happens to be. But in our day, some of these institutions are grinding people down faster than the most valiant efforts can recover them. Some of the effort now devoted to caring for the hurt of people should be diverted to caring for institutions, with a prime concern for how they are structured and how they are led.

A close look at these institutions reveals that they generally adhere to hierarchical structures with an unhealthy concentration of coercive power at the top and without an adequate leaven of persuasion to make them acceptable as vital units of our social structure. Furthermore, the coercive power of government is increasingly used to try to force them, particularly businesses, to become more socially responsible. The main recourse for alleviating pain in our low serving society seems to be to tighten administrative structures and pass more laws. We are burdened with a compulsion to deal with the adverse consequences of coercion with more coercion. Where will it end? Most of the efforts to reduce the pain of the hurt of persons are reactive: combating injustice, opposing harmful actions, limiting the power of the powerful, checking violence. Necessary as these actions may be, they are mostly reactions against hurtful initiatives that someone has taken. In an imperfect world with fallible people, some of these reactive strategies will continue to be needed. They help make life tolerable, but they contribute little to building a better society in which there are fewer harmful actions. The benefits of reactive measures are seldom cumulative. A dilemma is faced by those who care for people and who want to lead effective caring lives: can the reactive and the proactive building strategies be combined in one effective lifestyle? Is not a preoccupation with reactive caring for the hurt of persons incompatible with a concern for a fundamental reconstruction of our institutions? If they are not incompatible, does anybody have enough energy and the required flexibility of temperament to be proficient in both? Those who are dedicated to institutional reconstruction may be more effective if they are wholly committed to change by persuasion. Reactive strategies, however noble their intent, usually carry at least a tinge of coercion. The attitudes, knowledge, and skills of reactors and proactors seem to be quite different, and those who undertake one mission or the other may be responding to dissimilar senses of obligation.

The brief view just presented suggests that more persuaders are needed. Some coercion may always be with us, and those who hold coercive power but restrain its use deserve kudos, as Shakespeare memorialized in his ninety-fourth sonnet, which opens with the line "They that have power to hurt and will do none." But the mere holding of that power seriously limits them as persuaders. Not much of ultimate value in human terms can be built with it. Persuasion is the prime building force.

A more just and loving society will not be built by reaction, although some of its more glaring hurts may be temporarily reduced by it, as aspirin reduces physical pain. A better society will come, if it comes, as the institutions that are its constituent parts slowly, painstakingly, one at a time, become more just and more loving because those who hold coercive power become convinced that persuasion is a better building force than coercion. They will then release able, committed persuaders within these institutions and make attractive careers for them. And they will both allow and encourage persuasion to take over as much as it can of the administrative function. Those in ultimate power will make this fundamental change, not so much because they think they ought to, or even if they sense that it will work better, but as they become convinced that an institution guided by persuasion will make life more meaningful and fulfilling for them, the holders of the ultimate coercive power. The transition from what now prevails to such a more benign state will not be easy, nor is it likely to be rapid.

What will the individual do, one who believes in persuasion, who is committed to its exclusive use, and who accepts a view of social change like that suggested here? One accepts that initiatives, all initiatives, are taken by individuals, not by institutions. Institutions can only respond to the initiatives of individuals.

Two kinds of initiatives are suggested. First, address, from the outside, the holders of ultimate coercive power in one institution at a time. Undertake to persuade them to the view suggested above. Second, establish oneself inside some institution, avoid a coercive power role as much as possible, and slowly evolve as a persuader wherever there is the opportunity. Both roles require diligent preparation. One should not assume, just because one's motives are good, that one is effective as a persuader. It is a very exacting role. This approach to resolving the issue of power in an institution has the virtue of being evolutionary rather than revolutionary, The holders of the ultimate power need not commit themselves to a new and untried ideology (although one may evolve that they will be committed to). They have an intent, rather than a plan.

What is important is that the holders of coercive power, who are probably going to be in charge for some time, (1) understand the value of persuasion as the prime moving force in the institution, (2) accept that they are inhibited from being persuasive because they hold coercive power, (3) resolve to liberate as much persuasive energy as they can, and (4) stand aside so that persuasion can do its work as long as it is effective. These are not wholly new ideas; persuaders have long been effective within authoritarian institutions. In our time, it has become urgent that their influence should be greatly expanded by persuasion. If one is able and dedicated as a persuader, one has, as always, the opportunity to carry, wholly alone, a proactive persuading role and to wield a benign and serving influence—power.

The opportunity is greater today, as contrasted with simpler times in which there was not the dominance of large institutions, because one has the chance, if one will brave the complexities of large institutions, to find a substantial multiplier for one's effort. One undertakes this with faith that some of the holders of coercive power can be persuaded that life for them will be better, more whole and satisfying, if they use that power to bring persuasion into a dominant role in the affairs of the institution. Just one able and dedicated persuader, standing alone, can be powerful.

Legend has it that a great philosopher and his son were trying to get a balky calf into the barn. One had a halter on its head and was pulling; the other was pushing from behind. The calf had its legs splayed out and, for all practical purposes, was immovable. A servant girl was watching this with amusement from the kitchen window. When the two gave up, perspiring from the effort, the girl came out, stuck her finger in the calf's mouth, and led it slowly into the barn. Such is the power of persuasion—when one knows how and is dedicated to its use.

Heed Abraham Joshua Heschel: "The greatest sin of man is to forget that he is a prince—that he has royal power. All worlds are in need of exaltation, and everyone is charged to lift what is low, to unite what is apart, to advance what is left behind. It is as if all worlds . . . are full of expectancy, of sacred goals to be reached, so that consummation can come to pass. And man is called upon to bring about the climax slowly but decisively."[5]

POWER IN THE EXECUTIVE OFFICE

THEOLOGIANS AND PHILOSOPHERS have speculated theoretically and at great length on the subject of power. I would like to share with you a few thoughts about power, simply as I have experienced it—both as the recipient and as the wielder of power.

Let us take the simple dictionary definition as our base: power is the possession of control, authority, or influence over others. All power as I will discuss it relates to this definition, whether it is financial power, market power, organizational power, or government power. It all winds up with the possession of control, authority, or influence over others.

We live in a time when the attacks on holders of power are pretty vigorous. This is sometimes cloaked with seeming altruism. But underneath is usually the desire of the attacker to get more power for himself or herself.

I cannot conceive why anyone would want to be in a position of leadership anywhere unless one is comfortable with getting and using power. The wear and tear on the individual who leads is too great, and nothing, in my judgment, but the satisfaction of using power would compensate for the personal investment. If an intelligent person just wants to live comfortably and enjoy life, he or she can do that in our society without

---

Note: From a speech ghost-written by Robert K. Greenleaf.

carrying the heavy burdens of a leadership role. Only the rewards and satisfactions in holding and using power will compensate for bearing any real burden of leadership.

One's motives in holding and using power are another matter. One may have altruistic motives and hope to do good—to benefit society—or one may have less noble motives. But not much happens in this world, for good or ill, except that somebody accumulates some power—some control, authority, or influence over others. Those who shout "power to the people" just want to shift things around so they can better influence how this "people's power" is used. Ultimate power, of course, always rests with the great mass of the people as they make their choices of what they will and will not do. But power as we are concerned with it here, and as the dictionary defines it, resides in that person who has control, authority, or influence over how the choices among these widely dispersed people are made.

With this general introduction, I would like to share with you a few observations from my own experience of sitting in the chief executive's seat of a large company and holding as much of a concentration of power in my hands as this kind of institution can corral. Our company is not General Motors, but it is big enough to present all of the problems of bigness.

It is one thing to have the kind of power one might have in a small business, where one person can see or understand most of what is going on and can evaluate, if so desired, the consequences of his or her decisions. It is quite another matter to hold this power in a situation that is large enough that one person cannot directly see or understand much of what is going on and where it is often very difficult to know what the consequences of one's decisions are. It is this latter situation in large businesses that I want to talk about, because that is where I sit.

I have a certain power to command, some control over money, and access to some information that others can't get so easily, and certain things are appropriate for me to initiate and not appropriate for others. These are some of the formal vestings of power that go with my office. But these alone do not take me very far. And chief executives who rely too heavily on such as these do not go very far or last very long.

The critical element in my job is that I sit in the spot where all of the contending forces converge, forces that can either help or hurt what I want to get done—and that is to build a great business, a business where all of these forces must be reconciled in an optimal way. "The buck stops here" is only part of the story. As I see it, the essential skill that my job calls for is the use of power (and I have some) to balance all of the power forces that can help or hurt my business and balance them in a way so that we come out best. Like all other people who are willing to pay the price that holding and using power entails, I want to win. I want to build a great business—the greatest business I can make of it. My concept of my basic role is that I sit in the center (the organization chart shows I sit on top, but that is mere convention). I see myself surrounded by a large number of contending powers of varying and shifting magnitudes. And the peculiar power of my office enables me to work at settling the conflicts among them.

In mechanics, there is a mathematical principle called *moments of force*. It is a way of resolving the mechanical forces that impinge on a point in space; the chief executive's job is something like that. What are the forces that the CEO deals with? You know most of them as well as I do. There is the market: your customers and the money market and the talent market. There are levels of government—federal, state, and local—and the many things they want you to do and not to do, not to mention the money they want in taxes. There are the public interest groups: Nader, consumers, environmentalists. There are your own people, both as individuals in your workforce and collectively. There are the members of your management group and the several levels of power they wield. And then your owners, influential ones of whom may sit on the board, and the public members of the board, who have a different kind of interest.

From my own experience, I am aware that it is one thing to know about power, as you study it in a case, and it is a very different thing to sit where you deal with power by using it and contending with its use. And I do not mean to use the power of the chief executive officer just in a countervailing sense. The chief executive has lost the war if he or she thinks of using power in an adversary sense to stalemate the others. The CEO may win an occasional battle that way but will lose the war if that is his or her predominant strategy; there are too many others with too much power to think in terms of putting them all down. Even a CEO who is the sole owner of a business with a patent monopoly on something will lose with a strategy that is mostly adversarial. This is especially true if it is a large business.

How, then, does a chief executive use power to achieve a balance of contending powers that supports what the CEO is trying to achieve with the business—in my case, to build a great business, a business that is great in every dimension?

The CEO has a range of "process" competencies—finance, marketing, technology, organization, management, and so forth. Without these, he or she would not be likely to get into the job in the first place. Beyond these, what separates the chief executive who wins the war from the one who sees it as winning battles? Here are some examples:

- The CEO enjoys using power to get other people's power turned to support what he or she wants to do. Some people apply the nasty word *manipulation* to this. But as long as you have leadership, you are going to have manipulation in this sense. It has to be legitimate, because you can't hold our society of two hundred million people together without it.

- The CEO uses power to know more, and in a wider perspective, than those whose power the CEO needs to bend to support his or her goals. The successful top executives I know simply work harder and have better information resources to tap than other wielders of power. And they use these to get a better total understanding of the context in which they are operating. Out of this, they may get a strategy for winning the war.

○ The CEO uses power to be heard. Because of the nature of power, if the CEO has something to say, people will listen more intently; even people who consider themselves adversaries will listen intently, but the CEO must have something to say. With this knowledge and perspective, the CEO gains power by being able to foresee the problems he or she must deal with long enough before other people see them so that the CEO can initiate and lead. This is the lead that a leader has. It is lead time, time to move before events force the CEO's hand and he or she is in the unfortunate position of only being able to react.

○ Because the CEO holds the baton, he or she can articulate a far-out goal and lift other people's sights, including those who see themselves as adversaries. The difference between mediocrity and distinction in any kind of institution is in the goals. The goals may never be reached (just as we in this country have never reached the goals spelled out in the Declaration of Independence, but we have gone farther having those goals than we would have gotten without them). Far-out goals take people farther faster than close-in goals. The CEO doesn't need to invent the goal, but only he or she can articulate it persuasively.

○ The CEO uses power to build stronger people, particularly higher-level executives. The CEO uses power to strengthen inner resources—even in executives whom the CEO may have to demote or separate from the company.

○ The CEO who wants to build a strong company will want all of the forces he or she contends with to be strong. We are in an interesting transition on one of these—the board of directors. Some executives of large publicly owned businesses have secretly preferred weak or compliant boards. Now some of us are beginning to realize that a strong company needs a strong board, and we are setting out to build up the power in our boards. This is one of the very healthy signs of the times. It is said of Alfred Sloan that in the early days of General Motors, he set out deliberately to make all of his key executives wealthy so that they would have independence of judgment.[6] A great company was built by this kind of thinking.

These are some of the attitudes and ways of working that separate the CEO who wants to win the war from the one who sees it only as winning battles. I have used "winning the war" and "winning battles" rather than "long run" and "short run" because it sharpens the differences between the two styles. Everybody has some short-range strategies. But winners in the CEO spot make it by long-range thinking. You can document this as well as I can.

Anybody who ventures to talk about power needs to make a nod toward Lord Acton's maxim, "Power tends to corrupt; absolute power corrupts absolutely."[7] I accept this. I also accept that power is in the equipment of all who lead anything. Therefore, holders of power should be constantly alert to its corrupting potential and guard against being corrupted by accepting the value to them in the various power sources with which they must contend and dealing with them so as to sustain their power.

LESSONS ON POWER

WHEN THE HISTORIANS OF THE FUTURE add up the score on the twentieth century, they may mark the late 1960s as the time when people around the world came to grips with the issue of power.

Not that the issue is new. Several thousand years ago, the prophet Zechariah proclaimed, "Not by might, nor by power, but by my spirit."[8] People have been concerned with power and the use of power for a long time, and there is an abundance of scholarly literature on the subject. But there is a difference, as I see it, between a literature born largely of the speculations of scholars and moralists and the abundant record of these immediate years of record of the self-conscious, articulate awareness of large numbers of people in all walks of life who are the users and objects of power.

Future literature on power may be concerned not so much with scholarly thought on the subject as with analysis of the revealed attitudes of large numbers of users and objects of power. These attitudes are revealed as people interact with one another and speak for the record with great candor about their thoughts, attitudes, and motives as they contemplate the use of power, or their protection from its use, and as they react to the consequences of its use.

Note: From a speech ghost-written by Robert K. Greenleaf.

One of the new awarenesses of our times is the realization of the centrality of language in the complex of forces that make a social structure. The shift from a restrained Victorian usage to gutsy language and the once-taboo four-letter words in our best literary examples, a kind of speech that once bore the opprobrium of the gutter, has no doubt helped make common currency of attitudes and feelings about power that once were repressed. This has been augmented by the candid television portrayals of the war in Vietnam, the race riots in our cities, and the eruption of our campuses, which have immersed the home, the family, and the emerging generation of young adults day after day, for some years now, in the stark realities of power carried to violence.

What makes this different from the occasional violence of crime, which has always been in the experience of men, is the moral confusion that surrounds this panorama of power carried to violence that is the daily diet of most people the world over. With all of these stark and brutal revelations comes the argument of "good" people who approve and "good" people who condemn, thus leaving to each viewer, young and old, experienced and inexperienced, the terrible task of sorting it out. Gone are the days when the "good" guys in the drama were clearly distinguishable from the "bad" guys, when the generally accepted norm neatly separated the right from the wrong action. Much of the moral certainty that guided the average person in personal conduct and in the judgment of events has been eroded. This is why I believe that when the historians of the future assess these times, they will cite the late 1960s as the years when large numbers of people around the world came to grips with the issue of power. It is not that our generation is naturally more reflective about it than previous generations or more willing to engage with power as an issue. Our times have simply been bombarded with the evidence of power turned violent, while the usual concerns about what is good and bad in the use of power have been seriously shaken. Perhaps the two are related.

What does one do then? The question is on the mind of every thoughtful person I know. The hard-won advances of such civilization as we have seem threatened on every side by people who say, "Change it to suit me—quick—or I will destroy what shred of order there is!"

I grant you that it is an imperfect world and that many radical changes need to be made in it. It is not my purpose here to give you my blueprint for remaking the world. You have already heard enough of that. Rather, I would like to share my own response to the contemporary disorder in moral thought and what may be a related phenomenon of power gone rampant.

First, I am hopeful. Disorder is always threatening. But it also opens opportunities that might not otherwise be sought. In my experience, opportunities do not present themselves; they are always there for the taking. Things happen when people seek out opportunities. And one of the by-products of moral disorder is that it spurs the individual search for a new, more enabling ethic.

In this sense, despite the threats of the times, you are lucky because you are more likely to be seekers and to emerge as creative contributors than if you were launching yourselves in the world in more placid times when the moral order was in better repair. So I am hopeful that out of the stress of these times, which are hard on all of us, will come a new searching, especially by this college generation. The fruits of this searching will be more meaningful to you because you have more of your lives to be shaped by it and it will be easier for you to make the adjustment to a new and nobler ethic than for those of us whose lifestyles were set in a quite different era. I will bet on you. I could not stay in education if I did not see it this way.

My second response to the contemporary disorder in moral thought is to scan the available historic wisdom about crises of moral confusion. There is an abundance of this wisdom because there has always been a moral crisis. It is only occasionally that society falls into a disarray like the present. In our Western tradition, from the Old Testament prophets down to now, there is a vast store of wisdom that is relevant to times of crisis like ours when the reckless use of power threatens society and the people who should speak with one voice about right and wrong are in a babel of confusion. I have not reviewed all of our store of wisdom by far, but I assure you that in the last couple of years, I have been spurred to a much larger than usual preoccupation with the great wisdom sources. Where else, really, can one go?

This much I would like to share from my own search; it is brief and reasonably contemporary, and if one is disposed to let one's creative powers respond to it, a pretty complete philosophy for these times can be constructed from it. The great historian Charles A. Beard was asked by a student, "Professor Beard, before you lay down your mantle, won't you write a short book summarizing the lessons of history as you see them?" "I can do better than that," Professor Beard responded. "I can give it to you right now in four sentences." His four sentences are partly paraphrased from what others have said. Here they are:[9]

1. Whom the gods would destroy, they first make mad with power.

2. The mills of God grind slowly, but they grind exceeding small.

3. The bee fertilizes the flower it robs.

4. When it is dark enough, you can see the stars.

There is a great symbolism here that one should live with and reflect on for a while. It is one of those things, like Robert Frost's poetry when a student once asked him what one of his poems meant. "Read it, and read it, and read it," he said, "and it means what it says to you." Professor Beard's summary is a sort of symbolic poem in the sense that it is not so much designed to convey meaning as to elicit it. So it is not so much what Professor Beard is trying to say in his beautifully succinct and symbolic summary as what your creative response is when you read it and read it and read it. In the context of this simplified and yet, I think, quite fundamental approach to meaning, I would like to share how my thoughts have run after reading and reading and reading these four sentences. Your response to this summary may be quite different from mine, but seekers need to share, and it is in my role of seeker after understanding that I offer my response.

Let us take the first one: Whom the Gods would destroy, they first make mad with power.

This suggests to me that there is a necessary legitimacy to power when one uses it "sanely." It is difficult to see how our vast, complex, and soon to be overpopulated society can carry on without some concentrations of power. It is being mad with power that will anger the gods. It is the reckless, insensitive, not socially oriented use of power that is censored by destruction. Probably what is changing in the whole world today is a growing sense—among all people—of what is a legitimate use of power. The long line of decisions of the U.S. Supreme Court delimiting the use of police power is a specific case in point. But there still seems to be a legitimacy in the idea of countervailing power—an expectation of justice to be gained by encouraging one coercive force to stand against other coercive forces that are judged to be harmful. I suspect that a forthcoming revolution in values will challenge the idea of countervailing power just as the unrestrained use of police power is now being challenged.

What is judged mad is not what is so classified by a technical medical definition. It is a social judgment, and as such, it changes, sometimes rapidly. Just as the recent Supreme Court decisions have made police work more difficult and calling for much more highly trained, judicious, and thoughtful people as police officers, so other holders of power—parents, teachers, government officials, university administrators—may find themselves, in ways both subtle and unsubtle, required to be more highly trained in the use of power and more judicious and thoughtful. If this be the trend, who will deny that the effect will be good?

The mills of God grind slowly, but they grind exceeding small. Again let us take the Supreme Court decisions concerning police power. It is nearly two hundred years since our constitutional guarantees were written. But case by case, the mills are grinding away, and in the eyes of the police officers of the nation, they are grinding exceeding small. There does seem to be something inexorable about it. The general trend is clear enough, it seems to me. This is the age when people the world over have come to grips with the issue of power. One by one, the holders of power will be held in judgment. Reckless, insensitive, non–socially oriented uses of power will be categorically condemned, and precise standards of legitimate, sensitive, socially constructive uses of power will take their place. And the mills will continue to grind exceeding small.

Now don't look at me and ask, "What are you, a college president, going to do about it?" I'm looking at *you* and asking, "What are *you* going to do about it?" You're going to be around longer than I am. Soon you will be parents, teachers, businesspeople and professionals. This ever-finer-grinding mill is going to do more to you than to my generation. And you have a larger opportunity to be in the vanguard of one of the great social revolutions, the coming to grips with the issue of power.

The bee fertilizes the flower it robs. What tremendous symbolism in this simple assertion! Never take anything from anybody, from any situation, without leaving something of greater value than you take away. Never enter a situation without respect for the integrity of personality of every individual involved. Take the wage worthy of your hire, if it is the job that supplies your livelihood, but leave a creative force in the situation where you work so that the effect of your presence is a sustained, living, growing, beautiful thing. You may have the power to destroy, to hurt, to demean; but you will remember the bee that fertilizes the flower it robs.

When it is dark enough, you can see the stars. What nobler thought can one hold when the clouds are lowering and the very air shakes with violence?

I leave it with you. When it is dark enough, you can see the stars.

BUILDING THE ETHIC OF
STRENGTH IN BUSINESS

IN THE YEARS SINCE I RETIRED from my active career, I have
had intimate exposure to a wide range of institutions: exten-
sively with businesses, large and small, in the United States, in
Europe, and in the Third World, but also with church organizations, universities, and foundations. As I regard my total experience, I wonder what the judgment would be if there were a
common scale of values that could be applied to all institutions
so that we might weigh, on a comparable basis, how each is
doing in terms of the *obligations* it has assumed and its *opportunities* to serve society. My guess is that we would conclude
that businesses, in general, do as well as the others. No category of institution that I know about, as a class, does very well.
Compared to other institutions and callings, businesses are less
clothed with professional sanctity; they are more exposed and
are therefore easier to regulate by law; they handle more money
and property; and there is a greater opportunity to wheel and
deal; some of their many derelictions are more newsworthy,
and at the low end of the scale, they tail off into the thoroughly
corrupt. But at the high end of the scale, in terms of the obligations assumed and what they do with their opportunity to serve
society, I would rate some businesses as comparable to the best
universities, churches, and foundations. The differences between institutions are the differences between people. There is
something about the quality of individual people and what they

do with their opportunities that transcends stereotypes that are associated with institutional categories.

Along the way, I had a conversation with the minister of a church who was vehement in his condemnation of business ethics. After listening to a good deal of this, I interjected, "I don't see how you can make these judgments when, as a minister of the Gospel, you are deeply involved with two of our most pernicious rackets."

"What are those?" was his startled response.

"Weddings and funerals," I firmly replied.

"Oh," he protested, "but those are deep in the culture. You don't expect me to change the culture, do you?"

"That," I observed, "is exactly the justification the corrupt businessman would give."

A few years ago, I found myself on a panel before a seminar in a medical school that was discussing the ethics of the drug industry. In preparation for the seminar, someone had put a movie camera before a television screen and over a period of days had photographed the commercials of nonprescription drug vendors. Some of these zany ads are hard to take when seen once in a while as the price of watching commercial TV. But to watch one after another for a half hour was a nauseating experience.

At the conclusion of this film, the conference erupted in indignation at the affront to intellect as well as to taste. When it finally simmered down, the gremlin in me prompted me to make the following remarks. "I don't see why you are so upset about this. When a nation decides, as a matter of social policy backed up with criminal sanctions—as we have done in this country over a long period of years—that an industry like this will be regulated by requiring dog-eat-dog competition, then you shouldn't be surprised with a result such as we have just seen."

This provoked another eruption of indignation. "Are you advocating the repeal of the antitrust laws?" they shrilled.

"I don't know what I would do," I replied. "All I have to say is this: if you decide to regulate this industry in this way, then it seems to me that what we have seen here is a to-be-expected result. The antitrust laws were not brought down off the mountain chiseled in stone. They are crude manmade devices invented in 1890 and 1914 in an effort to curb what were then regarded as unwanted business practices. But all laws, like all drugs, have side effects. And what you have seen here today is, in my judgment, one of those side effects. If you don't like this particular side effect, then you should examine whether the remedy that was applied around the turn of the century is still the one you want to employ. Maybe, by now, we could find a better one."

This raises an interesting question about the similarity between laws and drugs. Both tend to have unwanted side effects because both are coercive. When one corrects a physical ailment with altered nutrition, there are not likely to be unwanted side effects. With a social problem, if persuasion alone is used to change what is thought to be a harmful practice, there are not likely to be unwanted side effects. But in an imperfect world with fallible people, recourse to drugs and laws is sometimes the best we know how to do. And people of conscience should know that if coercion is used, no matter how idealistic the purposes, no matter how logical the justification, no matter how bland the manifestations, there may be unwanted side effects that, on strictly utilitarian grounds, sometimes exceed whatever advantage there may have been in the primary action.

One issue of questionable ethics has recently been raised about the exploitation by universities of the current boom in business education. I only know about it what I read in the papers and hear on the air, but the accusation has caused quite a stir. It seems that because business education can be conducted so as to make money in these times, some universities are offering inferior master's degree programs in business administration in order to get a little extra cash.

Part of the public concern about business ethics today grows out of our failure as a nation ever to face, through the legislative policy-making process, the fundamental question of what kind of industrial society we want. When the framers of the Constitution did their great work nearly two centuries ago, they did not foresee an industrial age and the now-pervasive instrument known as the corporation. Corporations get their constitutional status from the willingness of the courts to construe them as persons under the Fourteenth Amendment. Beginning with Chief Justice Marshall's landmark decision in 1819, we have had a succession of court decisions and a patchwork of laws regarding business and its corporate form of organization. As a result, we have a patchwork business ethic in which some of what is labeled unethical now is a consequence of laws made in quite different times.

I am not stating this to deliver a jeremiad on our present society, although I do feel it is coming apart a bit at the seams. But for understandable reasons, we seem not to have a quality of leadership for our times that approaches what the Founding Fathers had for theirs. So I do not anticipate that, for the foreseeable future, we will take on the question of what kind of industrial society will serve us best. Consequently, we will probably continue for some time to muddle along with a patchwork of court decisions and inept laws with their uncalculated side effects, as we have for the past 150 years. As we do this, we will accommodate the unceasing demands for instant perfection and crash efforts to wipe out all injustice. In dealing with these pressures, new injustices will be created as we try to erase old ones, and we will likely find ourselves with more tortured decisions like the one the Supreme Court delivered in the Bakke case [finding that affirmative action discriminated against white Americans]. (No criticism of the Court is intended. The nine conscientious judges probably did the best they could do under the circumstances. Some policy guidance would help them too.)

As I reflect on this view of things, I am of two minds. First, I am glad that I am as old as I am and that somebody else will have to cope with the unending confusion. But my other mind turns to ponder these questions: If I were coming of age today and could have the guidance of a mentor who had lived through what I have experienced, how could I prepare to deal with current and upcoming conditions? How could I learn to take hold of some small piece of the world, work to make a constructive contribution to it, and grow with my experience? Or, put another way, if I were ten or twenty years along in my career with many potentially good years ahead of me but found myself burdened with the feeling of being ground down by present circumstances, could I be given a perspective that would help me gain outward poise and inward serenity so that despite the pressures, I could deal creatively with the opportunities I have? Let us discuss the issues raised by these questions, beginning with the word *ethics*.

Ethics, as a word, is suffering from overuse. It is a loosely defined word, and for some reason it has become the custom to start an agitation about ethics for every ill of our society. This tends to confuse the issue for those who are trying to use their efforts constructively. There is a place for an explicit concern with ethics. But this popular clamor is thwarting that concern, too.

Ethics, as I see it, is like humility. It has been said that if a person is self-conscious about his humility, he hasn't got it. It is a natural thing. Either you're humble or you're not. The same holds for ethics. The person who says, "Now I am being ethical," should be regarded with suspicion. The institution that seeks to remedy its faults by making a big to-do about ethics should be dealt with at arm's length. The basis for trust is not there. A friend of mine tells of his first boss in business, a rough, uncut-diamond sort of man with limited education but a lot of common sense. In commenting on a particularly difficult character they were trying to deal with, this boss observed, "You know, if a fellow is an S.O.B., if that is what he really is, deep down inside, he had better just go ahead and be one, because if he tries to be something else, he'll wind up being both a hypocrite *and* an S.O.B., and that's worse!"

This is the kind of overstatement that makes a point. Obviously, some of our impulses must be restrained. But there is also a sort of primitive integrity about being what we are. If the cards are bad, difficult to work with, I would rather they be dealt on the table than under it.

A lot of the talk about evil in the world smacks of the notion that it ought not to be there rather than as something to be dealt with realistically. I am a lot more concerned with helping good people deal with evil, and keep their integrity, than I am in eliminating evil. I am not enough of a theologian to know why evil is with us, but I know it is here. And I will be frank to admit that this would be a pretty dull world if there were no evil.

Ethics, in the abstract, does not interest me. But ethical people trying to do their creative, responsible best do interest me.

At this point I will abandon the word *ethics* because of the connotations that somebody knows what others ought to do. I am not denying that there are norms, gleanings from thousands of years of experience, that we would all do well to heed. And I grant that some people have a better understanding of those norms than others. But on arriving at maturity, the major problem of most young people is not that they do not know or care enough—that is, care to serve and not to hurt. (There are some, of course, who arrive at maturity not knowing and not caring, and they deserve a kind of help that is not in my experience to give.) For those who know and care and who are capable of a reasonably disciplined approach to life—both the emerging adult in college and the young adult in business—the need is to learn to grow in *strength*.

Let me take a moment to explain how I view the person who has cultivated *strength*. This is not a person who lives by codes and rules but rather one who knows the resources of inspiration and wisdom on which to draw and sees his or her own experience as an extension of that tradition. Somewhere an influence has shaped the attitudes and motives of this person so that he or she feels responsible for doing well in any chosen undertaking—

and for doing it in such a way as to become a plus value in both the immediate environment and the wider society.

This person has a strong feeling for his or her uniqueness and for potential greatness, if life is used well—and he or she wants to use it well. The person of *strength* may or may not profess a formal religious belief and may never make a speech on ethics, either publicly or privately. He or she may be rough or smooth on the exterior, may be mild or brusque of manner—but has courage. This is the way I see the person of *strength,* and this person may not have chosen, consciously, to be that way. He or she has been so influenced by upbringing and environment.

But some things this person *has* chosen: to be competent and industrious, to build inner strength, to do things that develop foresight, resiliency, insight, wisdom, and an imaginative response to all that presents itself. The person of *strength* may not be able to do all that he or she would like but realizes that if one is right inside, one can do more by trying than by not trying. An internally "good" person without the developed abilities I have mentioned is probably more of a social asset than an internally deficient person—a so-called "bad" person. But not much better. A well-motivated incompetent can do as much harm as a poorly motivated competent person. There is a tremendous obligation on the "good" person to develop personal competence because a mediocre "good" person can be more of a liability than an asset. And there is a like obligation on society, and on all the institutions in it, to know who the "good" people are and bet developmental resources on them.

Such people can be helped to learn to manage their lives so that when confronted with the opportunity for a decision or the chance to initiate a constructive action, they will be able to find the best course of action among several choices and stay with it as they carry increasing responsibility and cope with the confusion and stress of our times.

"Faith," Dean Inge once said, "is the choice of the nobler hypothesis."[10] Not the *noblest*—we may never know what that is—but the *nobler,* the best possible at the time the choice is made. I would expand the good dean's definition to include the ever-present belief that in the moment of decision, whenever it comes, one will be composed enough to see a range of choices and tough enough to choose the nobler one, the best possible one among available choices.

Now let's describe this person's qualities in terms of competencies. *Strength,* as that term is used here, is first, *technical competence* in whatever endeavor one is engaged in. But so many are technically competent who are not strong; in a clutch, they do not have enough choices or the toughness to choose well. What, then, are the competencies that distinguish the strong from the merely able? The list is probably long, but high on the list of competencies I see analytical sharpness, intuitiveness, foresight, persuasive ability, and comfort in dealing with power.

Disciplined analytical sharpness includes value analysis—the ability to weigh available choices on a scale that is bounded by *serving* and *hurting* people.

Intuitive fertility comes from constantly reviewing one's experiences and storing in one's internal computer the data from which choices are made. Then, in the moment of need, having pursued conscious analysis as far as it will go, one is able to withdraw from the analytical search and allow the unconscious resources to deliver, as on a computer screen, a range of choices. Faith, as noted, is the belief that in the moment of need and regardless of the stress, one can compose oneself and an adequate range of choices will be delivered.

Foresight, a facet of intuitive fertility, is simply seeing an event before it happens and preparing for it. The "lead" that a leader has, the possession of which is one of the bases of trust of followers, is that she or he cares more, prepares better, and foresees more clearly than others.

Persuasive ability includes respect for the integrity of the persons one would persuade. One is persuaded, I believe, when one has arrived, through one's own intuitive sense, at one's own feeling of rightness about a position or action. The person being persuaded takes an intuitive step from the closest approximation to certainty that can be reached by formal logic (which is sometimes not very close) to a state where one may say with conviction, "This is where I stand." Persuasion, thus defined, may help the one being persuaded to order the logic and take the intuitive step. But the person being persuaded must take that intuitive step on his or her own, untrammeled by coercive pressure, expressed or implied. Persuasion is one of the critical arts possessed by those who would be strong.

Another is the *ability to use and deal with power.* Anyone who possesses strength as discussed here has power—to hurt as well as to serve. It is important to use one's power to avoid being hurt oneself by others' use of power, but it is more important to use one's power affirmatively to *serve,* in the sense that those being served, *while being served,* become healthier, wiser, freer, more autonomous, and more likely themselves to become servants.

The difficulty in acquiring competencies like these, that build strength in persons who are able, is that classroom instruction contributes little. A university would not produce much of a football team if all it did was teach academic courses about the sport. The same reasoning holds for preparing young people to gather the competencies that make for strength in carrying responsible roles. The good practitioners of these competencies— and I have known quite a few—were not born with them; they learned them, but not in a classroom. The question is, can technically able people with the potential to learn such competencies be helped to learn them? Are there ways that we can favor the emergence of more strong people?

I think there are two ways that I am quite confident about. One opportunity is in the undergraduate years; the other is in the early years in business (other institutions, too, but my experience with the process has been in business). The exploitation of both opportunities will need the initiative of businesspeople.

First, the colleges and universities. What can be done there to help students who have the potential for it to start the process of building strength? The answer is the same as for any other important task: *find the right person to do it.* Here and there among the colleges and universities is a faculty member or an administrator who has the talent and the dedication to service to give this help to students. It is hard to know how many there are because there are so few signals within the academic establishment that the opportunity is there. What is needed is the initiative of a faculty member or an administrator who is willing to undertake it, possibly without the support of the institution and perhaps in the face of opposition from colleagues.

The effort is best made, I believe, outside the curriculum and among students who will respond to the opportunity without the incentive of grades and credits. I have had enough experience with such efforts to support the belief that there are professors and administrators who have the ability *and the strength* to give such help to students and that their lives will be greatly enriched if they take on this service. Furthermore, there are many students who are aware, by age eighteen, that they have the potential to develop strength, as I define it, and they will come forward and invest the time.

They can be helped, by a nonacademic coaching process, in a way that will greatly accelerate their growth. I have written a guide for both the interested professor or administrator and the interested businessperson who might support the work.[11] To the latter I would say, do not count on the college or university to identify the professor or administrator or support the work. It might happen, but, again, it might not. If you think it should be done, *you* take the initiative to find the professor, and *you* support his or her work, including getting in and working with students—personally. You may find your own life greatly enriched if you take on the initiating and supporting roles. But it won't be easy!

The other opportunity, giving help to those within a business who have the potential for growth in strength, will not be easy either, but it is manageable. And a stronger institution may result.

The best way I know to give this help within a business is to organize to identify those who have the potential to grow in strength and see that they have a substantial early experience under a boss who has the capacity to coach such high-potential subordinates so that they grow in strength. The only point at which classroom training may be fruitful is with the bosses. *Put your training money on the bosses of high-potential people.*

The work of building strength begins with someone at or near the top of the business who has the insight, the skills, and the drives—*a strong person,* one who will identify both those who have the potential to grow in strength *and* the bosses who will coach them and who will arrange for the training of the bosses. In a large business, this may require the attention of a specialized staff person. But large or small, what is important is that the top management of the company determines, as a matter of long-range policy, that it wants to make the effort to build a strong company by encouraging the growth of strong people. It is not expensive to do, but it does require an uncommon perception of how *strength* is built. I have a hunch that a top executive of a company will do better in his company if he invests part of himself—and some money but not a lot—in helping a professor in some college start the process of strength building in the undergraduate years. The executive who undertakes this will do better by acknowledging that there is more to be learned about the growth of people than the best of us will ever learn by working at it all of our lives. And some of what every executive would profit by learning is best learned by working with and supporting a sensitive professor as he or she coaches students to encourage strength building.

An asset to this approach to building *strength* in a company is that there is no penalty—in fact, there is a bonus—if one brings along more strong people than the company can hold. It is strength-building to lose strong people for the right reasons: they like you and appreciate the growth opportunity you have given them, but there is another place that needs them more than you do and will put them on a faster track. A friend of mine who is head of a moderate-sized company is a director of a much larger one. One day in a conversation with the head of the larger one, my friend mentioned that he needed a new controller and was having a hard time finding one. The prompt response was, "I will give you the names of five of our people who I think would serve you well, and we will be pleased to have you take one of them." When the one selected was deliberating on the offer he was told, "Make your own decision, but if you take this job and it doesn't work out, we will welcome you back." That attitude gets around—and builds strength.

This is not a discourse on management in general, only the facet that has to do with building *strength* as defined here. If one accepts the premise that "only those who have choices can make good decisions, and only the strong have choices," with the corollary that "the strength of any institution is gauged by the influence wielded by strong people," what can top leadership do not only to encourage the emergence of strong people but also to sustain their influence?

Reflecting on my own experience, I have seen much that is destructive. Some strong people emerge despite formidable discouragement because they have it in them to grow by contending with great adversity. But if the aim is to encourage enough strong people to make the company strong and to minimize the emergence of intensely competitive people—in an interpersonal sense, people who destroy *strength* in others—then to rely heavily on overcoming discouragement as a means to develop strength is not a sound approach. What, then, does one do? Beyond the suggestions made so far, the strong business seems to me characterized by two additional features:

> *Clear and compelling goals* that excite the imagination and give people something to hope for—goals that have meaning in human terms
>
> *Frequent face-to-face conversation* between top executives and lower echelons in which there is full discussion of

right actions, actions that comply with the law even when
the law is absurd and that serve and do not hurt people

Every time I hear of a major default by a lower-level manager, I wonder what kind of goals the business has placed before its people and how long it has been since someone higher
in the company talked with this manager about how to hold
one's head up in this crazy world and get a job done. Too often,
I have observed, top management just puts the screws on for
competitive performance; it sincerely hopes that the job will be
done in a way that brings credit to the company but is prepared
to disown the person who brings disgrace. That is not a
strength-building stance.

Why do so many businesses that have the technical competence and the financial resources to survive, perhaps even to
prosper in the competitive race, lack that quality of strength
that brings distinction? Why, despite "success," are they likely
to be judged "ordinary"?

I know of no single comprehensive answer to that question.
But I suspect that a common trait among them is *arrogance,* arrogance that results from the place top leadership occupies in the
traditional hierarchical structure, a situation in which the single
chief stands in the morally dangerous position of having no colleagues, only subordinates. And the attitudes that are likely to be
generated by that isolation of the single chief may color the
whole management structure, even in a very large institution.

The chief executive who recognizes the danger in this
arrogance-breeding role is not usually amenable to redesigning
the structure so as to minimize the risks because to do that, the
ultimate power now held by one person would need to be
shared. Short of this radical step, if the risk of arrogance is recognized (and some people in the role do recognize it but regard
it as inevitable and do not know what to do about it), is there a
remedy that might be acceptable and that would help free the
top executive for the kind of discussions with lower-level managers that are imperative?

The best I know is for the chief executive to consider the suggestions already given. (1) Nurture many strong people in the institution, people who are strong enough to challenge the top person. (2) Find a way personally to support a professor who is dedicated to encouraging strength in students. Make a major time investment in it; learn to talk to students, to understand them, and get on equal terms with them; see through them the shape of the future society that all of our institutions will adapt to, and get their perspective on the world. The executive who learns well from this involvement may then be better able to talk with subordinates—and find it a rewarding experience. Building strength in a business comes naturally when the top leader accepts that the process is best started at the top.

MANAGEMENT

INDUSTRY'S MEANS FOR
PERSONALITY ADJUSTMENT

TWO MAJOR FACTORS OF INDUSTRY—financial stability with more efficient use of capital investment and technical developments in materials and processes plus elimination of waste— have been subjected to a process of refinement in the past twenty years that has been unparalleled in the history of industry. But the third major factor, the human element, has failed to keep pace. There seems to be a growing conviction that further improvement in the mechanics of industry will net rapidly diminishing returns unless this improvement is more closely paralleled by a corresponding advance in the art of employing and utilizing people.

A more fertile field for personality training than industry affords in its training process probably does not exist. This may seem to be a bold assertion. But when the extent and intimacy of the contact between a worker and his foreman are considered and are compared with the same characteristics in other forms of association that might influence personality, substantial grounds for such a statement can be found. People of long experience in responsible positions of industry say they can trace the effect of the training of individual supervisors, the personality that these people have somehow impressed on the people they have trained, long after the association has ended and into activities that differ widely from the circumstances under which the training was received. Unfortunately, a survey of this kind does not always reveal favorable results, for the effects of poor teaching and the transference of undesirable habits and traits are sometimes as conspicuous as the propagation of constructive habits. Then the effect of this training is cumulative over a long period of time, for with expansion and normal turnover, some of the workers who under one supervisor were students ultimately become the teachers of the new employees.

But the problem is no small one. The responsibility for industrial training is spread over a large number of supervisory people, from corporation presidents to foremen directly in charge of workers, and any appreciable improvement must be made through the improvement of the ability of each individual supervisor. Most of our supervisory people are too practical to admit that personality training is a phase of vocational training, yet the great majority of these people make an effort to supply whatever training seems to be needed, mostly on an individual basis, for complete development of each worker.

Apart from the training of employees, there is another important means for the adjustment of personality in the hands of the supervisory people in industry. It is the matter of direction and motivation. Probably most of you have seen cases where an employee was judged a failure by one supervisor and the record of achievement actually indicated failure, but a transfer to another supervisor reversed the judgment and the same person's record indicated success. Undoubtedly, you have seen cases where people who have acquired disagreeable dispositions have had these tendencies rectified through changed incentives under different supervision. It may be difficult to see wherein the matter of incentives will assist in training or adjusting personalities, but if you will judge such an activity by its fruits, the results will be tremendous.

A capable supervisor is necessarily a student of motives, not necessarily versed in the jargon of the professionals but nevertheless is ever watchful of the effect of each order, suggestion, or word of advice on each individual. If he is practically minded, he may liken the supervision of people to the adjustment of a crystal detector on one of the older-type radio sets. This crystal, a small piece of galena mineral, was mounted in a cup, and a small hair wire was brought in contact with it. This instrument, when placed in the circuit, had the necessary electrical properties to serve as a detector of radio signals. But it was a very delicate instrument and required fine adjustment. Some crystals were spasmodic in their operation and required continuous adjustment. Some crystals had more sensitive spots on them than others. Some functioned with very little attention, but no crystal was so perfect that it would function continuously without adjustment.

Dealing with people harmoniously and effectively is a process of continued adjustment, for as producers, they behave much as the crystals. The old hard-boiled boss is rapidly becoming a thing of the past. This negative sort of supervision had as its criterion the discovery of *weaknesses and limitations* in people, a sort of pessimistic philosophy, for limitations are mighty easy to discover, and when in search of them, many fine qualities may be obscured. The evolution from this type of supervision to one more in keeping with the times has been a long and strenuous process. It is nowhere near complete, but it seems to be swinging in the direction of a more positive approach to supervisory problems. A search for the *capabilities and possibilities* in people is gradually supplanting the search for their limitations. It is a more optimistic philosophy.

But the basis for such a change in philosophy is far from sentimental, for it is the wise supervisor who realizes that the grist for his mill is contained in the possibilities in people and not in their limitations. With such a positive and aggressive approach, enlightened supervisors will proceed to search in their people for qualities that, when welded into a cooperative effort, will yield a superior product. The development of the individual worker in such a process is, of course, a secondary objective inasmuch as it serves the ends of the industry, which are primary. But the advanced thinkers at supervisory levels are beginning to see the possibilities in the idea that an industry that sets the development of the potentialities of its people as one of its primary aims is ensuring the accomplishment of the end and aim of the industry.

The analogy of the radio crystal is misleading in that the crystal is impersonal; it has no interest in the messages being transmitted through it, and as long as the mechanical and electrical adjustment is satisfactory, the instrument will function. But with people in industry, we must go further than the day-by-day supervision and direction. If an industry contemplates staying in business indefinitely, it has the problem of production, not only for today, but also for next week and next year. Thus we have another major problem in dealing with people, that of *sustaining* a force of competent workers capable of adapting themselves to improved methods, materials, and machines and ready to supply supervisory material as required by growth and turnover.

For a long time, industry viewed labor as a commodity, and the tendency to do so has not entirely disappeared. Every worker at some time or other becomes a philosopher, if only for brief and rare periods, taking stock of things as a whole. Many an interesting philosophy of industrial relations can be gleaned from the lunchtime conversation of a gang of laborers. And it is not the philosophy that more sophisticated people read in books. In fact, they do not call it philosophy at all.

Workers have lots of time to reflect on policies that management may formulate hastily or without careful consideration. They see at first hand the actual execution of a plan, the details of which may never be known to the person who originally conceived it. They are confronted directly by the ultimate manifestations of policies whose source may be far removed. Out of these observations and reflections grows a working-class philosophy that may be antagonistic, passive, or cooperative. The body of industry is its workers; the management can only direct. Volumes could be written concerning the achievements that have been realized when those directions struck the responsive chord of cooperation. History is replete with the accounts of disasters that have resulted from sustained antagonism.

One of the chief criticisms leveled at our present industrial system is that it reduces occupations to drudgery, makes mere cogs of humans, and deprives them of the sense of achievement that was present in more primitive forms of industry. There is but one answer: the increased production of goods and services and individual achievement must give way to group achievement. But the organization of industry has become so complicated that an individual contribution is almost lost in the process. To correct this tendency, a positive and sustained effort must be made to accomplish the following three objectives. (1) Every worker must be given the basis for a feeling that he or she is an integral part of the business. (2) Every worker must be given the basis for the belief that one of the ends and aims of the industry is his or her own personal benefit. (3) An opportunity must be given for every worker to claim satisfaction of achievement in the product or the industry.

There may be some question regarding the omission of any formal program for personality training and adjustment in industry. This omission is intentional because of the futility of attempting to accomplish permanent good with such an organization in any but very special cases. Modern tendencies in personnel work have come to consist chiefly in putting the personnel job where it belongs—with the line supervisory organization that bears responsibility for the utilization of the personnel. Any considerable improvement in the adjustment of the great mass of workers must of necessity come as a result of an improvement in the ability of supervisors generally to handle that problem.

It must therefore be apparent that the fruit of any research in the field of personality development, if it will be of appreciable value to the present industrial order, must be such that it can be readily understood and intelligently applied by the large number of ordinary people who are responsible for the supervision of the people in industry. The industrial order has become too large and complicated for any single agency to effect any considerable improvement in that structure without taking advantage of the tremendous opportunity for multiplying the results of efforts through the regular channels of supervision that industry offers.

BEHAVIORAL RESEARCH

A Factor in Tomorrow's Better Management

TWO PREDICTIONS ARE VENTURED as reasonable probabilities for American business in the next few years:

1. Change—radical change; technological, social, political, economic change; change that will require ceaseless adjustment and readjustment

2. Variation, some of it startling, in the capacity of businesses to adjust to change

Some businesses will adapt to or even capitalize on change and prosper; others will fail to adapt and fall behind.

This is an overly simplified view of the future, but it is essentially the pattern of the past fifty years. There is a good prospect that the pattern will repeat itself, perhaps on an accelerated scale.

What every businessperson who has a long-run view would like to know is, what does it take to adapt to change and prosper, and how does one know if one has "it"? The following attempt at a partial answer to these questions is not original thinking on my part. Rather, it is a synthesis of many people's thinking, presented as a point of view for consideration, a reference point in discussion.

What does it take to adapt to change and prosper? Insofar as thinking and acting done today will assure the future, it seems to me that the answer is managers who manage well. If we had a generally accepted definition of the word *manage* and a single best way of developing the ability to manage, this discussion might well end right here. But such is not the case.

What Is Management? A Working Definition

Since no one seems to know for sure just what the process of management is, anyone who ventures to talk about it is obliged to select from among the many definitions of the term the one that best suits the framework of thinking he or she intends to construct. For the purpose of this discussion, I have chosen Irving Lee's definition (although I'm not sure I interpret it as he does), a definition that views managing as three kinds of activity.[12] Just about everything that managers do while they're "managing" can be put into one or more of these three categories:

1. *Planning*—looking ahead, estimating future developments, and inventing alternative courses of action

2. *Deciding*—choosing an alternative to gamble on, for either immediate or future action

3. *Communicating*—getting and giving ideas, attitudes, convictions, insights

Managers often spend time on quite specific activities such as designing, auditing, inspecting, supervising, selling, and negotiating—all important and necessary for the current operation of a sound business. These activities may involve some planning, deciding, and communicating, and to that extent they may be acts of managing, as defined here. But they can be successfully carried out on the basis of someone else's planning, deciding, and communicating. Therefore, these are actions that can be taken by specialists who are not managers—according to the definition I have selected. They can be performed with superlative success today while the seeds of tomorrow's business failure are germinating if the planning, deciding, and communicating has not taken adequate account of the future. Thus, it may be argued, poorly "managed" businesses may be successful today according to some standards of success; and struggling near-failure businesses may nurture the makings of almost certain future greatness if their "management" is good.

Criteria of a Sound Long-Run Business

If you were the chief executive officer, a board member, the concerned owner, an employee, a customer, a creditor, or a supplier of a business that you hoped would continue as a sound enterprise for a long time, what would you look for in its current operations to ensure that your expectations would be met? In other words, what are the criteria for judging the long-run soundness of a business? What things can you see in the business now that augur well for its future?

In the past two years, these questions have been posed to 125 executives from businesses large and small from all parts of the country who have gathered to study the subject of management policies and functions.

Having watched these mature executives search for the answers to the questions, two observations are relevant here: (1) the questions are new to them, and they are initially skeptical about the utility of struggling with them, but (2) once they realize that the accepted criteria for current success may not be completely reliable in predicting long-run soundness, they work out the answers with comprehensive thoroughness. When the matter of future soundness is seen in terms of what managers are planning, deciding, and communicating today, "management" takes on a more dynamic and challenging aspect.

While there is not unanimous agreement on the criteria, the following fifteen points in brief outline represent a reasonable consensus of what these 125 executives said they wanted their business to *do now* in order to give maximum assurance of its long-run soundness.

1. Make a satisfactory profit
2. Protect our assets and use them efficiently—provide capital and access to capital for the future
3. Maintain good stockholder relations
4. Maintain and improve our position in the industry and the economy
5. Develop new products, new fields, new techniques, new demands
6. Conform fully with laws and ethical standards
7. Satisfy our customers and help keep them sound
8. Maintain good relations with competitors to improve the industry
9. Earn the respect of communities in which we operate
10. Favorably influence the climate in which all business operates
11. Effect growth of people in the business—in terms of morale, attitude, ability, initiative, self-reliance
12. Effect welfare of people in the business—in terms of economic security, health, safety, family stability, community responsibility
13. Improve our knowledge of and control over our business
14. Contribute something to the art of management
15. Provide for future top management of the business

What does it take to adapt to change and prosper? My assumption is that it takes management—planning, deciding, and communicating in a way that ensures substantial accomplishment of the first fourteen points and is developing future managers who will do even better in these respects.

If this assumption is sound (it has stood the test of considerable critical scrutiny, but it is still an assumption), how does one go about developing a management that can plan, decide, and communicate so as to build a business that will adapt to change and prosper?

There are many familiar answers: bringing potentially good people into the business, a good management selection and development procedure, sending managers to schools of various kinds, proper organization structure, adequate policies and operating procedures, and so on. Any good text on management principles will tell what they are. And they are all important. Because they are so well covered by other sources, I'm not going into them here.

Rather, I want to discuss an approach that has perhaps been overlooked in the literature of management. I want to discuss this approach against the background of the concept of adapting to change as the key to the long-run prosperity of a business; the definition of *managing* as planning, deciding, and communicating; and the fifteen criteria for judging whether a business is doing *now* the things that will ensure its long-run soundness.

The Research Approach to Better Management
Concept of Behavioral Research

I have selected the highbrow label "behavioral research" for the approach I want to discuss. I chose it because I intend to be fairly theoretical.

Let us go back to the fifteen criteria for judging the long-run soundness of a business. The value of sharpening one's awareness of the full range of these criteria is that they give one the basis for knowing how one is doing now. With that knowledge, a manager can plan, decide, and communicate about what one ought to be doing tomorrow.

It might be said that the growth of management as a teachable art has been paced by the development of ways of knowing how one is doing. Only by knowing the score can deficiencies be corrected or advances made. So the past fifty years, during which management has begun to emerge as a calling distinct from entrepreneurship, have seen the gradual development of certainty of knowledge of performance. Few, if any, absolute certainties have been established, but there has been a substantial movement away from standards of performance that are subjective, if not whimsical, in favor of standards that are more objective and rigorous. But there remains a relatively unexplored frontier in which standards of performance are still largely subjective. This is the area in which judgments and predictions must be made as to how people will think and feel and act and grow in response to some contemplated action. *Behavioral research, as I view it, is, in part, the search for greater certainty about how we are doing in matters that concern how people think and feel and act and grow.*

The Importance of Knowing

The importance of knowing how people think and feel and act and grow can be gotten by taking the fifteen criteria item by item and asking, How much of this "people" element is in here?

Take item 1, for instance, "Make a satisfactory profit." It probably isn't quickly evident, but those few words represent a lot of struggle for an area of agreement among all sorts of businesses. Wrapped up in the word *satisfactory* is the judgment of what is "right" or "reasonable" or "adequate" for a particular business at a particular time. It might be a very large profit, relatively, or it might be a red figure. One or the other may be "satisfactory" for a particular business at a particular time. Satisfactory to whom? Satisfactory to the *people* who have their capital in the business, to the *people* who are creditors—in fact, everybody who has an interest in the business is in on the judgment to some extent. And whether the business has a bright long-run future ahead of it depends a great deal on how people think and feel and act in response to the current profit performance of the business. This, in summary, is the judgment of the 125 who struggled with the criteria.

A similar examination of each of the remaining criteria will reveal that to know how one is doing requires some way of getting at how people think and feel and act and grow. The proportion of this factor varies from one item to another. But in items 3, 7, 8, 9, 10, 11, 12, and 15, it is largely controlling.

Obviously, a fair amount of executive competence goes into ways of knowing about people; otherwise, the business development of this century would not have taken place. But it is equally obvious that "people" knowledge has been an important factor in competition in the past. Other things being equal, a business that has a lot of such knowledge has been in a stronger position than a business having less.

A large contributing factor in the rise and fall of business has been sharpness and dependability (or the lack of it) of "people" knowledge. It is my hunch that it will be an even larger competitive factor in the future. The current interest in motivational research in marketing is a portent of a possible trend.

The Status of Behavioral Research

Despite a substantial increase in formal research at university centers, a growing number of professionally trained researchers working in business, and a large literature, in my judgment, most businesses that are striving to be sound in long-run concerns are not sufficiently concerned with behavioral research. They are not sufficiently concerned to give solid assurance of their long-run soundness.

Professionals in the field of behavioral research face a dilemma. If they do not make extraordinary claims, they are not heeded; if they claim too much, they are frauds. When businesspeople seek the help of a professional researcher, they all too often want a quick answer. When research in the physical sciences is involved, most executives know that there is a long series of time-consuming and costly steps between the initial hypothesis and a commercially usable result. Not so with behavioral research: here we seem to expect miracles.

I don't say this to criticize; there simply isn't much encouragement or leadership for doing otherwise. Judgment on what is good research is hard to come by. The average business conference doesn't deal with it to any extent. A cursory review of the curricula of business schools doesn't indicate much emphasis on it. Business literature doesn't point up the way businesspeople might become more aware. In other words, we face a new frontier with not much to go on. Some progress is being made, but it does not seem to measure up to the need.

The businesspeople I know—and this includes about 350 I've had in classes over the past five years, classes in which we were concerned with the development of executive ability and in which there was opportunity to assess both awareness and competence on this subject—are being substantially penalized for want of a little bit of behavioral research know-how.

Part of my basis for this opinion stems from the responses of these executives when asked the following simple question: What are the *results* you are responsible for? In other words, what are the tangible and intangible end products of the operation you head up? There followed a lot of discussion to make clear what this question meant. "If you were your boss and somebody else was in your job, what things would you look at in order to make up your mind about how well this job (the one you now have) is being done?"

Of the 350 who have been confronted with this question, those who haven't had a tough time with it can be counted on the fingers of one hand. And after considerable discussion, experimenting, and coaching, they generally weren't very comfortable about the answer they had to give. This might be viewed as very disturbing, asking a business executive what he's trying to do on his job and discovering that he can't tell you! But try an experiment. Ask anybody who has an important role in society, "What are you trying to do?" Ask for specifics:

"Give it to me in nice crisp statements, one, two, three, four, items that you would evaluate if you were passing judgment on the work of another person in your job." Then sit back and watch a person in real trouble, ninety-nine times out of one hundred.

The difficulty here, as I see it, is not that they don't know what they are doing. There is too much good work being done to support that premise. I believe the trouble is that they do not know in a way that permits them to communicate about it.

The status of behavioral research might be summed up this way: businesspeople do not have a research point of view toward their work as managers, because it seems to me that wherever a research point of view has penetrated an area of a business, people can communicate freely about that area with others "in the know."

I do not believe that the business that takes the long-run view and wants to adapt to change and prosper can afford to leave the answer to the basic question "What results are you responsible for?" on as fuzzy a basis as my experience says it is in the mind of many executives. It may be more comfortable to let the matter rest there, but I am willing to postulate that the planning, deciding, and communicating that will mark the better management of the future will require that managers communicate better with one another about what they are trying to accomplish.

I have used this example of executives not knowing what they are trying to accomplish because I have recently tested it on enough people in enough businesses to be reasonably sure that it is a general condition. But I would like to support my position further that businesspeople do not generally have a research point of view on their work of managing and that they are penalized substantially for it. For several years, I have been closely associated with staff people in a number of businesses, large and small, who share my interest in better knowledge of how people think and feel and act and grow. And I have the strong suspicion, as a general observation, that when actions are taken to *improve* how people think and feel and act and grow, very few such actions are taken with anywhere near enough certainty that the desired results will follow or that they will be worth what they cost. Viewed in retrospect, too few of these actions clearly accomplished what they were intended to accomplish. That is the penalty.

Dr. Melvin Anshen, writing in the September-October 1954 issue of the *Harvard Business Review,* makes this statement:

> Great credit should be given to the creative imagination that underwrites the current intense efforts by schools, professional associations and businesses to raise the level of executive performance through formal training. In the judgment of this writer, however, there is no other function or activity to which top management is today devoting so much attention and money with so little understanding or the return on the investment. . . .
>
> We have too little understanding of what actually goes on in executive development programs, too little knowledge of what these courses really accomplish. Granting the need for such programs, do the present courses adequately or efficiently meet the need? Are they on the target? Is the best use being made of the money, time and talent invested?
>
> We do not have adequate answers to these questions. We need some better basis on which to accumulate experience and provide stepping stones for the future. There are no precise tools for appraising programs of this sort, and it may never be possible to get clear-cut answers to the questions raised here. But the real current limitation is not in the tools of appraisal; it is the absence of a strong motivation to improve our knowledge of what is going on. This inhibits the development of better ways of knowing.[13]

What Dr. Anshen has said of executive development programs might be said about all activities aimed at improving how people think and feel and act and grow. "The real . . .

limitation is the absence of a strong motivation to improve our knowledge of what is going on." I have defined behavioral research in part as the search for greater certainty about how we are doing in matters that concern how people think and feel and act and grow. How can we go about "knowing" with greater certainty?

There is a disturbing note from the past on this, a warning. A new way of doing business has never been welcomed by those who have learned to operate without it. The young Charles Schwab was making disturbing gestures with a new metallurgical science. He was reproved by an old steelmaker, who said, "This damned chemistry will ruin the steel industry."

The Problem of "Knowing"
How Do We Know?

A poet once spoke of "knowledge never learned in schools." That is probably the kind of knowledge that good managers have that they have difficulty communicating about. They know it, but they did not "learn it in school." They did not learn it so that they can convey meaning about it to someone else.

These men may have had some formal training, and it may have been very good training. But there are important factors in successful performance that they did not get that way. There will, no doubt, always be a great deal of this, some "art" that people develop out of trial and error that cannot be communicated. The big question is, how much of this can a business afford to carry if it accepts a probable level of change in the next few years comparable to or greater than that of the past twenty-five years? How will *better* management evolve if people cannot, in the course of their routine relationships, pool what they know about the "art" and achieve greater certainty?

May I turn for a bit to another professional field for an illustration?

A noted medical teacher recently observed, "The problem in my field is how to make doctors out of people trained in medicine." A medical school has recently introduced training aimed at teaching the medical student to listen to his patients. A new development!

There are factors in successful performance that good performers often do not know about—consciously—and, conversely, poor performers do not know that they lack it. The medical school that is training students to *listen* to patients is trying to get at one of those things. Why is the school doing this? Because the ability and the willingness to listen to patients has been discovered to be a factor that distinguishes good doctors from poor doctors. In the research, some doctors had it as a natural gift or else it evolved somehow out of experience, but the ones who listened turned out to be better doctors. This is one of the ways in which a subjective factor that differentiates performance becomes "known" so that it can be taught, thereby helping to bring poor performers more in line with good performers.

It is my guess that doctors so taught will, in the future, be able to give a little bit better answer to the question "What are you trying to do?" than doctors not so taught. This seems an awfully late date for a medical school to discover that listening to a patient is an important element in the skill of a successful practitioner, since doctors have had the benefit of formal training longer than any other professional group except clergymen. But this is also true of some of the behavioral research findings being made available to industry today. It seems very elementary.

It seems that we have known these modern findings of behavioral research—or should have known them—for a long time. Yet only a cursory review of the performance of managers indicates that there is a lot that is "known" that is not being practiced—and could be practiced profitably.

Why is available knowledge that would help a person operate and live better not used when the need for it is great? The search for the answer to that question has been on the minds of serious thinkers for as long as we have a record of human thoughts, and I am not going to presume the wisdom to try to answer it. But I have come across a few ideas that have a bearing on this question as it relates to the interest that businesspeople ought to have in behavioral research. It sums up under four main headings:

1. We don't "know" a lot that we "know."
2. We're not so sure about much that we "know."
3. "Knowledge" gets lost and has to be rediscovered.
4. "New knowledge" threatens the "secret" of a business's success.

We Don't "Know" a Lot That We "Know"

The mind of man has been likened to an iceberg, four-fifths underwater and one-fifth above. What psychologists call the conscious mind is the one-fifth above the water, and the unconscious or subliminal mind is the four-fifths under the surface. Near the waterline there is a little communication between the two, as in dreams or in rare moments of insight. But generally we have little awareness of what's underwater. Yet there is a growing certainty about the vastness and importance of these underwater resources.

Generally, businesspeople don't talk about things like this. But there needs to be some awareness of these submerged resources that feed us impulses, hunches, sometimes whole judgments, that act as an automatic calculator with data we put in the conscious mind. Here, I am sure, is a lot of the "knowledge" on which successful people operate. But it is individual and personal, and it isn't transmitted from a person who has it to another who does not, at least not in the way that knowledge of arithmetic is passed along. This is probably what we have in mind when we use the word *wisdom*. Wise people, as distinguished from people who are merely brilliant, may have better access to those vast resources below the waterline. The same might be said of creative people.

In every business, there are the people who "know" materials, design, people, politics. For the most part, they are gifted. They probably have much experience. But there are many who have the experience to the few who have the gifts. They "know" something and are therefore wise. Other things being equal, the business that has the wisest person in its key spots will do better at adapting to or capitalizing on change and prospering. But nobody "knows" what the wise person knows. The wise person probably doesn't know himself. If a business is so fortunate as to have one in a key spot, how does it develop a successor? How would it develop a man or woman who "knows" what most people don't now "know," consciously and rationally?

Up to now, businesses, like other institutions, have accepted wisdom where they can find it and get along without it if it isn't readily at hand. The buyer of coal who doesn't have access to a person who "knows" coal will guess and let it go at that. But with the mounting complexities, is this going to be adequate for the future? I don't think so.

I will readily admit that wisdom cannot be taught as one would teach arithmetic. But I believe that it is learned. We write it off as a "gift" because we don't know too much about how it is learned. But we could know more about how wisdom is learned and what can be done to encourage its growth if we wanted to.

We're Not So Sure About Much That We "Know"

The persistence of the old story about the farmer who wouldn't buy the book on farming because he wasn't farming half as well as he knew proves something. Maybe it proves that he thinks the book is mostly more of the kind of knowledge that he now has and isn't using, and maybe the reason he isn't using the half of what he knows is that he isn't sure that it is valid and practical. It isn't a part of his tested experience. In other words, the half he is using is solid, dependable experience—as he sees it.

The other half is theory, largely hypothesis. Maybe it's true and maybe it isn't. More of that is what he thinks is in the book. If he is getting along and isn't intensely curious, obviously he has no use for the book.

For a long time, people have been theorizing and writing books. Much of the theory has some roots in experience. Under a certain set of circumstances at a certain time, a certain thing happened—and a general principle of universal application blossoms forth. Or there may have been no experience. Somebody saw a place for a theory and just dreamed one up.

I'm not condemning theorizing. There has to be a hypothesis before there can be an experiment or a validation. But much theory finds its way into a pool of available knowledge without experiment or testing. And all of it isn't dependable, usable knowledge.

For example, the handbooks on personnel practices contain many copybook maxims. These are some heard frequently:

> "Every person should know where he stands. Every person should have a periodic progress review with his boss."

> "Good work should be noticed and commended."

> "Never reprimand a person in public."

> "No one should supervise more than X number of persons."

I don't know whether these are trustworthy generalizations or not. But I suspect that the time will come when flat statements like these will not be made. What an effective boss will do in a certain circumstance with a certain person will depend on a lot of things. There may be a few extreme situations that a general rule will fit, but they will be few.

Maybe one reason that so much unused knowledge is lying around in business (pretty much everywhere, in fact) is that people who are smart enough to run a business—or a part of one—and keep it afloat are smart enough to know that a lot that passes for knowledge is questionable. And rather than get fouled up with stuff that doesn't work, the successful practical operator, whether in business, medicine, or religion, will draw the line that separates what he or she will use from what is in the book he or she will not buy. This person will draw that line way over in conservative territory.

By this reasoning, the farmer may not be lazy when he says he isn't farming half as well as he knows. He may simply be protecting the 50 percent that he uses and lives by. The urge to be secure is a powerful motivation.

There is a story on being sure about what one knows. President Eliot of Harvard enjoyed telling of an experience he once had, illustrating proper caution in drawing a conclusion. When he entered a crowded New York restaurant, he handed his hat to the doorman. As he came out, he was astonished to see the doorman promptly pick his hat out of hundreds there and hand it to him. In surprise, he asked, "How did you know that was my hat?" "I didn't know it was your hat, sir," was the answer. "Why, then," asked Mr. Eliot, "did you hand it to me?" Very courteously, the doorman replied, "Because you handed it to me, sir." This precise limitation of inference pleased the president.

Knowledge Gets Lost and Has to Be Rediscovered

Vilhjalmur Stefansson, the anthropologist and arctic explorer, who should know something about cold and frostbite, reports that the ancients "knew" that a person who gets too cold should take himself as quickly as he can to where it is warm. They "knew" it because it checked with common sense and because people living in cold countries had tested it for centuries. And yet it was only ten years ago that the Red Cross handbook dropped the recommendation to treat frostbite with snow and even more recently dropped the recommendation to raise the temperature of frostbite only slowly.

Thus a false theory can cause sound useful knowledge to be lost, and the rediscovery of sound knowledge is slow and difficult.

But knowledge can be lost in other ways. The importation of a *custom* can do it. Some of the potential of American industry was lost when the native good sense of small business organization was supplanted by military custom in organization thinking as businesses grew large. That happened about one hundred years ago, and we are just beginning to see the reemergence of what was probably a very sound idea in early industry, now called *job enlargement*. Sears, Roebuck's "flat" organization structure is something that might have come much earlier if military custom had not been imported.

Attitudes can also cause knowledge to be lost. I came into business early enough to see the last vestiges of serious opposition to technological changes. Important people would raise strenuous objections to new technological developments, not for economic or scientific reasons (and there could be and still is controversy on those grounds), but because they were emotionally disturbed by the new development. This is the kind of thing that in a more primitive society becomes a *taboo;* then knowledge is rejected and truly lost.

Today, we don't see much in the way of emotional objections suppressing knowledge on the material side of business, but we do still see it with knowledge concerning how people think and feel and act and grow. In that area, primitive thinking still shows through on occasion.

So knowledge cannot be viewed as strictly cumulative. Important knowledge can be lost, and the process of recovering it can be long and costly.

"New Knowledge" Threatens the Secret of Business Success

Most new business ventures fail, even in times of sustained high levels of business activity. Perhaps one in five is a reasonable long-term ratio of success.

Some of the reasons why some succeed and others fail are obvious—insufficient capital, poor timing, technical incompetence. But many of the reasons are not obvious. Some businesses fail when they seem to have everything, and others succeed with everything seemingly against them. One business flourishes and outstrips its competitor, whose leadership seems equally endowed with ability and resources. Why? Nobody knows—least of all the most successful. So every business that survives and performs its economic function over a period of time has something unique about it—and that uniqueness seems to defy analysis. So far, we don't know much about these "secrets of success." Some day, if we make the effort, we may know more.

When Hamlet said he would "rather bear the ills he had than fly to others that he knew not of," he was speaking for all thoughtful persons in the race of innovation—new knowledge.[14] I am prepared to concede that until we know a lot more about what makes a successful business tick than we now know, the resistance of men and institutions to new knowledge is a good thing, a sign of a healthy outlook. There are precious unknown attributes in every successful venture, and they should not be risked recklessly for the exploration of every passing idea.

The problem of knowing is a tough one, particularly in business, where the pressures on our time are so great. I have tried to point out that the essential management "skills" that have grown through experience are rarely passed on to successors. The strongly intuitive persons, those who are able to draw on the source of wisdom "below the waterline," cannot import that wisdom, not by "teaching." The management literature is full of interesting generalities that sensitive managers question; there is also the problem of trustworthy knowledge being lost and false ideas being accepted. Finally, there is the risk of losing the valuable essence of a successful business through the application of new "knowledge."

Behavioral Research: A Way to Know
A Manager's Research Point of View

The picture I have painted looks a bit discouraging. The road to improving knowledge and using it wisely is long and hard and rough. But there is nothing new in this. Human organization has been beset with handicaps like this as long as we have any record. The problem for business organizations is that when they cease to be adaptive, they fail. Other types of human institutions are often supported by sentiment long after they have ceased to be adaptive. But not businesses, not in our American situation, where competitive forces operate as freely as they do and creativity is relatively unhampered.

The business that takes the long-run view, that wants to do things *now* that will help it adapt to or capitalize on change and prosper into the indefinite future—that business, it seems to me, will want to be concerned about the effective use of knowledge in a *formal* way. Just as we have already done this with material technology, we must now do it by making our "people" knowledge more certain. So I will amplify my previous definition of *behavioral research* as the search for greater certainty about how we are doing and how we might do better in matters that concern how people think and feel and act and grow.

I am not a professional, and I am not going to propose to you any new human technology that a business ought to adopt. Able professional resources are hard at work on that, and I will leave to them the job of explaining and justifying any new theories by which a business ought to operate.

Unfortunately, as I see it, the problem of businesspeople is not simply one of being willing to go to a professional source and buy a package of behavioral research to take back to the plant or office and put to work. I have burdened you with quite a discourse on how the use of knowledge gets blocked because I believe that the business person must develop a research point of view himself. For one thing, the professional sources may not all be in agreement. Wise people of the past who have written down what they think could help more if they were in agreement, but they aren't. Too, the motivations of a professional are not necessarily identical with those of the businessperson. Their obligations are different. And professional researchers, like all other people in the world, have biases. The problem is to deal with those biases, because in behavioral research they can be more subtle and harder to trace than in material research.

Many fine resources for behavioral research findings are available to business, and there will be more when now-classified military research becomes available. These resources will become increasingly important to businesspeople. But the research point of view that I feel the businessperson should have is going to be the difficult hurdle, and I don't believe the person will get it only by studying resources outside his or her own business.

Benchmarks First

Lincoln once said, in a moment of crisis, "If we but knew where we are and whither we are tending, we might better know what to do now."[15] He stated the dilemma of all administrators.

Tools are available for assessing every one of the fifteen criteria for judging a business. Insofar as one wants to know how one is doing in matters that concern how people think and feel and act and grow, the tools are crude and cumbersome. But it is possible, for people who have the urge, to begin to pick up the bits and pieces of data that are indicators. These can be supplemented by formal surveys and studies, and a reference point can be established. Business operators may want some professional help to make sure that the way they set benchmarks is sound, but my suggestion is that managers get pretty deeply involved in this with their own staff. Otherwise, managers are not likely to develop a research point of view within their own businesses.

But at this stage of the "art of knowing," getting a good benchmark on all of the criteria is a difficult and trying job, and a person may well say, "I'll wait awhile until the art develops a little further." This would be all right if criterion 14, "Contribute something to the art of management," were not on the list. The businesses that adapt to change and prosper will be strong businesses. And one of the very important ways of being strong, one of the surest signs of vitality and an earmark of a long-lived business, is the constant effort to contribute something to the art of management. Surely, part of the motivation will be the desire to do one's share. But that is not the most important reason. The really important reason a business ought to be trying to contribute something to the art of management is that this is one of the best ways for a business to develop "muscle tone." So many other things fall into place when the urge to contribute to the art is vigorous and sustained—and sensible. So the businesses that make the effort to develop the ways of knowing about how they stand on matters that concern how people think and feel and act and grow are not only going to know first—and therefore act first and reap a competitive advantage—but they are also going to be stronger for having made the effort and better able to take another step.

But this poses the problem that in every action there is risk, and the more one exposes oneself to the incentives to act, the more risks one takes and the more one needs to build into the operation a mechanism for caution.

Research Through Practical Eyes

Since we have the evidence in modern times that sound, useful knowledge can be displaced by error through the intervention of false science, I don't believe that I am "looking under the bed" when I suggest that under the impact of modern behavioral research, some of our present useful business know-how may give way to error. One need not necessarily be a Jeremiah to be constantly aware that some of the past aberrations in people's thinking can be reenacted by us now. Despite the quip that "the only thing men learn from history is that they do not learn from history," I believe that a few people do learn and that their survival qualities (and the survival qualities of institutions they lead) are better than the average.

So having made something of a case for the value of behavioral research, I also concede that a businessperson can be misled by it and wander down the garden path. I think the danger is enough within the range of possibility that a built-in mechanism for caution needs to be devised. Just as the purchaser of coal, when confronted with all of the scientific data on samples of coal, needs the judgment of a person who "knows" coal, so the purchaser of behavioral research will need the advice of a person who "knows" the business, who "knows" a right action from a wrong one, who "knows" a good theory for a fallacy, for a particular business at a particular time.

The best approach I know of to get the benefits of behavioral research (which I see as indispensable to long-run soundness) and to minimize the risk of error (which I see as real and substantial) is to carry on research using people in the business who "know." The help of professionals is important, and sometimes professionals "know." But the only way to establish that a person "knows" is to apprentice one to the trade of management and subject one's practical decision-making ability to extensive tests where the stakes are real. My own experience is limited to research that bears on the selection, development, organizing, and direction of people inside a business. There I am sure beyond any doubt that we are on sounder ground when the research data are gathered, appraised, and interpreted by persons who "know." I suspect that this experience has some relevance with respect to research on how people think and feel and act and grow who are in the relationship of customer, creditor, owner, competitor, or public. But I have had no experience in these fields.

Being Practical About Behavioral Research: Team Research

If I were the head of a business and had followed the reasoning to this point and wanted to test it out, here is how I would proceed: I would ask myself and check with my colleagues in order to locate the *two* persons in my organization who are thought to have the most mature judgment on matters covered by behavioral research—two who "know." I would ask myself, "Of all the people in this organization, whose judgment would I respect the most to bring me conclusions or recommendations in this area?" I would establish reasonable assurance of the believability of their findings before I give them the assignment. They need not be the best all-around managers. They are simply people who "know" especially well on matters like these and so are respected by others who "know."

I would try to pick two who meet the qualification but are of somewhat different training, experience, and personality. This I would do to broaden the base of judgment and to get some cancellation of bias. But I wouldn't pick more than two. I wouldn't want a committee. I might want a committee to weigh the findings but not to serve as the research team.

The task for this pair would be, first, to do the work to establish in the top-management group an agreed-on statement of the criteria we were trying to satisfy to ensure that this would be a sound long-run business—a list something like the fifteen cited earlier. If a good professional was available to advise with my researchers (not to do the job for them), they should retain that professional.

When the criteria are clearly stated, I would ask my team to set up—with the advice of their professional—how to go about assessing where we now stand, establishing benchmarks for each of the criteria. Depending on the size of my business, the availability of personnel, and the urgency, I might break the job down and establish more teams to conduct the assessment in different areas of the criteria.

Just what would a team do? The best single source of suggestions on this is a little manual on research and reports put together by the Amos Tuck School and published by McGraw-Hill.[16] I would want my team to study this. Then, with some consulting help, the researchers should work out a "study design," a plan for getting and analyzing the data they need and setting up their conclusion.

The advantage of a two-person team shows up most clearly in the conducting of interviews. Because a large part of the data on a research study is gathered through interviews, the conduct of the interview and the judging of the significance of what comes out of the interview are very important parts of the job. In my experience, two persons, one conducting the interview while the other takes notes, get a better story. But the valuable contribution of the team comes out of the "huddle" after the interview. This is where the biases are canceled out and deeper insights and convictions are developed. The notes on what was said in the interview have value. But the contribution of the "huddle" judgment of two who "know," who were listening with penetrating insight—that is priceless.

If a company is limited in resources for this kind of work, a priority of importance would need to be established, and the various criteria would be assessed one at a time. A couple of people could spend a lifetime on this, but I wouldn't let them. I would limit them to a few months. With more time than that, they will go stale—if they are the right people for the job. I would rather take what they can produce in a few months and then appoint a fresh team, if necessary. But before too long, I would have an appraisal on how this business was doing on one or more of the criteria. In the absence of similar estimates on other businesses, I might not know for sure whether my benchmark was high or low. But if a reasonably good job had been done in putting the assessment in quantitative terms, at some future time I could take another look and see whether I was gaining or losing. Ultimately, I would acquire a feeling of certainty about my assessment. Then I could be said to "know."

In any event, the very first report by my first team would probably contain specific recommendations on where work could profitably be done to improve performance. I would select the most likely one of these for further study and put another team on the job of working out what to do to effect the improvement. On a later assessment, I would look for verification of the rightness of my action. Out of this, ultimately, I would expect something in the way of general principles, but I wouldn't press for that. I would press for more certain knowledge on how we are doing now and how we might do better. I would let generalizations sort of extrude themselves out of this process as a by-product.

I would go into this on the basis of making this kind of research a constant and continuous process. I would feel it just as important to have behavioral research going on this basis all the time as I would to have product development or basic material research going all the time. That is, so long as I wanted my business to take the long-run view, adapt to change, and prosper, I would want my research program to be adequate to the needs of my business.

There are, no doubt, other ways to get the results that I hold out for this type of team research. But this is the best one I have found to date.

I have not attempted to give a complete or documented procedure for studies of management by management. Rather, I have tried only to give a broad outline of how a business could go about developing a research point of view in its own staff, with a minimum of risk of being misled. Despite my considerable experience with research of this kind, I am unwilling to try to outline specific procedures. Every business must develop its own know-how within the framework of its own way of doing business.

Management for the Long Run

At the outset, I stated that I was going to reason from a definition of management that viewed it as planning, deciding, and communicating. I chose this limited definition because I wanted to be concerned wholly with how to help a business adapt to change and prosper. There is plenty of current literature on how to run a successful business today. There isn't so much on how to build for the long run—which means dealing with change. There is, of course, much more to building for the long run than I have discussed here, but I submit behavioral research as an important factor for the period of history we live in.

Management and Planning

I have a theory that I cannot prove, but it forms such an important support for my belief about what I have already said that I feel obliged to state it, realizing that it may be challenged and I can't defend it. It is this: extensive management experience, building as it does the priceless "knowing" on which all successful action rests, does have a negative aspect. It diminishes or limits or fails to keep alive the natural creativity that is the happy endowment of so many young people before they assume management responsibility. And I do not believe that it necessarily should be so.

Creativity is the heart and muscle of planning. Only as one can free one's mind to invent can one conjure up the estimate of a situation and produce a range of alternatives from which to choose. And sustained heavy responsibility does not seem to me to maintain freely functioning minds in all able people. One reason why I am willing to go out on a limb for behavioral research is that I believe that an occasional assignment on a research team, free from the pressures of specific responsibility, will put the necessary element into management experience to sustain, if not enhance, creativity.

Beyond the stimulus to creativity in the members of a study team, the findings of good studies made by the right people help sharpen the focus on a problem for a large number of people. They certainly stimulate people to look ahead, estimate future developments, and calculate alternative courses of action to a greater extent than if the study had not been made.

Management and Deciding

As I have watched people struggle with important decisions, occasionally I have seen a person make an important decision and seem to achieve a quiet serenity for having made it. For a long time, I wondered why. And again, I have only an unsupported theory: he had a strong belief or faith that something probably penetrated the waterline and connected up with the resources underwater—deep-rooted, firm, strength-giving. When those resources are available to help resolve a vexing problem, the decision seems to produce a sort of release from the pressure or the circumstances that required the decision.

It is my observation that participation in a team research project strengthens the kind of basic beliefs that underpin sound business decisions. Also, it furnishes for many people a firmer basis for decision making in the area of the study. One thing in particular I have noticed: when a good study is made by the right people, a lot of decisions get made in a lot of places that seem to have some connection with the findings of the study.

Management and Communicating

Communication, as I view it in a business definition, is the total process by which the ideas, attitudes, convictions, and insights that help a business reach its goals come to operate through the right persons at the right time. Probably a very minor part of the total communication process is people speaking or writing to other people. Everything that is going on communicates. Actions communicate. Failures to act communicate. Attitudes communicate.

The trouble with much communication, verbal and nonverbal, is that the communicator has no clear estimate of what ideas, attitudes, convictions, and insights—if widely held by persons having an interest in a business—would actually help the business reach its goals. Unless one has a real sense of this, one hasn't much chance of doing a constructive job or improving the operation through better communication.

I believe that the first step in good communication, anywhere, is listening. In planning, deciding, and communicating on matters concerning how people think and feel and act and grow, one has only two general ways of getting at the data needed to manage: observing and listening. And a great deal must be gotten by listening. I have a hunch that most managers are poorer listeners than they are observers.

Listening is one of the primary tools of a behavioral researcher. (The attitudes and skills of a good listener were discussed in "The Ethic of Strength" in Part One.) One of the principal by-products of team studies is that the researchers generally become disciplined listeners (but usually it is quite a struggle—good managers "train hard" on listening). The raw data—verbatim notes taken by good listeners—make powerful communicating material. There are few things more convincing than a simple quote from someone who spoke honestly, courageously, and insightfully under the influence of good listening.

Behavioral research offers some ways for checking the accomplishments of conscious communication. But it is a discouraging business if rigorously carried out because it shows that so many of our "best-laid plans" have either neutral or negative effect.

There is a "moral law" of communication that should be framed as a motto on every manager's wall: "He who would communicate should be certain that he is the right person to be communicating; that the ideas, attitudes, convictions, and insights being proposed are appropriate; and that the time is right." Why do managers need constantly to be reminded of this motto? One reason is that managers, like everyone else, occasionally get frustrated in reaching their goals. When that happens, sometimes the urge to communicate gets pretty strong—"tell somebody something"—and the wrong things get said to the wrong people at the wrong time.

Behavioral research, in which managers themselves are deeply involved, helps keep an organization reminded of this law. It helps because any study of how an organization is functioning picks up so many reverberations of bad communication.

Once an organization develops a research point of view and has a clear notion of what the ideas, attitudes, convictions, and insights are that help it reach its goals, there is a large body of communication experience and principles that can be drawn on with profit. Short of a sound research base, the effort to improve on operation by overt communication is apt to be hit-or-miss.

Management and Behavioral Research

I have tried, in brief outline, to show how behavioral research contributes to the elements of managing: planning, deciding, and communicating.

This is an embryo idea, this idea of behavioral research as a part of the development of a manager, as a way to bring more management know-how into rational focus, as a way to stimulate creativity and to develop certainty, and as a way to facilitate decision making and communication.

These desirable goals can be pursued in many ways; behavioral research is but one of them. In presenting this idea and arguing for its potency, I want to make clear that I am not opposing other ways in which progress in management effectiveness can be achieved. I simply want to lay *this* one on the line and urge its consideration as one of the means available.

As I have watched behavioral research at work, applied by teams of mature management people, it seems to me that it has some noteworthy virtues:

1. It makes possible the emergence or greater certainty and greater rationality of management know-how. It makes this possible out of the management team's own effort and without a directive from someone in authority. New and better knowledge evolves without dogma.

2. If behavioral research of this sort is a continuous process within a business (and I think it should be), management know-how is continuously evolving in the direction of greater clarity, comprehensiveness, and specificity.

3. Reference is made to the traditions of the business and sources of knowledge outside the business, and people who "know" conclude what is right for this business at this time. But nobody is compelled to accept their conclusions. Their conclusions are influential because the team members were chosen as persons of influence before they started.

4. As the insight of the study team develops, a wonderful blend of two contradictory qualities emerges: courage and caution. Study teams will reach conclusions and make recommendations that persons in high positions of authority would hesitate to reach and make! The study team members can do this partly because they do not have formal authority—no one will be coerced by their recommendations—and partly because they have been commissioned and have been freed to develop the insight out of which firm conviction is born. Therefore, they speak with the kind of authority that only wisdom bestows.

5. The management team becomes more alert to and interested in the research findings from professional sources. Team members can do this safely because they have some research maturity themselves. They do not look at these research findings as valid just because they came from impressive sources; neither do they dismiss them because they come from strange or unfamiliar sources. They accept them as grist for the mill and proceed to grind them up into a mix with practical know-how. The result is a well-blended and palatable dish of vitamins, minerals, proteins, calories, and roughage—manna for a hard-hitting organization.

6. If a study team is well chosen, a curious development takes place. The team attacks the problem with more than twice the determination and zest than either member would have separately. Because every judgment is a joint judgment, team members are more rigorous than either would be alone. They jolt each other out of ruts, and they have more fun (lone pursuits become tiresome).

7. A study report made by a team of people who know, whose believability was established, communicates something that mere words on paper cannot communicate. A study team does its best communicating orally. Something of the members' conviction and firsthand insight gets into the general stream of management knowledge.

8. Finally, people grow in the process of making a research study. I really believe that it is our surest tool for helping develop the full potential of a manager.

This, I submit, is a fairly formidable list of virtues, and more could be added. But there is a catch. This type of research is very difficult to do. It requires a certain wisdom and maturity and trust in an organization to get it started. It requires a willingness to set aside hard-to-replace and expensive management people. It requires the ability to select the right people for a team. And it requires the guidance of a staff that knows how to advise the team in the pursuit of its mission. The sum of these requirements is substantial.

But despite the stiff requirements, I am sure that behavioral research as outlined here, or some other approach that gets the same results, will find its way into the organization fabric of every business that achieves a measure of greatness under the challenging prospect of change that confronts us all.

I believe we are entering a period in which the institutional struggle to survive will usher in the "age of the development of human potential." Institutional leaders everywhere will become importantly concerned with how people think and feel and act and grow. They will become so not mainly for materialistic reasons, although that motive will be present. Nor will they do it mainly for sentimental or altruistic reasons, although that motive will also be present. They will do it, I believe, because people who are willing to bear the burden of heavy responsibility get their greatest satisfaction from creative achievement. And the frontier for the second half of the twentieth century will be creative achievement with the thinking, feeling, acting, and growing of people.

There is some creative urge in everybody. Every person is struggling for personal significance to some extent. And those who carry heavy responsibility—or aspire to it—are powerfully motivated to seek it.

So I have tried here to sum up from my own experience and from the experience of my associates in my own business and elsewhere the best ideas I know of to help those who lead a business—or any human institution, for that matter—make a best effort in the struggle for significance. As I stated at the outset, what is outlined here is a synthesis of many people's thinking. It is presented as a point of view, a reference point in discussion. It is not advanced as an "answer," neither final nor tentative.

I leave you with a thought from Rousseau: "Remember, ever remember, that ignorance has never been productive of evil, but that error alone is dangerous; and that we do not miss our way through what we do not know but through what we falsely think we know."[17]

THE OPERATOR
VERSUS THE CONCEPTUALIZER

An Issue of Management Talents

THE ESSENCE OF MANAGEMENT lies in the exercise of two major talents. One of these is operating talent: the ability to carry the enterprise toward its objectives in the situation, from day to day, and resolve the issues that arise as this movement takes place. This calls for interpersonal skills, sensitivity to the immediate environment, tenacity, experience, judgment, ethical soundness, and related attributes and abilities that the day-to-day movement requires.

The other is conceptual talent: the ability to see the whole in the perspective of history—past and future—to state and adjust goals, to evaluate, to analyze, and to foresee contingencies a long way ahead. Long-range strategic planning is embraced here, as is setting standards and judging performance. Leadership, in the sense of going out ahead to show the way, is more conceptual than operating. *Conceptual* as used here is not synonymous with *intellectual* or *theorectical*. The conceptualizer, at his or her best, is a persuader and a relation builder.

Highly developed operating and conceptual talent are not, of course, completely exclusive. Every able leader-manager is skilled in both areas, though only one or the other area will tend to be exceptional.

Both types of managerial talent, in balance, are required for sustained high-level performance in any large institution. They are not antithetical; in fact, in the right balance, they are complementary. When people who possess either talent to a high degree are intensely practical, dedicated, and responsible, the two talents work well together in a closely teamed relationship that gives great organizational strength. Both the operator and the conceptualizer are result-oriented. The operator is concerned primarily with getting it done. The conceptualizer is primarily concerned with what ought to be done—when, how, at what cost, in what order of priority, and, after the fact, how well it was done.

Enterprises that prosper over a long period manage to get people who specialize in one or the other of these talents into the right places; large enterprises in particular always have both talents functioning with influence and in balance in their top management so that neither dominates the other but each respects and depends on the other.

The achievement of this balance is hindered by a stubborn fact: whereas conceptualizers generally recognize the need for operators, the reverse is often not the case. Therefore, an operator in a top leadership post may not, without some help, see to it that able and influential conceptualizers function as they must. But a conceptualizer in a top spot is more apt to see that good operators are placed where needed.

One of the advantages of large decentralized organizations is that they can accommodate conceptualizers as a major influence in the central organization where they are most needed while placing operators in the dominant roles in the decentralized units. But teamed with each operator-head of a decentralized unit should be a conceptualizer working not as an assistant or as a staff person but as a close associate. This arrangement greatly facilitates the flow of ideas, both ways, between several conceptual specialists in the central office and the affiliated units.

Some able people, while they are young, probably can develop exceptional strength in either talent, but not both. Long concentration on one of these talents diminishes the possibility that a switch can be made successfully to the other. A substantial penalty may ensue if a person who has devoted several years, successfully, to one of these talents moves into a key spot that requires an exceptional level of the other because, once established as an operator or a conceptualizer, a person is apt to make any position fit his or her habitual way of working.

The issue of the balance of these talents in an organization is sometimes confused by the conventional designation of "line" and "staff" functions. Most positions that are regarded as line require a predominant operating talent. But some that are identified as staff positions also require it. They are simply operating services that are ancillary to the main body of work of the institution. The functions of personnel and purchasing, particularly in the affiliated unit of a large organization, are generally regarded as staff, but they may best be manned by operators.

Highly developed conceptualizers who are effective in top management seem to be much rarer than able operators. This may be partly because the number needed is substantially less, partly because they do not emerge naturally out of low-level management work, partly because it is harder for an operator to identify a conceptualizer (and therefore reward that person), and partly because the need for able conceptualizers is not generally recognized. The American railroads are the classic example of a large, important industry in which the need for conceptual talent has been traditionally unrecognized. The contemporary American university also shows signs of a similar neglect in its administration. Some institutions have risen to eminence because they accidentally evolved at least one able conceptualizer into a key spot. But then they lost eminence when they failed to maintain this talent at a high enough quality and in proper balance in its top management. (They probably lost it because they were not guided by an organization theory that required it. Not knowing that they had it, they were not aware when they lost it.)

Able operators are always required for good performance in any institution. An organization may perform well in the short run, as the railroads did, with an all-operating management. But for the long run, able conceptualizers, rightly placed in top management, are absolutely essential. To build and sustain a great institution, one must be able to identify (or develop) these talented men and women and see that they are always in places where their influence is needed. Providing able operators is an important and larger-scale task, but it is the more obvious and easier to do and therefore less likely to be neglected.

The purely operating motive, unsupported by strong conceptual talent, is likely to settle for doing well within the established pattern. Conceptualizers usually emerge when an institution makes a strong push for distinction.

One attribute of our time is that if any institution is to be judged distinguished, it must pull much farther ahead of the ordinary than has been required heretofore to attain this status. The effort to do this will bring the search for conceptualizers into higher priority.

THE MANAGERIAL MIND

THE LAWS UNDER WHICH corporation charters are granted generally stipulate that ultimate control of the resulting institution rests with a governing board of trustees or directors. By judicial decree, the power of the chartering governmental unit to govern comes to an end with the issuing of the charter of incorporation. That power then shifts to the board of trustees or directors. Churches, which are not generally incorporated, sometimes vest ultimate control in a trusteelike body. Other unincorporated institutions, through committees, sometimes evolve a comparable governance.

There is little question about the ultimate control of an institution being vested in a governing board of trustees or directors. What "ultimate control" means, beyond the power to appoint active top administrators when needed or to remove them if they default, is never very clear. There is little agreement on what trustees do, except that in nonprofit institutions they generally give or raise money. In some cases (maybe even most), trustees and directors are really regarded, deep in the attitudes of operating managers and staffs, as necessary evils or nuisances.

The United States of the late twentieth century may be rightly called a managerial society because the role and expertise of experienced managers have come to be generally regarded as wholly sufficient for the satisfactory operation of an institution. Except for the few limited functions described, trustees are sometimes seen as contributing little and are advised to keep out of the way and let the managers manage. My intention is to challenge these common assumptions and to suggest serious limitations on the managerial mind. Trustees then have a significant role that they can play best because they are able and informed people who are *not* managers. In short, I argue for an arrangement in which trustees provide the vision and purpose of what is to be done and managers get it done.

Managers are important people, and we need many of them. Perhaps their generally high compensation is justified, because getting things done requires such high skill, energy, dedication, sometimes even courage. If there is flak in the air, they have to take it. I think they generally earn their big money.

But there is an important occupational disability in the managerial craft that limits able managers in the generating of visions that are absolutely essential for purpose and direction for the institution. If purpose and direction are flawed, the very best managerial effort may fail.

Why is the managerial mind limited? Why is it not likely to generate the absolutely basic visions that give purpose and direction? The managerial mind is limited by its first priority to get things done—in the immediate—and to keep the institution afloat from day to day. To be good at getting things done, a manager must concentrate on the short range: where we were yesterday and where we are going tomorrow. The long range, the indefinite future framed against a good view of the distant past, requires a different kind of thinking. Maybe some geniuses can do both, but I suggest that they are rare. I have known a lot of managers intimately and have never known one of these exceptions.

Managers may argue that they get this kind of thinking from their staffs. I spent many years on such a staff, and I can testify that even if you think like a visionary (and I tried to), you had better talk like a manager or you won't be listened to and may not survive. I do not fault managers for this condition. After many years of reflection on my experience, I conclude that this is the way it should be. The job of managers is to manage well.

There is a great line in *The King and I,* when Anna is getting the king mixed up with some "modern" ideas and the old king gives the table a resounding crack with his fist and shouts, "If you're going to be king, you've got to be king!"[18] In this he was speaking for all managers. There are some ways of managing that work better than others. But in the end, they are all managing. And a commitment to a career of managing disqualifies one from another kind of thinking that is just as essential to the long-range success of the institution as managing. That other kind of thinking is best done by trustees because they hold the ultimate power and they have to be listened to.

Both trustees and managers are more effective when they use persuasion rather than coercive power. In an imperfect world, I accept that the power needs to be there in both cases.

I did not pull my contentions out of thin air. They rest on considerable experience as the member of the corporate staff of a huge bureaucracy and in a variety of trusteeships, both capped by extensive consulting experience to both trustees and managers.

GROWING GREATNESS IN MANAGERS

THERE CAN BE LITTLE DOUBT that in the years ahead, more management ability is going to have to grow out of persons who are potentially capable of development than in the past. The reasons are fairly obvious.

1. Unevenness in the population distribution—fewer people in their "good middle years" in proportion to oldsters and youngsters
2. Continued expansion of business
3. Increasing technical complexity of business
4. All of which adds up to scarcity—already evident
5. Plus a world of continued social, political, economic, and technological change that will make managing anything more difficult

We're going to need to produce more managers from the pool of potential, and they must be more capable managers than had they been born a generation earlier.

If more, and more capable, managers are going to grow out of the available potential, something has to change. It might be interesting to speculate on what has to change. Two changes are already evident:

1. Sending managers to school in both university courses and courses within business

2. Rotating potential managers in a wider range of jobs than formerly

Both of these developments are good—within limits, the limits being that going to school, even a good school, is a fairly passive experience, and schools for managers can give both trainee and boss a false assurance that the trainee's development is taken care of. Job rotation can be perfunctory, or a person can stay such a short time in any one place that he or she never carries real responsibility anywhere until the rotation is stopped; at that point, the trainee is supposed to be developed but clearly is not.

The limitation on most of the management development ideas I hear about is that they are dealing with a past that poses no real problem—the part of a person's equipment that is largely knowledge and experience. These things are important; they take time and money and effort, but we know how to provide them. I have no fears about an adequate amount of this kind of competence for the future. My reservations about the future, and they are substantial, are in the area of motivations, attitudes, perceptiveness, creativeness—in the capacity to make the great decisions that great issues demand. The business manager of the future, as I foresee this person, either foreman or president, will need qualities of greatness if he or she is to be judged adequate, qualities that business has been able to do with less of up to now, qualities that we have difficulty describing in terms of our own experience because we don't know just what the manager of the future will be up against. Yet I am sure that this durability of what we have built here depends on our laying the groundwork for horizons of challenge and opportunity that we perceive only dimly.

So I feel that it will take a new approach, a fundamental change, to make a material difference in the growing of managers, to bring the accomplishment more in line with the needs of the future. It will take a much more fundamental change than sending managers to school and rotating them through a lot of jobs.

I believe we need to view this at a different level, to think in terms other than the "devices" we hear most talked about. Too many of us are thinking in terms of doing something to people, something that we haven't done before, or doing more of something than we did in the past, something that is supposed to be good. I don't want to quarrel with this approach, but I want to take a different look.

If more, and more capable, managers are to emerge, people adequate for the requirements of the future, the change that has to come, it seems to me, is a shift from the point of view of *doing* something to people to thinking of *permitting* something to happen to them. This may sound abstract and a little vague, but anybody who makes this change in point of view toward someone for whom he or she feels responsible has made a profoundly revolutionary alteration in thinking. This holds whether it is parent viewing child, teacher viewing pupil, or boss viewing subordinate.

I suppose that any person in the position of mentor must ask, "What is most important to me in providing for the future? Do I want to leave my business with my great achievement and a person capable of administering my achievement, or do I want to leave a *great person* capable of dealing creatively and decisively with the problems to be faced, someone who can help another great person to grow as his or her successor?" There is no question in my mind about the choice of these. The business I have helped build has a very insecure future, insofar as my efforts influence its course, if I am trying to project *my* achievement into the future.

If my idea as the senior manager is to help great people grow, as the best guarantee of the future, then I need to know something about what I mean by growth in greatness.

If we had a crystal-clear answer to this and if we were all agreed on it, we could usher in the millennium right now. But we have no such answer; yet we need some sense of it if we are going to make the best of our opportunity, and I venture my opinion as to what it is.

I believe that people grow in these moral, perceptive, creative, and decisive qualities *as they achieve the freedom to become themselves.*

The seed of greatness, which all people share, was put there by the Creator. As parent, teacher, or boss, I cannot bring it to germination; I cannot even direct its cultivation because I do not know the character of the unique need in this unique individual. And the individual cannot "will" this germination either, because he or she doesn't understand its unique qualities any better than I do. Germination and growth are things that people can encourage by climate and conditions, but they cannot direct, shape, or influence them if true greatness is to emerge.

Thomas Jefferson's development is a case in point. Jefferson was a very bright man by inheritance. That part of him was born near Monticello, and with that part alone he probably would have been well known among his contemporaries. But the qualities of greatness that *we* know him for were born in George Wythe's house. George Wythe was the lawyer under whom Jefferson read law. He didn't take young Jefferson under the customary agreement of those times in which the law clerk was virtually indentured as an apprentice. He took him as a unique person with potential qualities of greatness, and he set up the climate that assured the maturing of those qualities. What went on in that formative period makes quite a story. From the perspective of his later years, Jefferson wrote of Wythe as "my second father, my earliest and best friend, and to him I am indebted for first impressions which have had the most salutary influence on the course of my life."[19]

I suppose that the difference between George Wythe and other lawyers under whom Jefferson might have studied is that Wythe saw his law clerk as an end in himself, a unique person with growth potential, and Wythe found adventure and satisfaction in watching him grow. Another lawyer might have viewed his understudy largely as *means*—as legs and arms to do the chores and learn some law on the side.

But in addition, Wythe apparently had a concept of freedom—the freedom that he must grant and the freedom that his understudy must achieve. The mentor's granting of freedom is fairly clear. He must not judge what his understudy will become. But how about the freedom that the understudy will achieve? What is it, and how does the climate set by the mentor encourage its growth? I would like to explore these questions within the context of contemporary American business because I think they are crucially important.

Let's say that I am a senior manager. I may be a president, or I may be a foreman, and I have work to do, obligations to customers, owners, employees, government. I have people associated with me to help meet these obligations. I intend to manage my part well today—and I intend to build all the strength for the future that I can build with the resources I have. I believe that the best I can do for the future is help younger managers grow so that they will be adequate for the future. I also believe that the important qualities they will need cannot be dictated or directed by me or by anyone but will emerge as a natural consequence of the total environment in which the person lives.

Now, as a business manager, I don't have access to that total environment. A lot has happened to this person before coming to work with me. And other influences—home, church, community, government—impinge even as the person is working with me. What can I do with the share of this person's environment that I can influence?

Like the native in the Deep South who, when asked by a tourist, "How do I get to Charleston?" thought a long time and then said, "Well, sir, you begin from here," we begin with what we have to work with. As a manager who feels an obligation for the future, here are some of the things I can do.

I can give my very best attention to the young people entering business. Give them responsibility. Help them get a feeling of what mature growth involves and assume some responsibility for their own growth. Give them the freedom to take reasonable risks. We discover more about ourselves through error than through success. Only the person who can take risks and tolerate the errors has a chance to achieve the freedom to become himself or herself.

I can watch the way incentives are handled. The reward for good work on a job should be in the satisfactions and compensation in that job. The opportunity for advancement should be held out to those of demonstrated competence who also give the indications of basic growth, growth in the achievement of their own freedom.

I can give research opportunities to people who show promise. There is so much to be known about the art of management that can only be learned by experienced managers turned researchers for a short while. There is no better way to give a manager the chance to feel a sense of freedom than to detach him or her from the job, assign a little bit of research planning, and allow two or three months to find the answer to a tough problem. You learn something about a problem, and a promising person learns something about himself or herself— something that can't be taught. It is probably the least expensive and most effective special kind of opportunity that can be given to a person capable of growth.

I can give a person challenge and opportunity in his or her work. Most of us are aware of some limitations on how much of this we can do. Yet in my experience, the most successful grower of people I know about did his most productive work through the Depression years when it was mighty hard to do. He was simply interested in growth, and he used the situation he had with the people he had and saw to it that the most challenge and opportunity was given to the most people.

I can state the goals of my operation with forcefulness and clarity so as to inspirit a person to build a personal concept of the future self within a larger framework than most people conceive. A person is more likely to emerge in mature years as a manager capable of carrying heavy responsibility if that person's own purposes are formulated early within the framework of an adequate goal for the company, something that gives a person a feeling of greatness.

I believe the kinds of things I have mentioned here are the things that any manager can do at any level of a business and at any stage of the economic cycle, from inflation to depression. I have seen them done, and it takes no genius of a person to do it. Any competent manager can do it with a firm belief in the idea that people grow as they achieve the freedom to become themselves. Once a manager accepts that he or she cannot compel or direct growth, energies can be directed into providing the indispensable encouraging climate and using the incentives available to recognize the emergence of true greatness.

And how will managers recognize true greatness as it emerges? I believe it shows in two ways: by the outward evidences of inward attributes that I call "moral"—the motivations and attitudes that make for a distinctive quality of executive competence, and by a consequent poise and assurance that mark the person who has become perceptive, creative, and decisive.

It is a difficult idea to express, but I believe I have some sense of how the moral side of a really great manager develops. We never fully understand a person's motivations, and yet we have some sense of them. They are growing in the right direction, it seems to me, when a person begins to think independently; begins to set goals beyond the self, beyond personal comfort and convenience, sometimes beyond one's own good; sets goals beyond the present; and takes personal satisfaction in the "freedom to become."

We can observe some of the attitudes, the sets of mind that guide a person's actions, which are a hopeful augury for a great manager. The person seeks to understand—an automatic reaction to everything. Wonder and interest mark this person's outlook. He or she develops a deep feeling of responsibility for the whole enterprise. The things that are good for the business make this person feel good, and the things that hurt the business hurt this person, deep down in the feelings. A manager emerging into greatness sees people as ends as well as means. This person knows that people must meet the practical requirements of business and are also unique personalities worthy of dignity and respect. This manager feels free to make risk-taking decisions when he or she may have to absorb the penalty of error.

If the climate of a business and the immediate work situation fosters the growth of motives and attitudes like these, then I am confident that what a person has in the way of capacity to be perceptive, creative, and decisive will emerge out of the normal experience of carrying responsibility. But until the motives and attitudes of a free person emerge, "training" in the skills of management is not likely to produce much in the way of greatness.

We who are mindful of our obligation to the future of American business enterprise work on a difficult frontier. Our vision of the future is dim, and our knowledge of human nature is feeble but growing. Frankly, if we did not have a good dose of old-fashioned faith, we would not make it. Trusting *all* to a process of human growth that we do not understand and cannot dictate calls for faith if anything ever did. Yet here we are with the greatest development of free economic enterprise the world has ever seen, and yet nothing but faith in the capacity of people to grow under freedom will assure its future.

Someone wryly observed, you are as young as your faith and as old as your doubts and fears.

I believe that this all gets back to two simple but basic questions: do you get the greatest fun of your business life out of seeing people grow, and do you see the assurance of the long-run success of your company in terms of growing great people?

ORGANIZATIONS

MY WORK AT AT&T

An Adventure in Spirit

IN MY GRADUATION TALK at Alverno College in 1984,[20] I noted that one of the five pivotal ideas that guided my work career was the suggestion of a professor of sociology in my senior year at college. His advice was that I get inside one of the big institutions of that day (none of which, in his opinion, was serving us well), make my career there if I could, and try to get into a position to respond to the criticisms that were made by people like him and become an influence, however small, that would help make that institution more serving. I accepted that advice.

I chose the American Telephone and Telegraph Company because it was the biggest at that time. I spent thirty-eight years there. I never became deeply involved with AT&T, either in its technology or as a business, nor did I ever hold an important executive post. Rather, I tried to get into a position from which I could learn about that company in depth and influence it with ideas. I believe that I accomplished some of what my old professor advised, and I am grateful to the company for providing me with a comfortable living while I carried out this mandate within its walls. Life there was not always easy or comfortable. There were some long, dry periods and a few dreadful ones that really tested my spirit. But as a total career it was rewarding.

I never announced my mission within the company. I probably would not have been hired in the first place or survived
long if I had done so. I always tried to the best of my ability to
do well the job at hand, but I also always had my own agenda,
from my first day to my last.

There were two periods, however, in which the top man
seemed to understand what I was up to and to appreciate what
it contributed to the company. The first was when I was between the ages of forty-seven and fifty-two, when a "caretaker"
chief was installed. This new chief was the only one in my time
who believed that the company did not have a good survival
strategy and wanted to do something radical about it. He had
the same time that Pope John XXIII had to act on his insight,
but he lacked what John had—a sense of history that might
have suggested a prudent course of action. He tried hard but
failed to accomplish much. He had the position from which he
could have led, but he did not have the ideas with which to
lead. I received a letter from him a few weeks before he died, in
his late eighties, in which he said, "I wish I could have done
more."

He once called me on the carpet to lecture me because, as he
said, "You aren't spending enough money!" I might have said
to him, "What are we going to do about those two fellows that
stand in the hierarchy between you and me?" or "Look, man,
this is your revolution. *You* spend some money." But I didn't
say anything like that; it would only have frustrated him, and
he would have blown his top. So I just said meekly, "I'm spending all the money I can prudently spend. I'm doing about all
that I can do within the constraints I work under." He was a
realist, and he accepted that. Much as he would have liked to
see me shake the place up, he knew it couldn't be done from
my position, he did not know how to do it from his position,
and I couldn't tell him. There are some things a leader simply
has to know. Without a sense of history, one cannot know and
really cannot be told. I needed the perspective of considerably

more experience to understand fully the tragic nature of this good man's dilemma.

The second period when I believe my role was understood and appreciated was my last seven years in the business, when I had a very close relationship with the president, who was the chief operating officer, or COO (the chairman was the chief executive officer, or CEO). Again, two fellows stood between us in the hierarchy, and there was constant strain over my closeness to the president. But we learned to live with it. With the perspective of more experience, I see that this was, in part, a counseling relationship. Within two months after I retired, this man had a serious episode of mental illness on the job, was summarily retired, and died soon thereafter. I have wondered whether I did the right thing when I left. I have had some experiences that have caused me to wonder how many of the seemingly strong people really are strong.

To go back to the beginning, I joined the Ohio Bell Telephone Company, a subsidiary of AT&T, in September 1926. My first two months were spent with a line construction crew. This was followed by a few months in an engineering office, just enough to learn some language so I could talk like I belonged. Then I was tapped for what proved to be the most formative experience of my adult life.

The company's first venture into formal management education was a two-week program called a foreman's conference. This was the construction and maintenance department of the company, at that time all men. I attended a five-week program to learn to demonstrate a foreman's conference and prepare me to lead one. For the next year, every other Monday morning, I received a group of twelve foremen. For two weeks, we sat around a big table and talked about the multifaceted job of being a foreman, the fellow who has to get the work done. There was no reading and no published agenda, although I had one. These fellows were where the buck stopped. The elaborate hierarchy of managers above them could think their great thoughts about what they wanted done, but what *was* done was what these fellows, who sat around my conference table, were willing and able to do. The pedagogical theory was that they would learn from each other, not from me; but I was the chief learner. My conferees ranged in age from thirty to seventy. I was twenty-three. I learned much from those wise and seasoned men. This was my graduate education, and I wouldn't have traded it for any other I know about. The course of my life work was set in that experience. It was there that I began to think of myself as a student of organization, of how things get done. The remainder of my thirty-eight years at AT&T and the focus of my postretirement work have been on that quest. It is a never-ending search; I have much yet to learn.

Before entering the AT&T system, all of my experience had been with small institutions—small businesses, small colleges, small churches. My initial impression on joining Ohio Bell was that this was different from anything I had experienced before. It wasn't just that it was big. It had a spirit and a sense of mission that was very compelling. The motto "The Spirit of Service" was posted everywhere. I was curious about how it got that way, and this led me to inquire into the history of AT&T, an interest that began in my first month and continued to the end of my tenure. If I had had the temperament of a historian, I might have written a history. When I retired, I left my voluminous file behind. It is a fascinating story. Some pieces of it have now been told, but the full story may never be heard because so much of it was in the heads of people who are now gone (they were still around as old men when I entered). Businesspeople are generally not literary folk who keep journals. I didn't keep one either.

The telephone was invented by Alexander Graham Bell in 1876. The two patents covering it are reputed to have been the most contested ever issued in the United States, so great was the desire to use that instrument and so restrictive was the policy of the patent holders.

The first telephone company was chartered in Boston in 1878, and its first general manager was a young man of thirty-three named Theodore N. Vail who had had a meteoric rise in the U.S. Post Office to superintendent of the railway mails, a subcabinet post. Vail stayed with the company nine years and left because of disaffection with the conservative policies of the Boston owners, who seemed to him more interested in the profitable exploitation of their patents than in building a business. A restless, creative man, Vail spent the next twenty years as an economic adventurer around the world. In that period, the patents expired, and a rash of duplicate telephone systems emerged. By the time of the depression of 1907, they were all in trouble.

In that period, another great builder emerged, J. P. Morgan the elder, who, before the establishment of the Federal Reserve System in 1911, was personally as close to a central bank as the nation had. He was a powerful, intelligent, and creative man who would be out of style today, but in the context of his times, he was a builder of quality institutions. (General Electric and U.S. Steel were put together under his aegis.) The Morgan companies were the first to issue financial statements with a certified public accountant's attest. (U.S. Steel in 1903 was the very first major company to issue one. These are commonplace today, but in 1903 the idea was revolutionary.)

Morgan started accumulating AT&T stock around 1900, when the company began to falter. By 1907, he had taken control from the Bostonians, moved the company to New York, and installed Vail as president. The modern company was built in the period from 1907 to 1920, when Vail died in the harness at age seventy-five. Those thirteen years make a great story. Vail was a great visionary leader, and the spirit that I felt when I started to work in Ohio was generated in that period.

On October 1, 1929, I moved to the corporate office in New York, a few weeks before the great stock market crash. There I discovered that the spirit I felt in Ohio no longer existed in the corporate office. Vail had been succeeded by his number two man, nearly his own age, who gave way in 1925 to a good young financial manager who presided over the company for the next twenty-two years. He achieved the reputation of a business statesman because he brought in the first public relations person. (Vail didn't have one of those. He wrote his own speeches, of which he made many, as well as his annual reports.) This PR man engineered an invitation for the new chief to address the National Association of Railroad and Public Utility Commissioners on the subject of AT&T policy. It was a newsworthy event, and references to that policy are still found in texts on business policy. I once asked the writer of that speech where he got the ideas that went into it. His prompt answer: "I found every single idea in Vail's papers." The moral I draw from that is that able PR folk can make reputations, but only genuine creative people with spirit can generate great ideas and infuse an institution with spirit. When I arrived in the corporate office, the chief who could (and did) do that had been dead for nine years, and the charge of spirit he generated had evaporated. I worked for the next thirty-five years in an able but dispirited organization. The spirit I encountered in Ohio in 1926 was the residual from the original infusion direct from Vail. AT&T headquarters, when I arrived in 1929, was living on warmed-over stuff. The words and the technical competence were there, but the spirit had fled.

My last title on the corporate staff was director of management research. With the help of a professional staff that I recruited, I had a broad charter to study and advise regarding the management of the business, including the values that guided it. In my last five years, I headed a summer course for young executives that we conducted jointly with Dartmouth College. Each of our students was somebody's nominee as a potential officer. We tried not only to educate for the officer level of the business, but as a faculty—the two Dartmouth professors and I—we tried to make a judgment about the potentials of our students for that level of management. Sometimes we offered advice regarding next assignments that might accelerate their growth. I recall one student who was born in New York and educated in parochial schools there and at Fordham University, with all of his work experience in New York City. Our judgment on him was: very bright, very able, and a good man, but parochial. When this was reported to the head of his company, we were asked, "What should we do with him?" We replied, "Send him out for two or three years as general manager of the state of Iowa." That advice was accepted, and he returned for a rapid rise to president of New York Telephone Company.

One of the courses in our program, taught by the chairman of the department of English at Dartmouth, was titled "The Language and Literature of Decision." The main subject matter of the course was four of Shakespeare's historical plays that were used as case studies of the language usage of kings. It was the most effective teaching of mature executives that I ever witnessed, and I have watched quite a lot of it.

I don't know what conclusion to draw from the following item; I leave that judgment to you. When I got within five years of my target date for retirement at age sixty, I began to dismantle my staff and get its members advantageously placed elsewhere. I knew that I did not have a successor. I had had a staff of twenty, and when I left, there was just one assistant with whom I shared a secretary. I have wondered why nobody asked why I did that. The course at Dartmouth was discontinued a couple of sessions after I retired.

Twenty years after I retired, AT&T was dismantled in settlement of an antitrust suit. Why, some ask, when the United States enjoyed the best and cheapest telephone service in the world? There are probably as many answers as there are thoughtful people who are informed about the company. My answer, from my bias, is because sixty years before, the company had lost its spirit. And why did it lose its spirit? Again a personal answer: because when the great visionary builder died in 1920, there wasn't a J. P. Morgan with the power to install another visionary builder as the new chief. Subsequently, the

bureaucracy of managers evolved one of their own and continued to evolve good, conscientious managers who did not have
the vision or the spirit to lead.

A parallel can be drawn with the Roman Catholic Church. If
the Curia, the governing bureaucracy, had had the power to select the new pope, they would never have installed John XXIII.
One of the great strengths of the church is that the power to select a pope is lodged with the cardinals, who are numerous
enough and varied enough that at least once in five hundred
years they can produce a great leader, and that may be often
enough for the church to survive. But for AT&T to survive the
new conditions after World War II, it would have had to produce a leader of Vail's quality at least every five years.

Up to World War II, AT&T had a sufficient monopoly on the
technology that a challenge to its telephone service was virtually impossible. But the war changed that. Coming out of the
war were several strong companies that could produce quality
telephone equipment, and they wanted in. They were not allowed in, so the first antitrust suit was brought. A few years
later, both satellite and microwave transmission appeared and
greatly increased the available circuits, which had previously
been dependent on the vast wire network that AT&T owned,
and the new companies that wanted part of the network business took the antitrust route to get in. The result was a negotiated settlement of both cases that left local telephone service in
the old monopoly position through seven separate regional
companies and AT&T as a competitive company specializing in
long-distance service, research, and manufacturing, with the
potential, if successful, to become a major world conglomerate.
I suspect that the AT&T chief who negotiated this settlement
got a deal that may prove to be a moneymaker for the investor.
The new competitors in the long-distance field may or may not
prosper. But at this writing, the public interest may suffer,
maybe for a short time, maybe for a long time.

What was lost that may never be recovered was a great
covenantal company, in the sense of an institution that carried

an enormous obligation for the nation's telephone service—its cost, its quality, and its availability. No single institution carries that obligation now. The field is occupied by a bunch of hucksters (including the new AT&T), jousting with each other in pursuit of a fast buck.

What, one may ask, would a leader with vision and spirit have done that the managers who operated the business after 1920 did not do? With Vail, the great visionary builder, in their past, they would have had a sense of history. I can document from my experience that the managers who followed Vail did not have that sense of history. Had they had it, they would have known that Vail faced a collision with the antitrust enforcers in 1913. With Morgan's backing, Vail set out to absorb all of the local independent companies that were largely in local service. He also acquired Western Union Telegraph Company and was on his way toward one unified electrical communication system. It could be argued that such would be in the nation's interest if it could be regulated in the public interest, but the tactics of achieving it were brutal. Morgan had enough control of the banking system to dry up the independent companies' credit, and Vail refused to connect them to the long-distance network. Vail was taking over the independents at a rapid rate. The national administration elected in 1912 took a dim view of all of this, and a settlement was negotiated with an exchange of letters. A formal case was never brought. AT&T agreed to divest Western Union, to cease acquiring independent companies, and to connect the independents to the long-distance network. The result was to freeze the ratio of Bell to non-Bell phones at about 80–20, where it remains to this day.

What a sense of history would have told modern managers is that when there is a change in conditions that requires adaptation, one takes the initiative while one has it and does not wait for the ponderous legal process to shove it down one's throat. If there is to be statesmanship in the relations between big business and government, the primary obligation is on business. Vail's prompt settlement of the issue in 1913 was hailed as business statesmanship. The post–World War II managers were not given those kudos.

A sense of history gives one more than an awareness of the past. It also makes one more alert to present circumstances and sharpens one's perception of the future. The managers of AT&T after World War II had nearly forty years to adjust to new circumstances and to take the initiative to work out compromises in which as much as possible of the old covenantal company could be saved. The record of the last ten years before the breakup does not reveal that that kind of thinking took place.

Let me document the assertion that AT&T's managers after World War II lacked a sense of history. After the first postwar antitrust case was pending, I had occasion to write a speech that the chief executive was to give at the business school at Columbia University. In my first draft, I wrote in an acknowledgment of the speaker's debt to Vail. At our first conference, the CEO literally growled at me, "I don't know anything about Vail, and I'm not going to make a speech about him!" I replied, "When you get to the Columbia Business School, if you will go into the big reading room of the library, you will see on the walls around the room twelve large photographic portraits of great builders of American businesses. And there, along with Ford, Carnegie, Schwab, Rosenwald, Rockefeller, and the others, you will find Vail. You may not know anything about Vail, but your listeners do. And they know what his unique contribution to management thinking was. What are they going to think of you if you show up to talk on this subject and do not acknowledge your debt to Vail?" After a moment of silence, he said, "OK, leave it in." How could this able, intelligent, and experienced chief arrive at the head of this giant company and literally know nothing of its history? The answer, I believe, is that history is not useful to a manager whose concern is mostly short-range. But it is imperative that one who would lead the institution and give it vision and spirit have a sense of history.

This chief, and a long series of able managers like him, ultimately lost the business. ("Where there is no vision, the people perish," we read in Proverbs.[21])

One further example: The centennial of the invention of the telephone was in 1976. Anticipating a big celebration, in 1974 the PR people commissioned a good business writer to do a journalistic history of the company to be published for the event. I had been retired for ten years, but I knew that this was going on. One day, I received a call from the writer asking to come and talk about it. When he came, he told me that he was having trouble finding anybody who could talk about the history of the company. He had gone to the president (the chief operating executive) with his problem. "I am a journalist," he told the president, "not a historian with a staff. And I have two years to produce a finished book. I can't find anybody who can sit down and tell me how this company came to be what it is." The president reflected. "I can't tell you. You had better go up to New Hampshire and talk to Greenleaf." Here was a business with one million employees, yet nobody the president knew could give the writer the information about the company he needed.[22]

I could give other examples of a lack of a sense of history by managers. I realize that I had that interest probably because I am not by temperament a manager. I have never wanted to be one, and I do not know whether I could be one if I tried. In my early days at AT&T, I had to elude efforts to put me in a manager's job. Fortunately, I knew that that was not what I wanted to do, that there were, for me, better ways of serving, and the company was flexible enough to let me serve it in the way that was best for me. I observed many who were not so lucky: managers stuck in staff work and staffers stuck in management. There are, no doubt, some people who can do both. I suspect that Vail was one of those.

MANAGER,
ADMINISTRATOR, STATESMAN

THE WORD *manage* comes from the Latin root *manus,* "hand," and has the connotation of control. *Administer* comes from *administrare,* with the suggestion of "to care for." The vast world of institutions needs many able manager-administrators. But particularly in large institutions, a quite different talent of statesmanship is of crucial importance. Whether the lead person is chief or *primus inter pares* (first among equals), it is probably best that the talent of statesmanship be possessed by that person. But if not, someone who is influential in the top group should have it. (In a large institution, the top person may not have to be a manager. And those at the top may lead better if they are primarily statesmen.)

A statesman, as I see it, is one who has a strong sense of history, both of the particular institution and its place in the evolving society. Along with this sense of history goes an awareness of where the institution is heading and a good estimate of where it is likely to be at certain points in the future. In short, this person sees things whole, or more whole than most do, and sees things whole in the future. This perspective gives that person a better view than most managers have of what the institution should do now in order to sustain its strength in the future. This thereby equips the statesman to negotiate (or direct negotiations) with other parties and institutions with which the institution has a relationship. The statesman, better than most, knows when to compromise, when to stand firm, when to stonewall, when to come clean and lay matters on the table, when to strike out with vigor, and when to surrender. And he or she has in abundance what all who lead need some of—spirit—plus the rare gift of respect for all people.

The person who has those talents may or may not be a manager. He or she may be able to manage but may not be interested in managing and may not perform well if put in that role for a long period of time.

A person in the theater once told me, "A professional actor may never quite equal a gifted amateur who appears for just one night. What makes a professional is that the person can be coached to a high level of performance and then, with occasional tuning up, may repeat that performance a thousand times, in rare instances for a lifetime, with little variation in quality due to ailments, foul moods, or headaches."

The able manager is a professional in this sense. He or she is able to sustain enthusiasm for managing and to attend indefinitely to the large amount of detail and personal leadership that optimal institutional performance requires. But if put in a position where statesmanship is required or where one must generate the ideas that sustained good institutional performance requires, an able manager may be inept, a failure. There are notable examples to this, as any student of organization knows.

To return to the theater analogy: the playwright may be the equivalent of the statesman and may not be a good actor. And the great actor may never write a play. Fortunately for the theater, the distinction between the two talents is recognized, and there are different criteria for judging each. One person may have both talents, but the adequacy of each talent is judged separately. There is also another separate calling, the director who puts the performance together and coaches the actors.

In leading and governing institutions, however, the distinction between manager and statesman is not so sharp and is not generally recognized. The rare person may be strong in both, and most able people may have a little of both talents. A strong, durable institution needs able managers to oversee its affairs, but it needs at least one able statesman to guide its strategic policy. That person should be strong in statesmanship and may not have the managerial temperament. He or she must be influential in strategic policy decisions.

An important weakness in the concept of the single chief at the top of a managerial hierarchy is that such a person is apt to be a manager and to assume, by virtue of having the position, that he or she has all of the talents it requires. Directors or trustees, who make or affirm the decision of who shall lead, generally have the same limited view of what is required to govern, and they are likely to install a manager and not take steps to ensure that *statesmen* shape policy. If, by chance (and it usually is chance), there happens to be a statesman somewhere in the institution, that person is likely to be a "crier in the wilderness." This biblical reference suggests that the dilemma of statesmen portrayed here is not a new idea and that the prevalence of low-serving institutions is not a new aspect of the human condition.

A gifted statesman is not necessarily a benign influence. There are good statesmen and evil statesmen. But a true servant who is also a gifted statesman has the chance to be influential in building serving institutions that are the foundation stones of a good society. This is written in the hope of aiding the process of nurturing more servant-statesmen.

There are numerous resources for training managers. They should be watched and, where these schools are preparing people to lead serving institutions, encouraged. The role of statesman, however, is the need of exploration; I doubt if it is yet known how to nurture people who have that gift. It is urgent that we learn to nurture statesmen because I fear that we are now losing some due to the prevailing notion that managing is all. And we need a new nonsexist label for the role. *Statesperson* would do.

These observations on managers, administrators, and statesmen rest on considerable experience working in and observing institutional governance. As I have watched with dismay the imminent dismemberment of AT&T, I have reflected on my thirty-eight years there and have pondered much on why this breakup is taking place.

The short answer to the question of why this is taking place now might be that the nation is no longer willing to accept that any vital public service institution as large as AT&T should be in private hands, even under regulation and even if, by breaking it up, the public may get poorer service and pay more for it (as may well be the case). A longer, more complex answer might be that for a company that big, rendering a vital public service, to be accepted under regulation, it must at all times be headed by a statesman.

In the crucial years from 1907 to 1920, when the modern institution known as AT&T was being built, it was headed by a great builder who was also a statesman, Theodore N. Vail. The first brush with the antitrust enforcers was in 1913, when radical concessions and new limitations were accepted and confirmed by an exchange of letters between an officer of the company and the U.S. Justice Department. A formal legal case was not brought but almost certainly would have been had the matter not been resolved informally. In *Telephone: The First Hundred Years*, the closest we yet have to a published and detached view of the company's history, John Brooks reports that the 1913 commitment was "hailed by President Wilson as an act of business statesmanship" and concludes that it "meant abandoning the dream of a national telephone monopoly." Further, Brooks observes, "it provides a striking example of the resolution of government-corporation conflicts by compromise, and sets the stage for the modern era of the telephone."[23] The next major event in this modern era was the passage by Congress in 1921 of a special act that exempted the merger of competing local telephone systems from the antitrust laws. While Vail died in 1920, this final step was the consummation of efforts begun before he died and carried to completion by the close associate who succeeded him. Almost all duplicate competing local systems were promptly merged after 1921, usually with the system having the predominant service in a city acquiring the other. This left the division between Bell and independents at about 80–20, where it was in 1913. (This fact may explain why the new law was accepted in 1921.)

The question is, why, in view of this auspicious start in its relationship to government and others who shared the field, has the company encountered such an acrimonious period since World War II, with two federal antitrust suits and numerous private ones, and with the resultant radical dismemberment of what is generally conceded to have been a great business that has been a national asset?

The easy answer is to blame it on an insensitive and cumbersome legal process, but this has been the situation since 1913. What has changed is that, at least since 1926 when I entered the business, AT&T has been headed by a manager who was not a statesman. The present incumbent may be a statesman (as I have defined that title), but I believe the war was lost before he took over, and I suspect he has salvaged as much as anybody could from what he inherited.

Alvin Von Auw, who served as assistant to the three preceding chairmen of AT&T, retired in 1981 and was commissioned to write the history of recent events. He is an able writer and was a participant in the events of these hectic years. In his recently published book, *Heritage and Destiny: Reflections on the Bell System in Transition,* he acknowledges the role of Vail the manager and his great contribution of the management tradition of AT&T, but he makes no reference to Vail the statesman and his handling of the antitrust issue of his time.[24] To me, this is a significant omission.

Immediately on entering the business in 1926, I became interested in the history of the company, and when I retired in 1964, I left a large file of what I had gathered. As I write this, I am depending wholly on my memory of events and the two books,

Brooks's *Telephone* in 1976 and Von Auw's *Heritage and Destiny* in 1983. In my later years, I lectured widely within the business on its history, and I was aware of an almost universal disinterest in that history among the managers at all levels in my time.

Without a sense of history, there is a lack of awareness of the present and perspective on what is new in the present. One new element in the post–World War II present was that after the war, several strong companies had the technology and resources to get into the telephone business who did not have these before the war. The vast needs for communication gear in the war and the close-down of nonessential industries had propelled many businesses into this work, and at the end of the war they were in hot pursuit of opportunities to exploit their new technology and production resources, which were no longer needed in prosecuting the war. They wanted a part of the telephone business, and they were determined to get in. They saw the antitrust laws as their entrée. Since AT&T, with its managerial orientation, was not disposed to let them in and had the power of size and some locks on the door (and was pretty much heavy-handed), the new eager entrepreneurs took recourse to the antitrust laws, and their stratagem worked. This eventual course of events was evident to a farsighted person in 1947.

What would a statesman at the helm or influential in the top councils at AT&T have done when this new situation first raised its head, which it did immediately after the war? A statesman would have taken the initiative to work out a design for the communications industry in which the needs and desires of these new communication companies would have been accommodated. The Bell System would have had to make radical changes, and sooner than it ultimately did, but it would have been spared the acrimony, and the great expense, of this litigious period. And perhaps some U.S. president might have complimented the company and its leaders on their statesmanship. The anxiety of one million employees and three million shareowners might never have been aroused as it has been. The investing public would not have lost its greatest "blue chip," a large, solid anchor in a volatile sea. One of the world's great research institutions might not be in jeopardy. And the integrity of a great corporation might have been preserved—an element for stability in the culture.

I have quoted elsewhere a line from Machiavelli that will bear repeating here. In his advice to the prince, he said, "Thus it happens in matters of state; for knowing afar off (which is only given a prudent man to do) the evils that are brewing, they are easily cured. But when, for want of such knowledge, they are allowed to grow so that everyone can recognize them, there is no longer any remedy to be found."[25]

The statesman, as we define him here, sees afar off and immediately starts thinking about how to respond, when it is appropriate to respond, to what he sees. By 1947, it was clear that AT&T faced new conditions to which the company should respond with something other than "Stay off my turf." Thirty-five years later, it did respond, and, in Machiavelli's terms, there was "no longer any remedy to be found"—not a good one, in any case. This was a clear failure of statesmanship.

In that period from 1947 to 1982, the business was well managed. Service expanded and improved, and the rise in cost to the consumer was kept well below the rate of inflation and was sometimes even reduced. Technological development was spectacular, with five Nobel Prizes awarded to Bell scientists. Earnings were good, and investors were amply rewarded. Employees were well cared for. It was a good place to work, and the company improved its stature as a public citizen. Why, the neutral observer might ask, was the government willing to dismember a business that was that good? There is no simple answer except that, perhaps, all three branches of government that were involved are dominated by lawyers and economists, and many in key spots are transients. And there is little in the equipment of either lawyers or economists that prepares them to think about what makes an institution effective. Rather, institutions—especially businesses—are seen as chattels and not as collections of humans who are searching for order, meaning, and light. *If there is to be statesmanship in the interactions between business and government, generally it must come from business.* Too few of the able conscientious people in government really understand what is out there, and not many stay in key spots long enough to understand anything as complex as AT&T.

My present view on statesmanship has been slow in evolving. One of the events in my later years at AT&T was the emergence as chairman of a man who had a phobia for efficiency. Like all persons in his spot, he had a real concern for maintaining the earnings of the company. Part of his strategy was to squeeze more out of the operation. I was among a small group of old staff people who looked askance at this but we were not in a position to challenge it. And the people who were in a position to challenge it were a bunch of mice. They knew as well as the rest of us oldsters that if this tactic were pushed too far, the result would be a disaster. It was, and it was.

One of the analogies I heard during the talks among old staff members was this: What if the mayor of a city decided that the fire department should be efficient? Instead of sitting around the firehouse most of the time playing cards, all firemen should be out fighting fires eight hours a day. The effect of this would surely reduce the cost of the fire department, but an awful lot of buildings would burn down. No service institution can be efficient in the manner of a factory assembly line (which was where this chairman got the idea in his last job as president of Western Electric, an assembly-line institution). Service requires a certain amount of slack in order that people and equipment are available to meet variations in demand for service. Telephone service is clearly in that category. Good service requires some idle equipment and people most of the time. But this chairman put on the screws and squeezed that slack out of the business. By the time I retired, the effect on service was beginning to show. There were occasional dial tone failures at peak hours in the nearby Wall Street area. There weren't too many and they didn't last too long, but they were occurring, an unmistakable signal that the machine was overloaded.

The service held for another two years until that chairman retired. Then the roof fell in on his poor successor, and there were major service failures in several big cities. The new chairman, an able manager, was in a real sweat to get the service restored, and many millions had to be spent that would not have been required if the previous chairman had not gone on his efficiency binge. And the business got a real black eye in important quarters just as it was entering a period in which it was going to need all the friends it could get. As the second chairman was nearing retirement, I wrote him a letter with the suggestion that in planning for the new management to succeed him, he should try to get more thinkers (I called them conceptualizers) into key staff spots in order to avoid in the future the kind of vexing service collapse that had plagued him. Clearly, he did not buy my suggestion, and this chairman was the smartest to hold that position at any time since 1920. But the man was a manager.

Alvin Von Auw's book on the recent years of turmoil in the company conceded that the time arrived when it was evident that field managers serving a tour at headquarters were not adequate staff for the stresses of that period. Thinkers were needed. Since Von Auw may have written the letter I received from the chairman, I felt somewhat vindicated.

I could have written a stronger letter. In my later years, I worked under the same able field managers who were brought in to key staff spots in headquarters. They were able, decent, conscientious people who had performed very well when managing units of the company under policy lines generated by the headquarters staff, of which I was a part. But when they assumed roles in which they had to produce, or pass on, policy lines for other field managers, the performance of some of them was dreadful. I had one immediate boss who died of a sudden coronary at age forty-eight. He had been one of our better general managers, but I am sure (and my view was confirmed by our medical director, who was working with this poor man) that the stress of this "thinking" role was what killed him. He was a manager and a manager only.

His job on the staff did not require that he produce ideas, but he administered a staff that did. And in that spot, he had to take responsibility for other people's ideas. He was an intelligent, sensitive, conscientious man, and this got him down. Once he took one of his problems to his boss and came back looking washed out and literally trembling. The big boss had dismissed him curtly with "When you have your mind made up, come back and see me." The big boss was a manager, too; he had the same problem, and he wasn't about to take on his subordinate's problems. But it left me with a job of counseling to do with my immediate boss.

The reverse of this situation can also be a problem, sometimes a dramatic one. Shortly after I retired, I was asked by the president of one of the Bell operating companies to come in and consult on the dilemma of a recently appointed general manager in one of their key units who was not doing well, a person with whom I was well acquainted. When the situation was described to me, I said, "I have been waiting for the other shoe to drop on this one ever since I heard what you had done with this fellow. You have taken one of your ablest staff people, one of the best minds in the business, and made a manager of him, and you will destroy him if you leave him there. The difference between this fellow and me is that I had sense enough to avoid being trapped in the kind of job you have put him in. You have plenty of work that urgently needs his talents. Get him out of that general manager's job and put him where he will be useful." They promptly did that, and he has served the company well.

A different perspective on statesmanship comes from work I did on a reorganization study I conducted with the American Institute of Certified Public Accountants immediately after I retired from AT&T twenty years ago. The institute is a significant organization (in addition to the usual trade association functions) because it conducts the certifying examinations for CPAs in all fifty state jurisdictions and also hosts the Accounting Principles Board, which is the rule-making body for the profession. For many years, the conclusions of this board were given the force of law by both the Securities and Exchange Commission and the Internal Revenue Service. What brought on this study was that there came a point when both of these governmental agencies had started to make their own rules, which did not follow the APB's findings; there was considerable confusion in the profession because these new rules, for the first time in years, were difficult to understand for the purpose of compliance. A blue ribbon committee of these CPAs had been set up to produce the reorganization proposal that might restore the influence of the institute. I was hired as consultant to that committee. It was an interesting assignment because I am devoid of accounting savvy and the committee was devoid of statesmanship. The principal learning for me in the two years I worked with the committee was something I was never able to share. But it is a useful cue to the importance of the statesman.

The staff work for the Accounting Principles Board had been done by a member of the institute's staff. This man (whom I never met because he had retired several years before I came on board) was probably the most knowledgeable accountant in the country in his time and was doing the work he most wanted to do. He was well acquainted with the SEC and the IRS, and when the need for a new principle arose, he first talked it over with these agencies. (I learned this from them. I'm not sure anybody in the institute knew about this procedure.) Then he worked out what he felt was the right answer and went to work with the APB (the members of which were all bigwig accountants) and deftly guided them so that they concluded what he had worked out. He did it so skillfully that they thought it was their invention. Then he went to Washington and "sold" it to the government agencies. And everybody was happy. The practicing accountants had rules they could live with, and the government agencies promulgated the kinds of rules that suited them.

When this man retired, he carried his unique gift with him. He was replaced by a pedestrian staffer who let the APB members decide what they wanted, and when he took their conclusions to Washington, the agencies would have no part of them. They wrote their own rules.

The members of the reorganization committee I worked with had "managerial" minds that could not comprehend the secret of the former successful way of working, and the institute had no means for producing another statesman for this role. They firmly believed that it was the superior thinking of the prestigious accountants who sat on the APB that persuaded the government agencies. I got my cue that this was not true from the most perceptive fellow that I met among the accountants. He was head of a large local firm in San Francisco who had served a term as president of the institute and knew the situation well. And I confirmed it in talking with the staffs in Washington. It was the gift of this statesmanlike staff man who understood both the parameters imposed by the thinking of the government agencies and the requirements of the profession. And it was this man's ingenuity in finding a solution that would suit both that made the work of the APB the success that it was during his tenure. At last report, the decision makers at the institute were still struggling with the problems. I believe they have a problem because they do not accept that anywhere a business touches government, there must be statesmanship—on the part of business.

Later I was working as a consultant with a company that was a polluter. When the environmental issue first heated up, I persuaded the head of this company, who was chairman of the government relations committee of his trade association, to take the initiative. Fortunately, he had a good deal of the statesman in him, and he went to the Environmental Protection Agency before it had made any moves, laid out the problem of his industry, and worked out the regulations that would make these companies' impact on the environment acceptable. To my knowledge, in all of the environmental furor, this industry has been spared from most of the litigation. Another demonstration of statesmanship in business.

My father, with whom I was very close and who devoted a lot of time to me, his only son, was a very bright, good man with but a fifth-grade education. He apprenticed early as a machinist and worked at that trade until he was fifty. Most of this was in a custom shop that built inventor's models. He could take a blueprint and build a whole machine. (Not many who call themselves machinists today could do this, and probably not many in his time.) He was active in the machinists union and in Republican politics. His first elective office was as city councilman in Terre Haute, Indiana, in 1910, when I was six years old. I recall attending evening council meetings with him, staying awake as long as I could listening to the often heated debates, then curling up in his overcoat behind his chair and going to sleep, to be carried home later.

A few years before Father entered the council, there emerged in Terre Haute a Democratic leader who was a powerful and charismatic but unscrupulous man. He quickly commanded a Democratic majority on the council and soon had every major officeholder under his thumb—all of the judges, the sheriff, the prosecutor, and, of course, the city police. He took the city to the cleaners; it was a tough time to be in the opposition, and under Indiana law at that time, there was no way the man could be challenged from the outside. But he made the fatal mistake of tinkering with the federal election in 1912. Father was in the delegation of Republicans that went to Indianapolis and filed the information with the federal prosecutor that brought an indictment of 116 local Democrats, virtually everyone in office. They were all tried in one trial and convicted, with the Democratic boss getting the longest term—six years, I believe.

Father was a prosecution witness in both the affirmative and rebuttal cases. The rebuttal was the more interesting because part of the defense was that the voting was by machine, and they produced a witness from the company that manufactured the voting machines who made the strong argument that the machines were "tamperproof." In rebutting this testimony, Father was put on the stand, with a machine, and demonstrated conclusively that the machines were far from tamperproof. (Later, when I was an adult and we talked about this, Father said that he didn't think the Democrats did tamper with the machines because they didn't need to. They had too much control over the vote tabulation. "Besides," he said, "I don't think they were smart enough.")

Father's four years on the city council (1910–1914) were probably his most significant, and the trial in 1913 was the key event in his career. It was the subject of many conversations in later years. In one of these talks, he characterized the Democratic gang as "a tough bunch" and himself as "their most persistent opponent. I have wondered, in view of their game, why they didn't 'rub me out.' I have concluded that it may have been because even in the most heated exchanges, of which there were plenty, I was always friendly and never attacked them as persons. I always saw them as likable folks."

Father next served eight years (1914–1922) on the school board, where he was a major force in modernizing the public school facilities. About 1920, he suffered a health setback and dropped out of politics. But he was active in his work until age seventy-seven and died serenely at eighty. His last words, taken down by my sister, who was with him, were, "I'm glad I'm going out rather than coming in." Now that I am at the age he was when he made that statement, I share his feeling.

After the Democratic boss had served most of his prison term, he made a strong bid to be elected mayor again and almost made it. He then dropped out of sight.

A few years later, about 1923, when I was a student at Rose Tech on the campus east of the city, I was thumbing a ride into town late one afternoon and was picked up by a workman in a jalopy with a dinner pail on the seat beside him. He was unshaven and in rough laborer's clothes. As we jostled along, he asked my name. "Are you George Greenleaf's son?" he asked.

I told him yes, and after a pause, he identified himself as that same Democratic boss. There was an awkward silence in which we were both recalling the same history. Then he put his hand on my knee and said, "I want you to know that I have a great affection for your father."

THE MAKING OF A
DISTINGUISHED INSTITUTION

WHAT ARE YOU TRYING TO DO? It is one of the easiest questions to ask, and one of the most difficult to answer. It is a particularly difficult question for one who heads an institution where achievement results from other people's efforts. It is much harder in a big place where the top person cannot see all that goes on. And if the head of a large institution wants to pull away from the pack and seek distinction, not just personally but for the institution, answering the question becomes most difficult of all.

By definition, not many people can be distinguished. But the pace of a developing society is set by those who strive for distinction. Ours has become almost wholly an institution-bound, administered society in which there is very little chance for the individual to influence the course of development. Distinguished *institutions* will nourish future greatness as a society. In fact, institutional success, in and of itself, just keeps the thing going.

What follows is addressed, in part, to those top people who have brought their institutions to a level called "successful" but whose own self-fulfillment needs will not let them settle for that. They must push on for distinction. They need not own the institution or be in an entrenched position of control. But they do need to be in the top administrative spot where the exercise of leadership toward distinction is appropriate to their role.

But mainly, what follows is addressed to those not yet in top spots, no matter how young they may be, who are resolved that if they ever achieve the top administrative role of anything, they will not settle for success but will hold distinction as the institutional goal. Furthermore, they will start to prepare themselves now. It is too late, usually, if one does not face this decision until one occupies the top position. The attitudes, the skills, the character development required to lead an institution to distinction are not suddenly bestowed with the mantle of office at age forty or fifty or sixty, no matter how competent and experienced the person at that point may be. Maybe this is why so many who occupy seats of power seem so old when they are not really old. They are simply not prepared for the leadership that would take their institution beyond success to the enriching influence on the larger society, an opportunity that is open to every type of institution, large or small.

This reasoning may also explain why Pope John XXIII, in all his radiance, seemed so young at eighty. He had spent his long life preparing himself for his role, with his attitudes, skills, and character development. If one has one's health, no age is too great for institutional leadership. But if success alone is the goal, in the modern world, most people are pressing their luck if they stay in a top spot past sixty.

What, a young person may ask, is the point of preparing for a top administrative position when the chance of getting into one is so remote? It is a good question. Clearly, there are many useful roles that do not lead to leadership positions. However, unless they shape the ways of institutions, they may not be as influential as they were before the age of organization.

One answer to the question "Why prepare?" is that the preparation will make a richer, fuller life regardless of whether one makes it to a top position or not. The crucial test was given by John Milton in his sonnet "On His Blindness." In the poem, Milton examines the plight of a gifted man gone blind, leading to the question, "Doth God exact day-labour, light denied?"

Reflecting on this question, he concludes with the affirmation: "They also serve who only stand and wait."[26]

The preparation for leadership to institutional distinction is morally hazardous if one cannot see oneself serving by standing and waiting. If one's life will not be sufficient unless one makes it marching at the head of some parade, one is locked into an attitude that can lead to a socially destructive role and perhaps personal disaster. Ambition is a great thing when the primary goal is growth of the person.

It is clear that Cardinal Roncalli was ready to be pope and had been for a long time. But he was perfectly happy not to be pope. Without this attitude, he could not have been Pope John XXIII as history knows him.

The greatest modern builder of institutional distinction whose life I know intimately refused the top position of a large business for five years until the conditions were met that would permit his leading it to distinction. Then, between the ages of sixty-two and seventy-five, he brought it from a tarnished, debilitated, disreputable state to one of true distinction by the standards of his day.

Confronting the age of organization, in which most people will do their work through and be served by institutions, the big question before the able young person who wants to use his or her life well is how to make the best contribution through an institution and how to prepare to lead one to distinction if he or she gets the chance. My purpose here is to try to illuminate the problem from my own long experience in one large institution, where I had the unusual opportunity for objective study of its ways, in process, from the inside, and my later opportunity to participate as consultant to a wide range of institutions around the world. I will not try to answer the question for today's young people because I am not of this generation. Rather, I will deal with the problem as I customarily deal with it in talking to the older generation now in control. But my primary purpose is to widen the perspective for young people who face these essentially moral choices of how to use their lives well in a progressively more structured, more complex, more organized world.

The Meaning of Distinction

Distinction, as applied to an institution, cannot be categorically defined. The lexicographers have not yet caught up with the opportunity. Furthermore, it is a different thing, superficially, in government, business, church, university, hospital, and philanthropy. It is somewhat different in big institutions from what it is in small ones. But underneath all of these differences lies a common set of qualities.

First, a distinguished institution is successful. Whatever the current criteria in its field, it meets them. With the exception of wholly endowed philanthropies (and there is a little question that even these are exceptions), all institutions must meet a market test. The competition between churches and schools for parishioners and students is just as real as among dealers for customers on automobile row. The government of the most tightly controlled autocracy is just as dependent on the consent of the governed as in the most liberal democracy. It might not respond as quickly, but it responds. The tests in all fields are the same: stay alive, hold your place in the market or better it, keep your clientele, maintain the support of those who have sanctions to control you. These are the primitive criteria of success in all fields, and an institution must meet these as the necessary platform from which to move to distinction. One must be in a race in order to win it; and on the literal race track, qualifying runs are usually required for admittance to the real race. Many people miss the opportunity for distinction because they will not (or cannot) pay the price of admission to the contest: success.

Distinction is what sets an institution apart from its successful contemporaries in a way that is sanctioned as right and good by those whose judgment in such matters predicts the future dimensions of a progressively more moral society. It is not synonymous with fame or display; in fact, it may be quite the contrary. It was once felt necessary for a bank to house itself in a Parthenon-like edifice. This has changed, and banks now tend to settle for attractive businesslike quarters. People now have better ways of judging the soundness of a bank. I predict a day when a church that builds an imposing edifice will be judged not socially sensitive in the use of money and a country club–like college campus will be thought to be a poor environment in which to prepare for the rigors of the real world.

Distinction is of the essence, especially as the institution relates to people. Its impact on its own internal society and on the larger society is of a quality that sets it apart as a noteworthy constructive influence. The answer of a distinguished institution to the question "What are you trying to do?" is in elementary human terms what makes for a decent good society. The answer raises the sights of people to the vision of a more moral world.

Note to the CEO Who Wishes to Build an Institution of Distinction

Building an institution of distinction out of a large business is not something the CEO can do alone, even with the help of ideas from consultants. A big company needs substantial staff work by an able staff person reporting directly to the CEO. This person would be specifically charged with the staff responsibility for advising the CEO regarding all moves that build the exceptional and sustain it for a long time.

The first step is to set up this new post, reporting to the CEO. Building the distinctive—the exceptional—should be this employee's main function. Some other functions should be assigned that will give the job a substantial content in the eyes of the organization. But these should not be so demanding that they divert the incumbent from the main task: building the institution of distinction. This position should have an appropriate title. The person in it should participate in all of the major decisions in the executive office. He or she should operate on the assumption that influence toward exceptionality is wielded most through involvement in the day-to-day top executive decisions. The main difference between this executive and others having specific tasks is that this one is charged by the CEO with a major concern for institution building.

The person occupying this position should have all of the usual qualifications for a top executive post. But he or she should also have the necessary drives, interests, and values to ensure performance with distinction in this special role. Furthermore, this person would be expected to acquire a sophistication about the performance required by gathering from the available wisdom, wherever it may be found. Such persons are rare, but they do exist, and most organizations could attract one. In fact, one may already be present in the organization.

This suggestion is advanced in the belief that the contemporary environment in which most large businesses operate is too complex for anything short of the kind of concerted move just recommended to be effective. The institution of distinction is not just a little bit ahead of the field; it is conspicuously out in front. And in these times, it will take an extraordinary effort to do this, one that most institutions are fully capable of making.

If this new staff job is set up as recommended, all members of the executive team would be more likely to bend their efforts consistently toward the exceptional because they are committed to the presence in their executive councils of an able executive who is explicitly charged with this goal. Then there is the peculiar problem of relationships in the top command of the organization. The presence of this type of staff person, committed to this special goal, would have a constructive effect. In other words, this suggestion is made with the intent of improving, immediately, the functioning of the executive office as well as building solidly for future distinction.

The distinctive are those who set the pace, who explore the limits of the possible. To the extent that the general run of people and institutions want to do better, the distinctive provide the models. Among people, the exceptional and distinctive are not necessarily the most intelligent, the best educated, the well known, or the successful. Among institutions, the distinctive are not necessarily the large, the prestigious, the powerful, or the influential.

RETIREMENT COMMUNITIES

AS A STUDENT OF ORGANIZATION (how things get done) and not a scholar or a theologian, I have reflected on the quality of a number of institutions. But there are only two that I have observed closely enough and long enough from the inside so that I can report a view that might be useful to one who is concerned with the theology of institutions. One is AT&T, where I spent thirty-eight years and had, from my position as director of management research, one of the best vantage points to observe the institution. I have already reported on this. The other is the retirement community where I have lived for nearly eight years. By constantly listening and watching as a resident, I believe I have a better view of what goes on here and am better able to judge what this institution accomplishes for its residents than could be gained by a staff member or a researcher who keeps regular office hours and is not really involved. However, there are four hundred people here, and one could probably elicit a different view from every one of them. So what I report is offered as one person's opinion. It is given, however, in a wider context of concern for institutions than most of our residents have. As I listen closely to what they talk about (and there is constant chatter to be listened to, even when one is not involved in it), I am not aware that there is much concern about my long-sustained interest in how things get done in institutions.

The community where we live opened on September 1, 1977 (we arrived on September 7), four years after its slightly smaller sibling one mile away. There are about four hundred residents here. We are all aged sixty-five years or over (with the exception of a few younger spouses), and the average is about eighty. Esther, my wife, and I are about on the average.

I have long believed that segregating the old in this way is not a good idea, either for the old or for the normal communities from which they are withdrawn, and this opinion was in print for several years before we decided to come here. Some people who know me asked, "If you don't believe in these places, why are you going there?" To which I replied, "When the signs of aging were clearly evident as we approached seventy, we concluded that this was the best option available to us, now that children caring for their parents is no longer in style, as it was in both Esther's family tradition and in our own home. In addition, the kind of place I live in, called a life-care community, is too expensive for those who arrive at old age without a substantial financial cushion. The assurances and benefits we have cannot be given to everybody, and they should be."

Now that I have lived here nearly eight years, I am even more convinced that it is not a good idea, and I believe that as our civilization advances (if it does), places like I live in will be abandoned, just as orphanages were abandoned fifty to sixty years ago when, as a society, we concluded that segregating orphans was not a good idea and we had a better one. In the meantime, the problem is how to do the best we can with an inferior idea.

Having said that, let me add that my wife and I are glad we are here because we have the assurance of being cared for. When one of us becomes disabled, we will not be separated, and we are among friendly people.

We have much to be grateful for. All the services are good, and we feel well cared for. The spirit of the staff is excellent, and our community is financially sound to date and looks good for the future, in sharp contrast to some others that have gone bankrupt. Our trustees (all of whom must be members of the

Society of Friends) and administrators are as able and dedicated as any who are likely to be found for an institution of this kind.

Yet there is an uneasiness and a tension here among residents that is unhealthy, especially in a community of the elderly, and I believe it reflects a failure to think through some assumptions that were made when these places were set up. I will try to state them in a way that will help frame issues to be addressed by a theology for a life-care community. In view of the fact that these communities are proliferating at a rapid rate, many sponsored by churches, the need for that theology is urgent.

One recent conversation points to the sources of this uneasiness and tension.

At dinner a few weeks ago with one of our most thoughtful and intelligent residents, the statement was made in these exact words: "The services here are good, but the public relations are terrible." On probing, what was meant was that the quality of life here is not good because there is distrust of our administrators, possibly our trustees.

I have not made a sociological survey and cannot say, statistically, how much of this kind of feeling is here. But from what I hear and overhear, there is a great deal of it. Of course, quite a few of us are "over the hill" and don't think much about anything. It is the thoughtful ones, like the one I mentioned, with whom I am concerned.

The residents here are mostly financially secure (or they wouldn't be here), and they have mostly had their heads above water. Yet this is institutional care, and with that comes the flavor that residents are objects of charity—yet residents are paying the bill, and a stiff one. I think there is resentment about that.

Then, when one signs the contract to enter here and pays a stiff entrance fee, one has, in effect, surrendered a major option. Most of us, after a few years when we might become uneasy about the place, not only could not afford to pull out but no longer have the energy to make another change. I don't want to pull out, but I am uneasy about the fact that if conditions here should become unbearable, I couldn't; I'm stuck with the place.

In citing these attitudes, I am not arguing against the nature of the contract. It seems a sound basis for this undertaking, the best option available to my wife and me, as we see it. But the presence of these attitudes suggests that our administration and trustees did not have an adequate theology to guide them when they set this up, and they seem not to have it now.

The evidence to support this assertion is twofold: one fault of omission and one fault of commission.

The fault of omission is that nobody in the administration talks to residents. In the nearly eight years I have lived here, I have not had one conversation with an administrator beyond pleasantries. If I write a letter when something is amiss, I always get a prompt and friendly reply. But how can the administrators know what I'm thinking if they never to talk to me? I believe I would be well served if I asked for an interview, but there has been no indication that they would like to listen to what I have to say. The only people listened to are the politicians, the officers of the residents' association, but they don't represent me. I have an individual contract with this institution. I represent myself. To be sure, there is a pair of social workers, and they are useful to needy people. But at any one time, that is only a few of us. Some people talk to the doctors and nurses (I don't), and I suppose there is a grapevine. They are young people. Like the rest of the administrators, they keep regular office hours, and they rarely show up in the evenings or on weekends.

When I told this to the headmaster of one of the Quaker schools, he was appalled. "How can they understand what they are dealing with if they do not share in the life of the community?" There may be an uneasiness among administrators about that. Perhaps it grows out of their awareness that among the residents are quite a few who have held, in their active days, much larger roles than our administrators. These residents may be more gifted in keeping their cool in debate. There seems to be a studied aloofness that suggests a feeling that it is the administrators' obligation to render the services and it is up to the residents to make their own community. That feeling may account for the tendency to deal only with the politicians and limit personal contacts to large meetings. Our administrators are friendly people and do well as managers of the employed staff. The employee spirit here is good, and that is appreciated by residents. But we are old and crotchety and often critical; quite clearly, sometimes we irritate them to the limits of their patience—and they show it. That really sandpapers the relationship. So with all of this, we seem much of the time to live in an uneasy truce with them.

I conclude from this brief statement that it is not realistic to expect all active administrators who are as good as ours are in maintaining the services to spend the time and have the skills and temperament that talking to residents as people would require. It seems to me that implicit in the concept of life care is a quality of life in community that is as good as it can be, while we are striving to make the best of a basically bad idea, one that we may one day abandon.

My suggestion for a constructive and manageable action is to install an associate administrator who would live in an apartment, eat meals in the dining room, attend functions, and get to know people as only a resident can. Such a person might be engaged at about age sixty as a staff member and at sixty-five become a resident (if he or she wanted to) in the other community. Such a person would, in effect, be the pastor to the community. The person chosen for this pastoral role probably would not have been a preacher because that person would want to carry on the traditional side and the local churches already provide adequate religious services. He or she could have been a lawyer, doctor, social worker, or member of some other calling in which talking to people was a comfortable and important role. I can think of a few residents here who might have been interested at sixty in taking that role and then moving on at sixty-five to become a resident and find the way to an unobtrusive kind of serving.

"But this will cost money," some will protest. Of course it will. But if it is accepted as an important element of trust (and I think it is), money will be found. Perhaps some other things will have to give a bit, as with any other high-priority undertaking.

When I discussed this idea with an influential friend in the area, the response was, "Don't expect Philadelphia Quakers to understand the need for pastoral care. That may be the root of the problem; they don't understand it and therefore it has not been provided for."

It seems absolutely imperative to me that residents of life-care communities be listened to, as individuals, by responsible administrators. But this, in itself, might not accomplish much unless the following act of commission is stopped.

The act of commission that should stop is the delegation of administrative authority to the residents' association. This practice is most destructive and creates hurtful tensions that are the last things a gathering of old people need, people in various states of disrepair.

I understand the logic for it; it gives residents something to do and may (although this is questionable) save some administrative expense. The delegation of authority seems to be part of the thinking I referred to earlier: that the obligation of the administration is to provide the services and that the community should build and regulate itself. I can only wonder why trustees who make a great investment of time and thought, as our trustees do, would want to make that assumption, which to me seems pernicious. But they seem to have made it. And by delegating administrative authority to their residents' association, they have compounded the error.

A clear fact of history is that our residents did not organize themselves. The administrators imposed this structure on them. I was involved; I know. I also know, from being involved from the beginning, what great harm was done to the quality of life here by this procedure. There are four reasons why delegating administrative power to the residents' association is harmful.

First of all, it politicizes the community. The politicians, the ones who get elected to office in the residents' association and are given power, love it. And in some of them—too many, I regret to say—it brings out their worst. We have had flagrant examples of arrogance, vindictiveness, and high-handedness. Is this to be encouraged in a community in which there are many foggy, only "partly there" people? How come the Quakers go for all of this voting and politics? I could understand the Methodists doing it, but I wonder if the Quakers have lost their direction.

Most of us who have had active careers have had enough of tension and conflict. We didn't come here to get more.

One could theorize from an old saying: "When people grow old, they become more like they are." Some of our politicians may have been these destructive types all along, but when they were younger, they kept their impulses under control. As old people, perhaps the controls are off. I call to mind our most flagrant example of the destructive wielding of power. That person held a position in the active years where the behavior exhibited at this institution would not have been tolerated. After leaving this institution's politics, with its attendant powers, that person is again pleasant and agreeable.

When Lord Acton stated that "power tends to corrupt, and absolute power corrupts absolutely," he might have had in mind some old people he had seen. The corruption with power of some of our old people has been disastrous. And how did they get that power? They were given it by administrators who receive it from the contracts we residents signed and the money we paid in. A travesty, to put it mildly.

Second, the power is sometimes not well used, not as well as competent administrators would have used it. I have in mind my experience with the arts and crafts room, a beautiful forty-by-seventy-foot open room with windows on three sides. The use of it was delegated to the residents' association right after we were organized, and I was made chairman of that room. I struggled for several months to get the board of the association into agreement on how that room should be used, but it was too big a problem for them. One day, I was on the phone with an old friend in a community like ours on the West Coast who was still doing his own work, like I was and still am. I asked him, "Paul, how do you live in one of these places and get your own work done?" He promptly replied, "There is only one way: have absolutely nothing to do with residents' activities. You are in a place like I am, full of people with time on their hands, and they will eat you up if you have anything to do with them."

I thought that over and resigned and have kept a considerable distance from all of this frenetic activity ever since. And the arts and crafts room, a truly beautiful facility, has stood there for nearly eight years with not more than 10 percent use, a great waste of resources. It will always be that way as long as its use is delegated to the residents' association. It is simply beyond the reach of a bunch of old politicians to take on a problem that involves a larger creative solution.

Much as I value my own work, I would gladly have stayed on and worked indefinitely with our administration to develop a good program for that craft room. It wouldn't have taken much of the administrator's time, just a small fraction of the time he spends talking to the politicians, from which very little of constructive good to the community results.

Third is the problem of contract violation. The contract between individual residents and the corporation is the basic document that controls everything for this place. It makes no mention of a residents' association, and the only reference to delegation of the executive director's authority is that it may be delegated to the staff. Now I think I know why that clause was put in there: to forestall the possibility that someone should demand that he or she personally handle everything. But if the meaning of language should ever be fully tested in adversary proceedings, I suspect that the governing consideration would be what the person contemplating signing that contract is entitled to read into it. And that may be what I read into it: the executive director's authority may be delegated only to the staff and not just to anybody and certainly not to a group of residents as a political entity. The one time I challenged our administrators on the extension of "staff" to include residents, he stonewalled the question. It seems clear that he did not know what this language meant, legally, but that he intended to keep on delegating to the residents' association as he was accustomed to doing.

The hazard in this attitude is that the contract could be the basis of a suit. A couple of times in recent years, residents have been sufficiently angry about how the residents' association was botching things that they would have sued (and they had the means to do it) if they had thought of it. I am not going to alert anybody to this option, but if the community administrators continue to ignore the possibility of a suit, they are likely to get one. And that will be a sad day—first to be dragged into court to wash the community's dirty linen, but more important, there might be a court order to stop this promiscuous delegation. I would not want to live in this community operating under a court order, and a lot of other people wouldn't either. The "blue chip" status now enjoyed could be lost.

The fact that a challenge on the meaning of this contract would be stonewalled and really not responded to or discussed suggests to me that our administrators, perhaps even our trustees, are not sufficiently aware of how crucial a matter this contract is to a thoughtful resident. If they were talking to all residents and not just to the politicians, they would surely know and would never stonewall any challenge to the way that contract is interpreted. Until that language on delegation is thoroughly tested in the courts, I will continue to believe that it means what it says and that the executive director's authority may not be delegated to a residents' group.

Finally, and most persuasive to me, is the matter of trust. The most elementary view of trust suggests that residents of this community, under the cloud of uncertainty and doubt that surrounds this relationship, are entitled to have all decisions that concern the use or enjoyment of these valuable resources made by a responsible administrator in his or her prime years and not by foggy old residents like themselves. When I wrote to our administrator this past year protesting the plan to locate a putting green in a spot that would mar our beautiful campus, his response was that the matter had been delegated to the residents' association and would I please take my complaint to that group. I wrote back refusing to do this, with the comment that this practice of delegation militated against achieving the quality of community life that is possible here. No response. But the putting green was placed in a less offensive location. I hold this administrator's attitude to be a clear breach of trust.

I have given four reasons why delegating administrative power to a residents' association is a destructive idea: (1) it politicizes the community in a harmful way, especially for old people; (2) it is, in some instances, an ineffective way to use resources and get things done; (3) it is a violation of contracts with individual residents; and (4) perhaps most serious, it is a breach of trust.

I have argued for a pastor to the community who is a member of the administration, partly to talk to people in a way that more fully relates them to the community and partly to learn more about how people are feeling and faring. The pastor should particularly talk to the more intelligent and thoughtful who are most in touch with the social workers and who probably do not say much to the doctors and therefore are probably not communicating with the administration at all as matters now stand.

Such a revision would leave plenty of scope for residents to be active in organizing work for themselves and planning and carrying out the many activities that now go on here. It would simply stop a practice I think is a contract violation—delegating administrative authority and control of facilities—and thereby remove administrative power that seems to be a corrupting and destructive element in the present way of doing things.

If the life-care community takes these two steps—set up a pastor to talk to residents and stop delegating administrative authority to the residents' association—it will have moved a long way toward accepting full responsibility for building community and raising the quality of life. A theology of life-care communities would help refine a concept of community that would have much wider application than life-care institutions and would help aim churches to (1) be more influential in preparing people for more effective leadership in building a better society and (2) guide their lives as corporations more carefully to meet their obligations of trust.

PART THREE

LEADERSHIP AND THE INDIVIDUAL

THE DARTMOUTH LECTURES

Bad organization theory is bad because in practice it pulls people down. But if I had to choose between a bad organization theory with a great leader and a good organization theory with a poor leader, give me the former any day.

The interest and affection that the leader has for his followers—and it is a mark of true greatness when it is genuine—is clearly something that the followers "haven't to deserve."

Every once in a while, a leader finds himself needing to think like a scientist, an artist, or a poet, and his thought processes may be just as fanciful as in those areas.

Robert K. Greenleaf

IN 1969, ROBERT GREENLEAF gave a series of lectures at Dartmouth Alumni College on the topic "leadership and the individual." These were collected into an essay and privately distributed. *Leadership and the Individual* is the last major essay Greenleaf composed before writing *The Servant as Leader.* In it we find most of the same themes, expressed in a conversational, accessible style: everything begins with the individual, leaders are chosen by followers, the only "lead" of a genuine leader is foresight, and a leader's impact is measured by his effect on followers.

Even though he is speaking before a university audience, Greenleaf is not complimentary toward universities as mentors of future leaders; indeed, he accuses universities of fostering anti-leadership attitudes. His prescriptions are practical: support the essential abilities required to lead—values, goals, competence, and spirit. Two criteria are used to evaluate the success of such training: (1) the ability to set and articulate goals and reach them through other people and (2) the ability to satisfy the people whose judgment must be respected even under stress.

The lectures explore the four essential abilities in great detail, encompassing discussions of strategy, creativity, foresight, listening, organizational structures, personal responsibility, and other powerful and practical themes.

Greenleaf contends that an individual sustains leadership by *spirit*. Here, as elsewhere, he refuses to define *spirit*. He stands before it in awe. He does, however, have a belief about what it does: it builds trust, even as it sustains both leader and followers.

Greenleaf ends with two soaring statements: "Nothing much happens without a dream" and "Virtue and justice and order are good, but not good enough—not nearly good enough. In the end, nothing really counts but love and friendship."

I

THE CRISIS OF LEADERSHIP

I HAVE CHOSEN to talk about leadership and the individual because we seem to be in a crisis of leadership. Taking the simplest definition of the leader as one who goes ahead to guide the way, a leader, as I will use the term, may be a mother in her home, any person who wields influence, or the head of a vast organization.

As I see it, we are in a crisis of leadership for two main reasons: first, because so many people who are concerned about the state of the world, or some part of it, and have the opportunity and perhaps the obligation to lead are perplexed and unsure about what to do; and some just don't try hard enough. As a consequence, the disparity is too great between the promise (what is reasonably possible with our resources of material and knowledge) and the performance (what our whole range of institutions actually deliver), and our society is vulnerable.

The second reason for the crisis is the rise of the anti-leaders, particularly within the universities. Not only do some of our best young people reject the Establishment and its ways, but they also believe that when the present order of society is destroyed (which they hope is soon because they don't want to live in it as it is), the more ideal society they hope to see replace it will not have leaders as we know them. What it will have is not clear, nor is there much thought about how we go from here to there without a civil disruption that could cost millions of lives. They are not without philosophical support for their position from the academic community.

Either one of these two conditions without the other would not produce a crisis of leadership, in my view. (And the second has probably emerged to fill the vacuum created by the first.) But the two in combination, interacting with one another, do produce a crisis of leadership. However, I am hopeful that good will come of it, which is the main reason I am interested in visiting with you about leadership and the individual.

My only qualification for talking on this subject is that I have thought a lot about it for a long time and I am currently engaged here and there with people who are concerned, including young people who hold the view outlined above.

I do not think of myself as an expert on anything—certainly not on leadership. I hold no professional degrees, I occupy no certified position, and I have no comprehensive theory to offer you. I make my way as a consultant now, more by asking questions than by giving answers. At least half of my motivation for being here is that I expect to learn something.

Let me state some assumptions that underlie what I will try to share with you in these five lectures. They may not be the assumptions *you* would make; but we will have a more fruitful time here if, in our discussions of leadership, *all* assumptions are examined. I state mine not to persuade you to accept my assumptions. I do it for two reasons: to clarify my own thinking and to encourage each of you to examine your own assumptions.

First, I have said we are in a crisis of leadership because so many people who have the opportunity or the obligation to lead are perplexed about what to do. My assumption here is that the suddenness and extent of the knowledge explosion plus the expansion of education and the communications media have presented new conditions for which traditional ways of leading are not so effective. Furthermore, many who have the opportunity and the obligation to lead are not inventive or adaptive quickly enough. In these times, there are few professions or vocations in which one can learn how to do it in one's youth and then spend the next forty or fifty years practicing as one was taught. It takes a real struggle to remain contemporary in these kaleidoscopic times, and leaders in all walks of life are getting a rude shock. Not enough of them have made the effort to be *contemporary*.

Second, our educational system is not designed to prepare for leadership (the fulsome statements of college catalogs to the contrary notwithstanding). I assume with John Gardner in his perceptive essay of three years ago that in fact our colleges and universities administer what Mr. Gardner calls an anti-leadership vaccine.[1] They tend to bias students toward becoming critics and experts and away from becoming responsible participants in society. I do not believe that, with all these institutions, there is the knowledge about how to shift the emphasis.

Third, the value system of the Western world that has been building since Moses brought the tablets down the mountain some three thousand years ago has been pretty badly shattered and, I believe, irretrievably so within the lifetime of the youngest person here. I assume that it will not be reconstructed as it was. It will be replaced, I believe, by something better. The new ethic may be delayed by counterefforts from my generation. But when a new ethic is built, and it will be built, it will be largely the work of people who are now young. The best that we oldsters can do is be hopeful and manifest our faith. I use the word *faith* as old Dean Inge defined it. "Faith," said Dean Inge, "is the choice of the nobler hypothesis."[2] Not the *noblest*—we will never know what that is—but the *nobler* hypothesis. If we remain open and flexible and struggle to be contemporary, we can *choose* the nobler ethic as it emerges. It will be hard. I know from my own experience that it will be hard, and a lot that is precious to me and my generation will be destroyed so that a new and nobler ethic can be built.

This is not a new idea. It has been on the walls in the basement of Baker Library for almost forty years in the Orozco panel that depicts the angry Christ chopping down his own cross. I saw that part of the Orozco murals in the early 1930s when the plaster was hardly dry and the scaffolding was still there. I am sure from the way that image has haunted me all of these years that something of what is now going on in the world is the result of the cumulative effort of images like these that began to emerge with the impact of World War I. World War II greatly accelerated it, and the Vietnam War has been the crowning, completing influence. The moral world of Moses is the principal victim.

My fourth and last assumption is that the forces for good and evil in the world operate through the thoughts, attitudes, and actions of individual beings. Societies, movements, institutions are but the collection or focus of such individual initiatives. What happens to our values, and therefore to the quality of our civilization in the future, will result from the conception, born of inspiration, of individuals. Perhaps only one individual will receive it. The very essence of leadership, therefore, derives from openness to inspiration, to insight, that either produces the nobler ethic or guides one's choice among alternatives.

I happen to be a Quaker by persuasion. I am a backsliding member as far as the contemporary Religious Society of Friends is concerned, but the Quaker tradition is the source of such religious orientation as I have. This permeates my assumptions, and you should know this. Out of this comes the image of an eighteenth-century Quaker, John Woolman. John Woolman is known to wider society for his *Journal,* which is a literary classic.[3] But in the Quaker tradition, he is the model of the great and gentle persuader. He was not a strong man physically, nor was he the leader type in the sense of holding important office. He never did a protest, nor did he go to jail or found a movement. His major mission was to rid the Society of Friends of slaves.

It is difficult now to imagine the Quakers as slaveholders, as, indeed, it is difficult for me to imagine anyone being a slaveholder. This prompts me to the uneasy feeling that two hundred years hence it may be difficult for those people to conceive that so-called good people could have been as we are today. It is a sobering thought. But the Quakers of that time were a solid, conservative, affluent slaveholding class in the early eighteenth century. (A sharp-tongued critic characterized the Quakers of that day as the literal fulfillment of the biblical injunction that the meek shall inherit the earth.) By 1770, almost a hundred years before the Civil War, no slaves were held by Friends, almost wholly the result of the single-handed effort of John Woolman, who, over a period of thirty years, traveled by foot and horseback up and down the East Coast talking to slaveholding Quakers one at a time, persuading them to free their slaves.

By committing his adult life to it (Woolman died in his early fifties), man by man, inch by inch, he rooted this monstrous evil from his beloved church, the Society of Friends. His main argument was not that it would be better for the slaves, although he believed it would be. His main attack was questioning the slaveholder: "What does slaveholding do to you, as a person? What kind of moral institution are you binding over to your children?" One wonders what would have been the effect on this country if there could have been fifty John Woolmans, dedicated as he was and as persuasive, ranging this land in the eighteenth century. There might not have been a Civil War with its six hundred thousand casualties and a resultant social problem that is at fever heat more than a hundred years later with an end not yet in sight. Could the emergence of such persons be nurtured by an institution? I think it could be. Professor Horace Williams demonstrated it by his consistent teaching over a period of forty-five years at the University of North Carolina. The civilization of North Carolina, as a result of this one man's effort, is different. It has some things that no other state in the Union has.

This is my closing assumption: the preparation of men and women who would lead as John Woolman led so as to build a society more in the grace of a nobler ethic could be the explicit accomplishment of our colleges and universities. They *need not* operate so as to justify John Gardner's opprobrious label, the administerers of the anti-leadership vaccine, and they cannot long do so if our free society is to survive.

These are the assumptions that will guide what I will say in the remainder of my lectures. I have not always held these assumptions, and I may alter them with further experience, but this is how I see them now. Since I have been asked to talk to you and you have been willing to listen, at least up to now, I feel obliged to share them, not, as I said, that you are asked to accept them, but rather that my statement of my assumptions will encourage you to clarify and state your own assumptions about leadership and the individual.

I don't want to be dogmatic about it, but I suspect that we will never have a firm, scientifically rooted definition of leadership. Man is an evolving creature, and societies in all their relationships are evolving; and this evolutionary development is far from finished. Furthermore, what it takes to *lead* will also continue to evolve. In the wide variety of human nature, effective leadership, in practice, is likely to be a great many things. It seems to me to make a more interesting world to view it this way. So I admit a slight bias not to be rigorously scientific about it.

My interest in this subject began in college. In the second half of my senior year, I happened to take a course in the sociology of labor problems. My professor was neither a great scholar nor an exciting teacher. But he was wise in the ways of men and institutions, and some of his wisdom came through to me. One day he made an observation like this:

> There is a "people problem" in all modern institutions, particularly in American business. It is a problem of how to lead the enterprise, particularly the larger ones, so as to elicit the best effort and provide the most satisfying existence to the people who work there. Some of you ought to get inside these institutions and work on this problem. Outside, you can write, preach, research, advocate, legislate. But if you really want to do something about it, you

have to get inside, establish yourself, and commit yourself in a way that makes it possible for you to be influential.

That did it for me. A short talk with the professor after class, and my career aim was settled. I have often wondered whether, on that fateful day, something unusual was said or whether I just happened to have my doors of perception open a wee bit so that a significant signal could come through.

In the past few years, I have been quite deeply involved in undergraduate education, and I am impressed by how difficult it is, in our untraditional society, to communicate this kind of wisdom to young people. And I have wondered for those young people today who are so intent on changing things, how it might be possible for them to hear my old Professor Helming's advice: that if you want to change something constructively (it is easy enough to destroy it), you have to take the *responsibility for leadership,* and this may mean committing yourself to some kind of institution, taking the bitter with the sweet, the dull and routine with the exciting and the challenging.

This was what I decided to do: commit myself to an institution. I left college with the intent of getting hired by the business that had the most people. I joined AT&T because it had the most people and because it was a complex, technically sophisticated, and politically involved institution. I wasn't really interested in being a businessman—still am not. Although I spent thirty-eight years on a business payroll, I never thought of myself as a businessman. Rather I kept my own interest in the institution as a social phenomenon, in the problem of leading and advancing it as an institution. It is some kind of tribute to the people in this particular institution that they would permit me to spend most of my thirty-eight years, in one way or another, working on this problem.

The best test of how it worked out came a number of years ago when the president of my company had a visitor from another company who was interested in some of our work about which I have some special knowledge. The three of us went out to lunch together, and when we were seated, our guest, whom I had just met, turned to me and asked, "And what is your role in the company?" The gremlin in me prompted me to say, "Gee, I don't know, why don't you ask the president!" The president gave me a cold look, turned to his guest, and said, "He's a kept revolutionary." I think this sums up my career pretty well.

In these few sessions, I want to share some of what seems important from my explorations. Keep in mind, please, that I am primarily a doer, not a scholar. I have been more interested in wielding influence than in abstract thought. I chose to get inside the institution, accept enough of its ways to survive in it, and work on the problem rather than stay outside and write, think, teach, or advocate. I had enough of the organization man in me to survive inside. In my next talk, I want to deal with strategy, which is, in part, the art of survival. A high frustration tolerance was required because there were many "dry" years. Now that I am at the point where I can view my career in retrospect, some things stand out that were not so apparent as it unfolded. Since I will be talking mostly from experience, what I will have to say in these talks will, at times, be quite personal.

I said earlier that the simplest definition of a leader is one who goes ahead to guide the way. This is the dictionary view of it. I would like to go a step further and examine the abilities that any sort of leadership calls for. I also said earlier that a leader may be a mother in her home or an informal wielder of influence or the head of a vast enterprise. It is not the vastness of the enterprise that tests the ability to lead. The great captain of industry may be all thumbs when dealing with a problem of his children in his home. Some people seem to be able to lead well in any environment they enter, but most of us do much better in some situations and not so well in others. Yet running through all of them is a common set of abilities. I have tried to distill what they are from many discussions over a long period of years with many kinds of leadership people—in business, military, education, religion, government. These, as I see it, are the essential abilities required to lead—*values, goals, competence,* and *spirit*—expressed in two sets of requirements: the ability to set and articulate goals and reach them through the efforts of other people and the ability to satisfy the people whose judgment must be respected even under stress.

Let us pause a minute on this word *stress.* Tolerance for stress is an interesting phenomenon. Stress is what makes life interesting by giving it its challenge. Few of us would be persons of consequence if we never encountered stress. Much as we try to avoid stress, we would not want to live in a world that did not have any. I have no formula to give you to achieve poise amid sustained stress. In fact, I think it is a matter of individual design that each person must work out for himself. Some of us are lucky and just grow into a stress-resistant ability without giving it conscious thought. But many of us, including me, have to work it out. Since one never really knows how well armored for stress one is, it is probably a sounder course in this ever-changing world for each person to design a stress management program for himself. It would be nice if it could be done when people are young and in college, and I am confident that this could be done there easily. But it is well to get at it whenever one feels the need, no matter what the age. I don't intend to try to teach a lesson on this subject here; but in my next talk on leadership strategy I will deal with some material that may be useful.

In summation, I would like to enumerate first some of the crises of our time that make all leadership more difficult—at all ends of society and in all relationships.

1. Wars cold and hot—of which there seem to be no end— with the rising tide of protest that accompanies them

2. The issue of nationalism with the forces of communication, transportation, and enlightenment fanning the flame and sharpening the conflicts and differences

3. Our sharpened awareness of an uneasiness about poverty and disease and suffering around the world

4. Rising divisiveness—age, economic, ethnic

5. The alienation of youth and their rebellion against the Establishment in all of its forms, which results in the denial of leadership as a role to be aspired to

The combination of these would give a pretty hopeless outlook for those who would be more effective in leading were it not for some emerging strengths.

A new kind of humanity is emerging. Perhaps it is coming out of our more widespread education and rising awareness from the candid portrayals of the mass media. The TV coverage of the war in Vietnam has brought home to many millions of people the horrifying details from which noncombatants have heretofore largely been spared. TV documentaries like the recent one on hunger in America have found an audience. The churches have made a radical shift toward social concern. Many more influences could be enumerated, but it is clear to me that our humanness has been aroused as it has seldom been before. The prospect that capital punishment might disappear in the United States and that our view of crime and punishment may change radically within our lifetime is a significant augury of this.

Burgeoning science and technology and the impact of this on all of our communication is bringing a pervasive rational element to all of education—to all of life—that should provide a progressively steadying influence.

The mounting interest, both scholarly and popular, in the study of man and the growing body of substantive knowledge about people and their relationships is a significant new strength for those who would lead anything.

The combination of these new strengths is leading to some disturbing new trends, however. Some of these:

A much greater candor in all communication. The four-letter words are going to be common utterances on the airwaves within ten years.

The reexamination—perhaps the first widespread critical examination—of such important assumptions as the Protestant work ethic, traditional morals, our views on property, and many others.

A persistent questioning of the old loyalties: nationalism, as manifested in rising opposition to military conscription; the revolution among the young clergy in the Catholic church; the general revolt against authority among the young.

It is difficult to imagine a more demanding challenge to leadership than such a summary presents. It is, as I see it, a challenge to individuals rather than to institutions. The challenges will ultimately be met by institutions: home, business, church, school, labor unions, government. But the initiating forces that bring a new level of institutional performance must come from individuals, not just "big, strong" people, but all people of conscience who will accept the obligation to lead as defined here— to go ahead to guide the way.

II

THE STRATEGIES OF A LEADER

I WANT TO TALK about the strategies of a leader. What ways of thinking and acting favor one's effectiveness as a leader? All of these strategies can be learned; therefore, they can be taught. Some people just naturally have them. Often they don't know that they have them, so they aren't much help to us. If we want to be more effective in a leadership role, then we are interested in those strategies that we can consciously cultivate. This is mostly what I want to deal with today, not in the sense of a formula that I can hand over to you, because I don't have that, and you should not want one.

What I offer as strategies are those that have seemed important to me as I have worked at this over the years. Each person should design his own strategies if he wants to be his optimal best. I simply want to stimulate you to think about it.

Goal Setting

What are you trying to do? This is one of the easiest questions to ask and one of the most difficult to answer. The fanatic has been defined as one who redoubles his effort as he loses sight of his aim. This is no joke. I have seen people turn to aimless frenzy when they became confused about their aims.

The effective leader always has a goal. It may change from time to time, but at any given time, the leader knows what it is. The dictionary defines the word *goal* rather generally. I will use it in the special sense of the overarching purpose, the big dream, the visionary concept, the ultimate achievement that one approaches but never achieves. It is something presently out of reach; it is something to strive for, to move toward, or to become. It is an aim or purpose so stated that it excites the imagination and gives something people want to work for, something they don't know how to do, something they can be proud of when they achieve it.

"Make no little plans," wrote Daniel Burnham fifty years ago; "they have no magic to stir men's blood and probably themselves will not be realized. Make big plans," he said. "Aim high in hope and work, remembering that a noble, logical diagram, once recorded, will never die but long after we are gone will be a living thing, asserting itself with ever-growing insistency. Remember that our sons and our grandsons are going to do things that would stagger us. Let your watchword be order and your beacon beauty."[4]

What started me to thinking about the importance of the goal, the design, was my early experience, forty years ago, in my old company, AT&T. I told you why I chose it—it had the most people. I had not been in it long until I realized that as an institution, it had a quality, a character, a momentum that was a bit unusual. The only institutions I knew much about before this were churches and schools and small businesses. This one was different. It was building something; the others were merely operating or maintaining something. I wondered what accounted for the difference, and the answer was not hard to find.

This business, as an institution, had in its early history a great visionary goal setter, a great dreamer. Emerson once said, "An institution is but the lengthened shadow of a man."[5] AT&T—in fact, electrical communication around the world—is the lengthened shadow of a man named Theodore N. Vail, who was the first manager of the first telephone company in 1878 at age thirty-three. He left in 1887 because of disagreement with the conservative nondreaming Boston owners of the company. He returned as president in 1907 when J. P. Morgan had wrested control of the then near-bankrupt and disorganized company from the Boston owners. Vail, with Morgan's support, built the modern institution over the next thirteen years, when he was between the ages of sixty-two and seventy-five. This is a condensed version of a fascinating story that would take a couple of hours to tell.

Vail's break with the Boston owners in 1887 was precipitated by his statement of the great dream in 1885 and his insistence that, as the operating head of the company, this was what he was going to do. Here is his dream exactly as he stated it: "We will build a telephone system so that anybody any place in the world can talk with anybody else, any place else in the world, quickly, cheaply, satisfactorily." At the time this was stated, it was an utterly fantastic goal. That was eighty-three years ago, and the world is still far from realizing this goal. Today, we are so close to realizing it in this country that it is difficult now to comprehend what a fantastic and visionary dream this was in 1885. No wonder the conservative Bostonians, content to sit comfortably and profitably as a smug patent monopoly, were disturbed by this wild dreamer who, incidentally, had made them all wealthy at that point. But it didn't disturb J. P. Morgan, who took the company away from the Bostonians in 1907, brought Vail back, as an old man, and backed him to the hilt to work on his dream.

Vail died forty-eight years ago, and AT&T is still his business. When I entered the business in 1926, six years after Vail died in office at age seventy-five, the overshadowing influence of this dream and the great man who dreamed it were plainly evident.

This is my best example of what a goal is and what it contributes to leadership strategy. Clearly, as I see it, *if* the goal is right, the rest of leadership strategy falls into place naturally. That is not to say that the rest is easy—far from it. But if the goal is wrong, or inadequate, the rest of leadership strategy is just a spinning of wheels; nothing worthwhile will happen, and much damage may be done. Time will not permit as much discussion of the remaining several strategy items in my notes. I have emphasized goals because if they are not right, nothing else counts.

The strategies that follow are not listed in order of importance, nor is the emphasis given any one of them an indicator of its relative importance.

Principle of Systematic Neglect

Because leaders are responsible, as they contemplate all the possible actions they might take to fulfill this obligation, it is clear that there are usually more things to be done, that ought to be done, than there is time or energy to do. This is equally true of the housewife and the captain of industry.

Once when I was pretty stretched out on my job and running hard, I sighed and said to one of my early bosses, "I wish I could add some hours to the day!"

"That wouldn't help you a bit," he said. "You would just use the time to find more things to do. It is just as important to know what to neglect as to know what to do."

That impressed me, and I decided to watch more closely how this boss did his work. He was never hurried, always had time to see his people, mostly kept regular office hours. Yet over a period of time, he was remarkably effective in accomplishing important things. The secret, I discovered, was that he had a list of things that needed doing, arranged in order of priority. The item at the top of the list was always at the center of his attention, and in a short period of time he could mark it off as completed. Then he took the next item and did the same thing. But there were a multitude of other obligations bearing down on him while this was going on. The secret was that he neglected them all, as much as he could get away with. It took a major emergency to get the center of his attention moved away from the top-priority item on his list.

Now, this wasn't easy. All sorts of people, including his boss, were beating on him constantly about the things he ought to do that he was neglecting. If they beat too hard, he would make a gesture to appease them, but seldom did this divert his major effort on the top-priority item. As a consequence, he was the man people complained about the most. He was also the one who, everybody recognized, accomplished the most. He was a very effective man. By watching him, I learned the law of systematic neglect—a most valuable strategy.

Listening

Persons who achieve *high* leadership positions are generally not good listeners. They are too assertive. They have to *learn* to listen. It is something they have to be taught, usually against their will. Mothers of children sometimes aren't good listeners either—for another set of reasons. Most people could profit by a conscious strategy of learning how and when to listen.

Listeners learn about people in ways that modify—first the *listener's* attitude, then his behavior toward others, and finally the attitudes and behavior of others. Listening is as important to a mother dealing with her children as it is to the head of a state. Sometimes the heat can be taken out of a child's temper tantrum with just a few seconds of intense listening. Of all the work I did in management training in listening, I think I accomplished more with teaching managers how to listen than with anything else.

Language as a Leadership Strategy

A leader must articulate the goal. The goal may have emerged out of a group consensus, but it could emerge only when an individual person articulated it. It may be called a "leaderless" group, but whoever articulates the goal that makes the consensus idea is a de facto leader.

ON BECOMING A SERVANT-LEADER

One important difference between the coach or director and the performer in sports, music, or the theater is that the coach has the language facility to communicate about what is to be done. He has both the concepts and the words.

Language is deceptive, however. Alfred North Whitehead once said, "No language can be anything but elliptical, requiring a leap of imagination to understand its meaning in its relevance to immediate experience."[6] Nothing is meaningful to me until it is related to my own experience. I can remember what you say, perhaps repeat it back to you like a computer does in the retrieval process. But *meaning*—a growth in my experience as a result of receiving the communication—requires that I supply the imaginative link from my fund of experience to the abstract language symbols you have used. The effective use of language includes some estimate of what the listener's fund of experience is plus the art of tempting the listener into that leap of imagination that connects the verbal concept to the listener's own experience. The limitation on language, to the communicator, is that the listener must make that leap. One of the great communicating arts is to say just enough to make that leap of the imagination feasible. Many attempts to communicate are nullified by saying too much.

The physicist and philosopher Percy Bridgman took another view of it when he said:

> No linguistic structure is capable of reproducing the full complexity of experience. . . . The only feasible way of dealing with this is to push a particular verbal line of attack as far as it can go, and then switch to another verbal level which we might abandon when we have to. . . . Many people . . . insist on a single self-consistent verbal theme into which they try to force all experience. In doing this they create a purely verbal world in which they can live a pretty autonomous existence, fortified by the ability of many of their fellows to live in the same verbal world.[7]

This, of course, is what makes a cult—a group of people who thus isolate themselves from the evolving mainstream and forfeit all opportunity to lead. Sometimes an established leader becomes trapped in one of these closed linguistic worlds and loses his leadership.

Most of us, at one time or another, some of us a good deal of the time, would *really* like to communicate, *really* get through to the level of meaning rooted in the listener's experience. It can be terribly important. The best test of whether we are communicating at this depth is to ask ourselves, first, are we *really* listening? Are we listening to the one we want to communicate to? Is our basic attitude, as we approach the confrontation, one of wanting to understand? Remember that great line from the prayer of Saint Francis: "Lord, grant that I may not seek so much to be understood as to understand."[8]

Then, when we speak, we might practice asking ourselves, "Just how much should I say, and how should I say it to tempt my hearer to make that imaginative leap that connects what I want to communicate to his own experience in a meaningful way?" The penalty, if we say more than that, unless our hearers are making a special disciplined effort to listen and understand (which we usually can't count on), is that, when we pass that optimal point, they turn off their hearing aids. Oh, if they are polite, they will know what we are saying and will be able to respond with a polite question or rejoinder. But our communication will not penetrate to the level of meaning, which is all that really counts.

In this process, one must not be afraid of a little silence. I know that some find silence awkward or oppressive, but a relaxed approach to dialogue will include the welcoming of some silence. It is often a devastating question to ask oneself, but it is sometimes important to ask it: "In saying what I have in mind, will I really improve on the silence?"

Some of our best communication, especially to the young, is done obliquely—let it be something they overhear rather than something beamed right at them. Most of us don't like to be lectured to, but we all like to eavesdrop.

Values

Al Capone was a leader. Adolf Hitler was a leader, a truly extraordinary one. This isn't what we want more of. What we do want is differentiated from these two very able leaders in just one dimension, but an awfully important one: values. In just three value choices, we can separate what we want from what we don't want in a leader. We want a leader to be *honest, loving,* and *responsible.* I want to explore only one of these three attributes, *responsible.* It needs a special definition because the generation gap hangs on how this word is used.

I am not using it in the sense that so many of my generation use it when what they mean is that they want the youngsters to behave so that the oldsters' comfort and sense of propriety are not disturbed. (And I will say, parenthetically, that I have had as much trouble coming to terms with this one as anybody.)

As I see it, responsible people build. They do not destroy. They are moved by the heart; compassion stands ahead of justice. The prime test of whether an act is responsible is to ask, How will it affect people? Are lives moved toward nobility? If you want to take on a tough mental exercise, forget what I have just said and ask yourself, "If *I* want to be effective in leading young people today, how would *I* define responsibility?"

Personal Growth

The leader must be a growing person. Nongrowth people are finding it more and more difficult to lead, especially to lead young people. One of the most tragic of modern dilemmas is that of the middle-aged parents who cease to grow and are rejected by their children. (One of the easiest ways to assure one's growth is to cultivate at least one mutual friend who

306

makes one stretch, intellectually, to the point of discomfort. Too many of us settle for *only* comfortable friends.)

Ours is a rough era for the nongrowth people. It has not always been so. Age was once revered for age. Not today. Did you see the film *The Graduate*? Do you remember that shocking scene when Ben holds open the door to the hotel ballroom while that parade of affluent, paunchy, sterile old people streams out? I can't get that picture out of my mind. And there isn't a person over thirty in that film who isn't a stinker.

Withdrawal

Leadership in any of its dimensions, from the home to the nation, can be pressure-ridden and very taxing—emotionally and physically. Anyone assuming a leadership obligation needs a strategy in his own defense against this. The best defense is to be able to withdraw, cast off the burden for a while, and relax. This presupposes that one has learned the art of systematic neglect, to sort out the important from the less important and just not to do the less important, even though there may be penalties and censure. It is better to be alive and be censured than to be a dead hero. This is not an overdrawn portrayal of choice. I have seen some people actually kill themselves with work when their lives would have been more productive had they run at 75 percent of maximum capacity (rather than the 125 percent they attempted) and lived a little longer as a result.

I am not advocating laziness; but I am advocating governing one's life by the law of the optimum, optimum being that pace that gives one the best performance over a life span, bearing in mind that there are always the occasional emergencies. The optimum includes carrying an unused reserve of energy in all periods of normal demand so that one has the resilience to cope with the emergency.

I am speaking now of leadership. I believe the approach of poet Edna St. Vincent Millay, who wrote about one's candle burning at both ends, is OK for a poet or an artist.[9] One's optimum may best be realized that way. But most who carry responsible roles of leadership should not regulate their lives in that way. A mother's major influence on the personalities of her children is probably between birth and age two, certainly by age six. But it is also pretty important that she be around to see them through their teenage crises. Burning one's candle at both ends may not permit that.

It is imperative that one be able to withdraw, sometimes only for minutes. But it is also important that one be able to relax in those intervals. Relaxation can be learned.

Tolerance of Imperfection

In order to reach goals through the efforts of other people, we must have a view, a view rooted deep in our interior, that people can be immature, stumbling, inept, lazy. Put all the sins you can name on the list, and the people one is obliged to lead are probably guilty of them all. Anybody can reach a goal through the efforts of other people if those people are all perfect, but there aren't *any* perfect people, not even me and thee. Yet even the imperfect people are capable of great dedication and heroism. They are, in fact, all we have.

Some people, a lot of people, in fact, are disqualified to lead because they cannot work through and with the half-people who are available to work with them. And the parents who try to raise perfect children are certain to raise neurotics, with much greater damage possible.

Being Your Own Person

I have mentioned the great teacher Horace Williams and his profound influence on the civilization of North Carolina. This begins with the concept of the university; as stated in its charter, it was conceived somewhat differently than most. Its charter states, in effect, that the university exists to develop the civilization of North Carolina. Horace Williams is one among many who took this charge seriously. Perhaps he is the best known.

One usually would not think of such an extraordinarily individualistic man as being a leader. In the sense of being the head of something, he wasn't. But as a constructive influence on society, he was a leader of great stature, partly because he taught so many who later emerged into titular leadership positions to "be your own person." And the effect of this one man's teaching over a period of forty-five years left a tremendous legacy of influence because it favored the emergence of leaders who were strong partly because they were conspicuously themselves, they were "natural" men and women who strongly felt that they owned themselves, and whatever talents they had for leadership were thereby immeasurably strengthened.

So we come to the last of my leadership strategies. I could name more, but I think I have given enough to suggest the range of ideas one might cultivate if one seriously intends to strengthen one's performance as a leader.

Acceptance

A very effective college president said recently, "An educator may be rejected by his students, and he must not object to this. But he may never, under any circumstances, regardless of what they do, reject a single student."

We have known this for a long time in the family. For a family to be a family, no one can ever be rejected. Have you ever read that great poem of Robert Frost's, "The Death of the Hired Man"? I once heard Frost read it here on this campus. The most moving lines to me are in the conversation on the farmhouse porch, the farmer and his wife talking about the shiftless hired man, Silas, who has come back to their place to die. The husband is irritated about this because Silas was lured away from him in the middle of the last haying season. The wife counters by pointing out that this is the only home he has. The husband doesn't want to accept that, and they are drawn into a discussion of what a home is. The husband gives his view that home is one place where acceptance is guaranteed, not so much out of love, but out of duty. If one must go home, family members must allow it. In my mind's ear, I can hear Frost, in his gruff voice with a New Hampshire twang, giving the husband's view. This is the male view. I have come to see it as the symbolic male—hard, rational, uncompromising. The wife gives the symbolic feminine reply—gentle, feeling, accepting. In answer to the question "What is home?" she replies that home is nothing we deserve. Home is like unearned grace; it is simply available, no strings attached.

Some women are hard and uncompromising, and some men are gentle and accepting. What Frost portrays for us here (and I don't know what his intent was) is the masculine and feminine principle. Because of the vagaries of human nature, the halt, lame, half-made creatures that we all are, the great leader (whether it be a mother in her home or the head of a vast organization) would say what the wife said about "home."

The interest and affection that the leader has for his followers—and it is a mark of true greatness when it is genuine—is clearly something that the followers "haven't to deserve." I have known some great leaders; it has been my privilege to work for a few. Some, not all, had gruff, demanding, uncompromising exteriors, but deep down, inside all those I think of as great—no exceptions—was a thoroughly feminine aspect, reflected in their unqualified attitude of acceptance of their people. You might get fired if you did not do your job. But as a person, you would never be rejected. Because their followers felt accepted, they tended to perform beyond the limits they had set for themselves. Initially, they may have excelled to please their leader but eventually they did so to please themselves.

I have suggested several leadership strategies: goal setting, systematic neglect, listening, language, values, personal growth, withdrawal, tolerance of imperfection, being your own person, and acceptance. A whole lecture could be devoted to each of these. In the next two lectures, I will deal at greater length with two of the key ones: knowing the unknowable and foreseeing the unforeseeable.

III

LEADERSHIP AND THE UNKNOWN

LEADERS OFTEN are not geniuses. One of the problems that geniuses have in the world is that they are sometimes led by people who are less developed intellectually. In fact, those of us who are not geniuses have some of the same feelings as we do toward the mayors of our cities, our governors, the presidents of our country, the heads of our firms, the presidents of our universities. They sometimes do not appear too intelligent by the usual standards; yet they are able leaders. Clearly, the requirements of leadership impose some intellectual demands that are not measured by IQ or academic intelligence ratings. The two are not mutually exclusive, but they are different things. The leader needs two intellectual abilities that are usually not formally assessed in an academic way: he needs to *know the unknowable* to *foresee the unforeseeable*. The leader knows some things and foresees some things that the people he is presuming to lead do not so well know or so well foresee. This is partly what gives him his "lead," what qualifies him to go ahead and guide the way. And this may be why the genius-level people must sometimes accept the leadership of people who are simply wise. As recently as fifty years ago, many would attribute these qualities of knowing the unknowable and foreseeing the unforeseeable to mystical or supernatural gifts, and some still do. Now I think it is possible at least to speculate about them within a framework of natural law.

The best way I know of to think about the human mind as a basis for discovering the special "knowledge" of the initiator, the leader, is the iceberg analogy. About seven-eights of the iceberg is underwater. The top of the iceberg is the conscious part of the mind where one "knows" and remembers, where two plus two equals four, and where the logical steps plus the access to memory are almost wholly conscious. There is a borderline area, the waterline, that shifts a bit, and the wholly submerged part is usually called the unconscious mind. Some theorize that the unconscious mind holds every sensory impression ever experienced and may even include ancestral memories. The body field theory suggests an interconnection and could explain thought transference; and some respectable physical scientists are willing to speculate on the durability of memory traces. This gives a "natural law" basis for explaining clairvoyance.

In far-out theorizing, every human mind, at the unconscious level, has access to every bit of information that is or ever was. Those who seem to have unusual access to this vast store of information are called "sensitives." There is a theory that once we were all sensitives and that telepathy was common, but as our analytical minds and knowledge developed, there was too much communication. Sensitivity became a liability, and natural selection weeded it out. This is confirmed by the prevalence of illness among sensitives today. What we now call intuitive insight may be the survivor of an earlier and much greater sensitivity. But it may bring us nearer the optimal balance between the conscious and the unconscious rationalities for living in the world as it is today.

Much of this is highly speculative, but none of it is clear out in limbo. It is within the bounds of what speculative, scientific minds are willing to ponder in the existing framework of known natural phenomena. Information recall under hypnosis is suggestive of what is potentially available from the unconscious.

I have come not to want to use the term *irrational*. I would rather think of every mental process as being wholly rational, perhaps at a level that would hold us in awe if we fully understood it; but we don't. What we now call the irrational thought or the irrational act I would rather attribute to the miswiring. The action is perfectly rational because the person is acting as instructed. It seems presumptuous for someone to say that something is irrational just because he can't understand it.

Now, what is the relevance of this somewhat fanciful theory to our problem at hand, the thought process of a leader? One of our contemporary business leaders put it this way: "If, in a business decision, you are waiting for all of the information to come in, it never comes." There always might be a little more information if one waited longer or spent more effort to get it, but the delay and the cost are not warranted. There is an optimum for every kind of decision: the most information for the least cost in the shortest period of time. You seldom have 100 percent no matter how much you spend or how long you wait, and if you wait too long, you have a different problem and must start all over. This is the terrible dilemma of the hesitant decision maker.

Leaders must be creative; and creativity is largely discovery—a push into the uncharted and the unknown. Every once in a while, a leader finds himself needing to think like a scientist, an artist, or a poet, and his thought processes may be just as fanciful as in those areas.

I once dreamed the solution to a business problem in a rather dramatic way. It has happened only once. I have had other dreams in which I received insights, but only one provided a fully developed practical answer to an important problem. It was a classic example of the creative act. All of the requirements were met: (1) a problem that required a new invention, a leap into the unknown; (2) an intense concentration on the conscious knowledge search and analytical reasoning until the conscious knowledge about the problem had been brought to the optimal point; and (3) withdrawal from the problem, relaxing (in sleep) from the conscious analytical process, thus permitting the unconscious process to function. The resolving insight happened to come in a dream. Usually it comes (if it comes) when the level of consciousness has been moved away from intense analytical concentration on the problem.

As a general observation, my intuitive knowledge comes when, after a period of intense analytical concentration on understanding a problem, I relax and, in one way or another, move into an altered level of consciousness, which may range all the way from what we call absentmindedness to deep sleep. Then the unconscious mind may take over and toss up a new insight, a hunch—a leap of thought into the unknown.

Benjamin Cardozo wrote an interesting book, *Nature of the Judicial Process,* and his chapter "The Subconscious Element in the Judicial Process" has something of interest to say on this question. Cardozo contrasts the views of Montesquieu and the French jurist Saleilles. Montesquieu believed that judges were neutral vehicles for the objective application of the law, while Saleilles argued that jurists willed the result at the beginning, then found legal doctrine to justify their positions. Justice Cardozo said of Saleilles' view, "I would not put the case this broadly. So sweeping a statement exaggerates the element of free volition. . . . None the less, by its very excess of emphasis, it supplies the needed corrective of an ideal of impossible objectivity."[10]

I hold with Saleilles rather than with Judge Cardozo's more cautious view. But then, when Cardozo wrote this, he was still a practicing judge. I am retired and a little freer to say what I think.

In summary, part of what gives the leader his "lead" is that he knows things that others who accept his leadership don't know. They may have higher IQs and possess more conscious knowledge, but they accept the leader because of his superior insights on matters of vital interest to them. For this reason, he's acknowledged as the one who should go ahead and point the way.

IV

LEADERSHIP AND FORESIGHT

A COMMON ASSUMPTION about the word *now* is that it is this instant moment of clock time. To be sure, in usage we qualify it a little by saying "right now," meaning this instant, or "about now," allowing a little leeway. We say, "I'm going to do it *now,*" which means I am going to start soon and do it in the future, or, "I have just *now* done it," meaning that I did it in the recent past. The current edition of *Webster's Unabridged Dictionary* admits all of these variations of usage.

For my purposes, I want to liken *now* to the spread of light from a narrowly focused beam. There is a bright intense center, this moment of clock time, and a diminishing intensity, theoretically out to infinity on either side. *Now* includes all of this—all of history and all of the future. As I view it, it simply gradually intensifies in the degree of illumination as this moment of clock time is approached. This central focus, which marks this instant of clock time, moves along as the clock ticks.

What we call foresight or prescience, a better-than-average guess about *what* is going to happen *when* in the future, begins with a state of mind about "now," something like I have suggested by the light analogy. *Action* in the present moment of clock time is sharply differentiated from what has gone on in the past and what is going to go on in the future. A sort of constant "moving average" mentality (to use a statistician's term) is operating all of the time. The process is continuous. The concern with past and future is gradually attenuated as this span of concern goes forward and backward from the present moment. But it is an unvarying profile of a span of attention that each of us carries forward with us from minute to minute.

What I want to do, as vividly and as forcefully as I can, is to distinguish the concept of foresight that I hold from the prevailing popular view of prescience, which is a sort of mystical gift that a seer calls into play now and then when he chooses to look at his crystal ball. Rather, foresight is a wholly rational process, the product of a constantly running computer that is regarding the events of this instant and comparing them with a series of projections made in the past, which are in turn being projected into the indefinite future, with diminishing certainty as projected time runs farther and farther on. As Wordsworth said of the Happy Warrior, "He sees what he foresaw."[11] It is a continuous, never-ending process. In our psychiatric casualties we see the failure of an individual to see what he foresaw. And in our long-lived dynamic institutions we see the opposite—a high level of seeing in the present moment what was foreseen in the past.

Machiavelli, writing three hundred years ago about how to be a prince, put it this way: "Thus it happens in matters of state; for knowing afar off (which it is only given a prudent man to do) the evils that are brewing, they are easily cured. But when, for want of such knowledge, they are allowed to grow so that everyone can recognize them, there is no longer any remedy to be found."[12]

Theodore Vail, the great goal setter who built AT&T, said that a leader must see problems soon enough to act on them *first*, in the right way. Otherwise, others will force the issue and the leader will be backed into compromise.

In my old business, after a lot of travail, we managed to get it stated that the *failure* to foresee is an *ethical* failure, because serious ethical compromises *today* (when the usual judgment on ethical inadequacy is made) are usually the result of a failure at an earlier date to foresee today's events and take the right actions when there was freedom for initiative to act. The action that society labels "unethical" in the present moment is often really one of *no choice*. A lot of guilty people are walking around with an air of innocence that they would not have if society were able always to pin the label "unethical" on the failure to foresee and the failure to act constructively when there was freedom to act.

Foresight is part of the "lead" that the leader has. Once in a position of leadership, the leader has the opportunity to use the superior information resources that his position gives him in order to maintain his lead. Once he loses this lead and events start to force his hand, he is leader in name only. He is not leading; he is only reacting to events, and he probably will not long be a leader if he does not recover his "lead."

The words *foresight* and *prescience* are poor words, but we have no better ones. They imply that the foreseer sees the literal dimensions of an exact event at a precise point in time in the future. It happens sometimes. A factory manager sees his inventory of parts declining with no replenishments in sight. Thus he can compute the exact day when he closes his factory. But this is not foresight in the critical sense; this is merely a computational problem, if one has all of the data. The leadership decision depends on "intuiting" the gap between the limit of the solid information and what is in fact needed for a dependable decision.

So it is with foresight. There is a gap between what trend predictions supply and the view of the future circumstance on which present decisions depend. This is what Machiavelli meant, I think, when he said "knowing afar off (which it is only given a prudent man to do)." The prudent man, as I see it, is the man who constantly thinks of now as the moving concept I spoke of—past, present moment, and future are one organic unity. This requires living by a sort of rhythm that encourages a high level of insight about the whole span of events, from the indefinite past through the present moment to the indefinite future. One is, at once, in every moment of time, historian, contemporary analyst, and prophet—not three separate roles. This,

I think, is what the initiator, the leader, is every day of his life. He is historian, contemporary analyst, and prophet. And over the whole gamut he is filling the information gap with a high level of intuitive insight.

So we come back to knowing the unknowable and the access to the vast, under-the-waterline resources of the unconscious mind in order that we may foresee the unforeseeable. It is partly a matter of faith. Stress is a condition of modern life. One takes on the rough-and-tumble of leadership roles with the belief that if one enters a situation prepared with the necessary experience (and knowledge at the conscious level), the intuitive insights necessary for optimal performance will be given. I see no other way, in the world of affairs, for one to maintain serenity in the face of uncertainty. It requires only that one understand the creative process, which requires that one follow the conscious analytical path as far as it will carry one and then withdraw, release the pressure, if only for a moment, in full confidence that the resolving insight will come. If the full insight does not come on the first try, one resumes the analytical pursuit again—withdraws and waits in confidence. Usually a slightly higher level of insight will come.

This is not a how-to-do-it seminar, but I will venture a few suggestions on how to prepare to know the unknowable and foresee the unforeseeable at a level that supports one as a leader even in the muddled, confused world we live in today.

1. To any problem one confronts, one's first response is, What questions can I ask about it? The shape of the future, seen in the present moment, can only be in the framework of questions asked. Thus one approaches a problem in the spirit of a search for understanding.

2. When one acknowledges that one sees the *present* in terms of *partial truth* only, the fragmentary knowledge of the future is not seen as so sharp a contrast as when knowledge of the present is seen as complete and solid. People who are dogmatic about the present are usually dogmatic about the future—and

wrong. This is a curious line of reasoning, but I believe it is valid. *To sharpen one's view of the future, one must first relax the certainty with which one views the present.*

3. Intuitive insights come with "clearing the mind." After any intense problem-solving activity, one might practice clearing the mind so that, with eyes closed, one sees only a neutral gray wall.

4. The best knowledge is not certainty (whether about the present or about the future) but progressively sharper insights. As one moves the past-present-future frame along, this is apt to be the result—progressively sharper insights. The end result, given enough time, is that one will be known as wise.

5. The greatest foresight, the most difficult and most exciting, is to develop young people as they come along to deal courageously and creatively with the future. You cannot bind the future to your present wisdom. By the time you have crystallized your wisdom, it is probably out of date. But you can help shape the future society and ensure its durability by the kind of people you prepare for the future.

6. Somebody needs to dream the big dream and tell the society—family, church, school, city, nation, business, perhaps the world—what it can be. Robert Browning said it in two short lines:

> Ah, but a man's reach should exceed his grasp,
> Or what's a heaven for?[13]

7. It is terribly important what one thinks about as one goes to sleep. Sleep is far more than knitting up the raveled sleeve of care that Shakespeare mentioned. It has many functions. For purposes of knowing the unknowable and foreseeing the unforeseeable, it is the rhythmic withdrawal in which the vast unconscious mind can order itself to serve us. What we think about as we go to sleep is a sort of programming of the computer. But that is a bad analogy, because the computer's program is a conscious instruction—literal and explicit—and the computer's response can be checked out. There is a subtle connection between

the conscious level of thought and the response of the unconscious mind. It resembles somewhat Whitehead's dictum about language when he said that a leap of the imagination of the *hearer* is required to establish the relevance of the language to immediate experience. In this case, one does not ask the unconscious mind for anything, and one does not *expect* a response. One just holds the thought and drops off, into sleep, reverie, or simply an absence of thought as if looking at a blank gray wall. The analytical wheels must stop spinning, and the mind must be in repose. Sleep is probably the highest form of repose, and the moments of awakening are, in my experience, the most fertile for intuitive insight. But not much comes if one is "hung over." You have to wake up with a clear head to do this.

8. All of this requires, I believe, living a schizoid life. One is *always* at two levels: *in the real world,* concerned, responsible, effective, value-oriented. One is also *detached,* riding above it all, seeing today's events in the long sweep of history and into the indefinite future. Modern man as a leader, it seems to me, must somehow effect a marriage between his Protestant-ethic conscience, which grows out of the Judeo-Christian tradition, and philosophical detachment about which the legend of the compassionate Buddha has much more to say.

I want to conclude this discussion of knowing the unknowable and foreseeing the unforeseeable with reference to the subject of awareness—not knowing the unknowable, but knowing the usually not known—usually not known because many people are not sufficiently aware.

Awareness means opening the doors of perception wide so as to take in more from sensory experience than people usually take in. It is not hard to achieve, and I think it makes life more interesting; certainly it strengthens one's position as a leader. First, there is more than usual alertness, more intense contact with the immediate situation, whatever it is, and a lot more stored away in the unconscious computer to serve us with insights when needed.

There is a great line from William Blake:

> If the doors of perception were cleansed everything
> would appear to man as it is—infinite.[14]

I have gotten my doors of perception open wide enough often enough to know that this statement of Blake's is not mere poetic exaggeration. Most of us move about with very narrow perception—sight, sound, touch—and we miss more of the grandeur that is in the minutest thing, the smallest experience. We also miss great leadership opportunities.

The opening of awareness stocks both the conscious and unconscious areas of the mind with a richness of resources for any need one faces. But it does more than that: it builds and clarifies values; it armors one to meet the stress of life with assurance that one will act rightly; and it augurs for serenity in the face of disaster. The cultivation of awareness gives one the basis for detachment, the ability to stand aside and see oneself in perspective in the context of one's own experience, amid the ever-present angers, stresses, and alarms. Then one sees one's own peculiar assortment of obligations and responsibilities—a detached view of oneself in the world that enables one to sort out the urgent and the important from the less urgent and less important and perhaps deal with the latter. Awareness is not a giver of solace. It is just the opposite. It is a disturber and an awakener. The able leaders I know are all awake and reasonably disturbed. They are not seekers after solace.

Let me sum up the relevance of all of this to leadership at any level—the mother in her home or the head of a large institution. One of the sources of stress is a lack of confidence in one's ability to cope with the forthcoming situation, so one goes into it stressed and tense and greatly increases the opportunity of performing badly. Confidence at a time like this rests on two major assumptions: (1) that one has an adequate strategy, as discussed in my second lecture, and therefore is prepared, and (2) that one will be able to compose oneself in the situation and receive the intuitive insight needed to deal with it. This is a kind of faith. One does not ask for miracles. They sometimes happen, delivering us from dilemmas that we are not really entitled to escape, but one cannot depend on miracles. One goes in prepared with strategies, with knowledge, and with as much as can be anticipated by foresight in the way of preparation. Belief that the needed insight will come, in the situation, is then the supporting faith that relieves one of stress in a way that permits the creative process to operate, that makes dynamic visionary leadership possible.

If one then couples this kind of confidence in one's ability to cope and to lead with a constant awareness of the imminence of danger, not in an obsessive way but in a rational recognition of the reality of the ever-present moral and physical dangers, one has the rudiments of armor that makes one a leader and reassures those who follow.

I want to close with a brief analysis of one of the great stories of the human spirit—the story of Jesus when confronted with the woman taken in adultery.

One of the decisions I made a few years ago was to be my own theologian. Then I discovered that there is a pretty good consensus among professional theologians that in the end, in the quiet of his own inner thoughts, every man *has* to be his own theologian because, at the very least, he has to decide whether to accept or reject or ignore someone else's theology. My decision was to regard all scriptures of all religions as great stories of the human spirit and take them for the insight they yield on that basis. I don't urge this view on anyone else; but this is where I come out. I tell you this so you will understand how I am using this one particular great story of the human spirit.

In this story, I see Jesus as a man, like you and me, with extraordinary prophetic insight of the kind we all have some of. He has chosen a new mission among his people to bring, among other things, more compassion to their lives. He is a leader, as I see it, in the fullest meaning of the term. He meets this situation prepared in a strategic sense—as we viewed it earlier. Without this, he could not have had the sustaining faith that the approach he used was a viable one.

In this scene, he is being challenged, taunted insistently, by the mob crying, "The law says she shall be stoned. What do you say?" Jesus must make a decision. Leadership depends on it. The situation is deliberately stressed. What does he do?

He sits there writing in the sand. I see this as a withdrawal device. In the pressure of the moment, having assessed the situation rationally, he creates the condition that will allow creative insight to function. He could have regaled the mob with rational arguments about the superiority of compassion over torture. A pretty good logical argument could be made for it. What do you think the result would have been?

He did not choose to do that. He chose to withdraw instead, and cut the stress, right in the event itself, in order to open himself to creative insight—and a great one came: "Let him that is without sin among you cast the first stone."

This story suggests something about the fourth element of leadership: spirit. I will take that up in my last lecture.

V

THE INDIVIDUAL AS LEADER

IN MY OPENING LECTURE, I presented four assumptions that I said would run through these discussions on leadership and the individual. I said that they may not be the assumptions you would make and that they were presented not to persuade you to accept them but more to help clarify my own thinking and to encourage each of you to examine your own assumptions. I would like to restate these assumptions briefly and add a short elaboration that takes account of the ground that I have covered in four lectures, plus ideas that have emerged in our discussion sessions and in informal conversations.

My first assumption is that we are in a leadership crisis because not enough of those who have the opportunity and the obligation to lead have kept themselves contemporary. Furthermore, the suddenness of the knowledge explosion plus the enlarged communications media have presented new conditions, especially among the youth and the disadvantaged, which call for an inventiveness and an adaptability that leaders heretofore have not had to have. Then we are confronted by the confusing argument, from some who are obviously and strenuously trying to lead, that there should be no leadership. So leaders in some sectors of society are getting a rude shock. In some respects, leaders in the business community, which went through its revolution of governance in the 1930s, seem less disturbed than those in education, government, and the church. But there is a pervasive uneasiness among all who lead, and it has its roots, I think, in their failure to keep abreast of the revolution in thought and in the conditions of society and to alter their attitudes and their strategies quickly enough. As someone said here this week, it is difficult to lead if you do not know where your followers are going.

My second assumption is that our educational system is not designed to prepare for leadership. John Gardner has made a strong case (to which I subscribe) that particularly our colleges *discourage* growth in leadership by an overemphasis on the training of critics and experts.[15] The realization of this comes at a time that a crisis of leadership overshadows the land. So we have the dilemma of domestic disorder that we should be able to turn to the universities to help solve. But when we do so, we find them pretty effectively engaged in heating the crisis rather than cooling it. During these two weeks, I have been asked several times what we can do about this. My answer is that it is difficult to see how anything can be done quickly because the crisis of leadership is probably most acute in university administration itself. The chief examiners of assumptions have left some of their own assumptions unexamined, and the chief haven of critics of society is now the object of mounting criticism.

My third assumption is that the value system of the Western world that has been building since Moses brought the tablets down the mountain three thousand years ago has been pretty badly shattered and, I believe, irretrievably so, within the lifetime of the youngest person here. It will be replaced, I think, by something better. As in any value revision, some of the old wisdom will no doubt reemerge with the new moral sanctions, but much of it will be *new*. The restatement of contemporary morality will, as I see it, be largely made by those who are now young. They are struggling to do it now in a way that shakes my generation—and me. The best evidence I have that the moral law is badly shattered is the babbling of conflicting voices from our contemporary theologians. To be sure, a lot of the old moral law still persists in the inertia of the attitudes of older people who know no other way, and they carry some of the youngsters with them. But as I see it, the necessary consensus to support the contention that there is a moral law no longer exists.

My fourth and last assumption is that the forces for good or evil in the world operate through the thoughts, attitudes, and actions of individual beings. Societies, movements, and institutions are but the collection or focus of such individual initiatives. What happens to our values, and therefore to the quality of our civilization, in the future will result from the conception, born of inspiration, of individual persons. Perhaps only one person will receive it. This has happened before in the history of the world. I gave you my example of John Woolman, the eighteenth-century Quaker who, one hundred years before the Civil War almost single-handedly talked the Quakers, one by one, into freeing their slaves. And I speculated on what the history of this country might have been if fifty dedicated people of his persuasiveness had ranged the land in the eighteenth century, dealing with the issue of slavery as Woolman dealt with it. I suggested a theory of social change based on one-by-one, person-by-person persuasion. Then I asked whether we had the educational skill to find and train enough people to deal with contemporary issues in this way to make a difference. And I said I thought we did because of the example of Horace Williams, a near-contemporary at the University of North Carolina who, over a long teaching career, released a force that has made the civilization of North Carolina different. I have done a little work with leaders in North Carolina, and their spirit is different from what one finds elsewhere. This is largely the result of the influence a few great teachers like Horace Williams chose to wield through forty years of teaching at the university. In one discussion group, Alcoholics Anonymous was cited as an outstanding modern manifestation of the one-by-one, person-by-person approach to social problems. It is one of the most significant social developments of the past thirty years. These were and are my four assumptions.

The title of these lectures is "Leadership and the Individual." I have stressed the word *individual* because of my belief that the only access we have to inspiration, those subtle promptings of intuitive insight from the vast unconscious storehouse of wisdom and experience, is through the mind of an individual. I was deeply touched by a quote from a late lecture by Camus. "Great ideas come into the world as gently as doves. . . . Listen carefully and you will hear the flutter of their wings."[16] Only the solitary individual in the quietness or his own meditation gets these great ideas intuitively. They don't come in stentorian tones, over the public address system to groups. That only happens *after* an individual has listened carefully to the flutter of their wings. The wings themselves do not flutter into the microphone. Yet, on the other hand, I must say that it is difficult for the influence of an individual to go very far without the mediation of an institution. And in the paper I gave you titled "Responsibility in a Bureaucratic Society," I argued as persuasively as I know how that all institutions tend to become bureaucracies, especially as they grow old, large, or respectable.[17] In my paper, I quote the dictionary definition of *bureaucracy*—a system that has become narrow, rigid, and formal; depends on precedent; and lacks initiative and resourcefulness—a pretty bad state of affairs. It is the feet of clay that tend to encumber everything that is organized. *All* institutions—churches, schools, governments, businesses, hospitals, social agencies, even families—all tend to become bureaucracies, regardless of the sheltering ideologies or the specific goals. Only the new and the small and the struggling seem to be relatively free of this dreadful disease.

Despite this gloomy view of the state of organized society, I am hopeful. I am hopeful because of the restlessness of the abler young people. I believe they are going to take us at a pretty fast clip to a new and nobler level of values. When they get us there, it will not be utopia. Man's fate will still be the same, and the human dilemma will still be with us. A generation from now, as a society (if we're still here), we will probably feel we have made some progress. But one thing I am reasonably sure of, is that this agitated younger generation is going to be in more trouble with their children than we are with ours simply because they are not preparing themselves to manage the consequences of the revolution they are determined to carry through. They may carry it through; I am betting my chips that they win. But as I see it, they are not going to be heroes in the eyes of the eighteen- to twenty-two-year-olds twenty-five years from now. And the fault will be ours—parents, schools, and our institutional life generally because we have been too uncritical of the pervasive bureaucracy, too unwilling to examine the assumptions that underlie our bureaucratic walls and to prepare the oncoming generation to manage a less bureaucratized society.

But still I say I am hopeful because of the exceptional quality of some of these young people, quality that wasn't evident in my generation when I was young.

Let me read the statement made by Professor B. D. Napier, dean of the chapel and professor of religion at Stanford University, about David Harris, age twenty-one, one of the better known of the recent student protest leaders, on the occasion of his resignation as president of the student body at Stanford:

> I don't know what Dave's reasons are for resigning, and maybe that's beside the point. His administration has taken its toll on him, and I think in the long run on official Stanford. But he's been there long enough to see his real stature, his authentic greatness. How often do you see a man who, in being himself, can help you be and find yourself; in whom you can detect no deviousness at all; whose compassion is no less compassion for being unsentimental; who cares like hell about the world he lives in and can somehow go on loving and believing in the people who inhabit it, even while he protests the ways we go on lousing it up! For all of his sharp, unrelenting criticism—in part, of course, because of it—all of us, and all at Stanford, and the

whole college and university scene in America are better for
having him where he's been.[18]

To which I would add, What more could one ask a man to accomplish by age twenty-one?

My generation and the intermediate one have been judged
hypocritical by the younger generation because of the surface
discrepancies between the promise and the performance. By
training the young to be critics and experts rather than responsible participants in society, I think we oldsters come off a little
better than we deserved by being called hypocrites. Had we
trained more of our able young people to become responsible
participants in society—really trained them as we are capable
of it, with our best resources—then I think more of them would
see it as I do. Their judgment would be that we are hypocritical
but also *immoral* because too many of the best of us refuse to
examine the assumptions we live by. And to refuse to examine
the assumptions one lives by is immoral.

How did our society get to be so bureaucratic? I believe that
it started with a man called Jethro who was the first management consultant of record, mentioned in the Book of Exodus.[19]
Jethro was the father-in-law of Moses. Moses, struggling to
keep order among his followers in the wilderness, was in an administrative snafu: he was losing his leadership. Jethro came to
visit, looked the situation over, and advised Moses to set up a
bureaucracy to handle the workload. So Moses gave heed to the
voice of his father-in-law and did all that he had said. Moses
chose able men out of all Israel and made them heads over the
people, rulers of thousands, of hundreds, of fifties, and of tens.
And they judged the people at all times; hard cases they
brought to Moses, but any small matter they decided themselves. Then Moses let his father-in-law depart, and like all
good consultants, Jethro, having given his advice, went on his
way to his own country.

Every student of management knows this story and knows
that this is the first statement of the hierarchical principle of

organization. This hierarchical principle has come down to us like the axioms of Euclid, except that three hundred years ago we began to reexamine Euclid's assumptions—to our great benefit. Jethro's principle of organization is as yet relatively unexamined. Everything that is organized has reference to it.

Since the stigma of bureaucracy is universal, I have thought about this for a long time. One day I visited a wise friend who is a distinguished rabbi and scholar. I reviewed with him the story of Jethro and noted that Jethro's reason for his advice to Moses is that the suggested new arrangement would ease Moses' burden by distributing the work, *delegating downward* all of the small matters and providing an orderly procedure for Moses' rule. There is no suggestion that it would be good for the people of Israel. Moses was wearing himself out on the job. His father-in-law wanted to save Moses, and his advice aimed to do that and, we might infer, nothing more.

We know that in the end, the Lord sacked Moses, rather summarily, right in sight of the Promised Land, and put in a new leader for the triumphal entry. The Lord's reasons for sacking Moses seem to me rather specious, the kind of reasons many of us have invented when we are going to do something unpleasant to somebody and prefer not to give our *real* reasons. *Could it be,* I asked the rabbi, that the Lord's real criticism of Moses that led to the substitution of another leader was that Moses had taken this stupid advice from Jethro and that the unfortunate bureaucratic consequences were already evident in the tribes of Israel? This, I suggested, and not the reason the Lord gave Moses, was the cause of the Lord's dissatisfaction. The long-term result, of course, for the Western world and ultimately the whole world, is that the world has been stuck with a lousy organization theory for three thousand years.

The rabbi listened intently with his eyes sparkling as I presented my proposition in a little more detail than I have given it here. When I had finished, he thought a minute and then said, "You can't prove it one way or another from the record, but that's as good an explanation as I've heard."

If we could get to the root of the unrest in our contemporary institutions, we might find that long-outworn ways of organizing are one of the basic causes. The hierarchical organization postulates the leader as the *superior* of his followers. In the Catholic orders, the word *superior* is an actual title. We now need a principle of organization that postulates the leader as the *servant* of his followers.

Bad organization theory is bad because in practice it pulls people down. But if I had to choose between a bad organization theory with a great leader and a good organization theory with a poor leader, give me the former any day.

As Henry Ehrmann was talking yesterday on university governance, I thought of a comment by the philosopher Sidney Hook. A great university, said Professor Hook, has a great faculty. But great faculties, by themselves, do not maintain themselves. To build and maintain a great faculty, there must be an administrator who is a great leader.

In the end, it is the *person,* the leader as an individual, who counts. Systems, theories, organization structures are secondary. It is the inspiration and initiative of individual persons that move the world along.

Two facts about Thomas Jefferson are relevant to our interest in the leader as an individual. The first concerns the drafting of the Declaration of Independence. This is clearly to Jefferson's credit. But had it not been for the valiant effort of Ben Franklin, the Declaration would have emerged the typical chewed-up committee document of the kind that nobody hangs on his wall. It got a little chewed up as it was, but nothing like it would have been if Franklin, then an old man, had not been the strong-hearted defender of the integrity of Jefferson's work. Let us think about that in relation to ourselves. If we don't see ourselves in a leader role, maybe then we can be the Franklin to some aspiring Jefferson and give the support that makes greatness out of what might otherwise be mediocrity.

The second point about Jefferson is what he did during the years of the Revolutionary War. His contribution to American civilization in that period, in my judgment, ranks ahead of drafting the Declaration and his later service as president.

Once the Declaration was proclaimed, Jefferson was famous, the war was on, and he was importuned on all sides to take an important role in the war. He turned everyone down. Jefferson was his own man. He probably knew he wasn't a great administrator (if he didn't, a short experience as governor of Virginia awhile later made it clear).

Jefferson believed that the war would be won, that there would be a new nation, and that that nation would need a new system of law. And he appointed himself to be the architect of that new legal system. So he went back to Virginia, which was the only place he wanted to be anyhow, and chose this interesting course of action. Much as he liked to sit in his ivory tower and think and write, that is not the way he did *this* job. He got himself elected to the legislature and began drafting statutes embodying new principles of law, and he took on the tough fight of getting his conservative colleagues in the legislature to enact them into law. In all, he wrote about a hundred and fifty statutes, and in four years of strenuous effort, he got about fifty of them enacted. (Over the next hundred years, when legislators were hard pressed on a thorny issue, they kept digging into that file of the remaining hundred to see if Jefferson had worked it out for them.) It was a tough struggle to get those fifty enacted. When Jefferson's effort was slowed to a halt, as it occasionally was, he would get on his horse and ride back to Monticello to rekindle his spirit, write some new statutes, and come back to make another run.

The consequence of this effort was that when the Constitutional Convention convened twelve or thirteen years after the war, important elements of the new constitution were already operating, and had been for some years, in Virginia. Jefferson wasn't even around then. He was serving as ambassador to France. He didn't *have* to be around. He had done his great work years before. Such are the curious and wondrous ways in which leaders operate.

So do not ask, as many of you have asked these past ten days, "Where is the great leader to come from to guide us from the present confusion? What system or way of approaching our problems will work best?" These are the wrong questions. Rather, let us ask ourselves, "What is the great dream I would like to see brought to realization? What talents do I have, what talents might I prudently acquire to help move some part of the world toward that dream? Where can I make my effort count?" Then let us go to work with our own two hands wherever we can get hold of the problem.

I want to turn now to the last word on our list, *spirit*. If you do what I have just advised, you will need it. Given the other three elements—values, direction, and competence—what is the element of spirit in leadership?

In my role as my own theologian, I do not want to define or explain it. There is, in my theology, a mystery before which I simply stand in awe. At the threshold of the mystery, I ask no questions and seek no explanations. I simply bow before the mystery, and what it wants to say to me comes as gently as doves as I achieve the quiet. Spirit is behind the threshold of the mystery. I don't know what it is, even though occasionally I get intimations about it, but I do have a belief about what it *does*. When a leader has it, it builds *trust*; it builds trust not only between leader and follower but also between followers. Humans have not always been trusting, but trust is the cement that makes possible institutional solidarity, from the family to world society.

Even trust must be qualified by the word *optimal*, just the right amount to keep between those two limits that Henry Ehrmann set for viable participative society—not so active as to destroy nor so indifferent or apathetic as to abdicate. Somewhere between blind trust and distrust there is an optimum of trust that supports leadership that moves toward what is richer, more honest, more fundamentally right.

The tests of leadership are realistic and exacting. Whatever the goal is, does the undertaking move toward it? And what does the scorekeeper say?

My introduction to this subject was intense and at a very primitive level. After my first three months in my old company with a line construction gang, a little crew of lineman and laborers (of which I was one) and a foreman and a truck, I spent a few months in the Engineering Department to learn a little language. Then I was sent to an intensive school to be trained to lead what we then called foreman conferences. For the next year, every other Monday morning, I received a new group of twelve foremen and we sat around a table for two weeks of guided discussion—no reading, no formal agenda except what I had in my head. My twelve conferees seldom included a high school graduate, sometimes included an illiterate. And we talked for two weeks about the problems of these foremen at the quite elementary yet profound level of leading people where the work of the world actually gets done. This was my graduate education. It left me with a tremendous respect for little people whose claim to what status they have rests almost wholly on wisdom and experience. Since the rest of my experience has been in pretty sophisticated society, I give you this much of my origins to help explain the choice of path through which these five lectures have gone.

Now I must close.

This has been a rich and rewarding experience. I have made new friends. My mind has been stretched. And my already deep roots in Dartmouth have been strengthened.

Three things stand out at this point as I add this experience to many others.

1. Nothing much happens without a dream. For something great to happen there must be a great dream—the dream of an individual person. "Make no little plans," wrote Daniel Burnham. "They have no power to stir men's blood and probably themselves will not be realized."[20]

2. Not much that is really important can be done with power—coercive power. Such power has its place. In an emergency, it is convenient to have had it established beforehand who has what power so that the emergency can be dealt with promptly. And some things that men fancy they value can be built with it—the Pyramids, for example. Beyond that, coercive power must be valued in inverse ratio to its use. As our civilization evolves, the liabilities of holding such power increase, and the real disabilities of the holder of power become more apparent.

This morning, as I listened to Reese Prosser's talk, for the first time I realized that by using the awful power we had in the first atomic bomb, we forfeited much of the great influence we might have had about its later use. There is a great line in Shakespeare's Ninety-Fourth Sonnet: "They that have power to hurt and will do none."

3. I must listen to the flower people, and I must listen to the Birchers. I do this not because it makes any particular sense in my conscious rationality to do so but simply because they are here. And I do not ask why they are here, because I see the "why" of why any of us is here as a part of the mystery. It is behind the threshold where I do not ask. Who knows, if I were able to ask and got a straight answer, I might find that their reasons for being here are better than mine. It is a humbling thought.

Virtue and justice and order are good, but not good enough—not nearly good enough. In the end, nothing really counts but love and friendship.

PART FOUR

IN PERSON WITH ROBERT K. GREENLEAF

[For twenty years] I've been free to do what I want to do, trying to do some things that won't save the world but may leave a little bit of it a little better than if I hadn't tried. At least, that's what I learned from my father, and that's been pretty much my lifelong credo.

The difference between organizations is how the people relate and how they actually function, which may not bear a whole lot of relationship to how the thing is sketched out on paper.

What I've been suggesting right from the start of writing The Servant as Leader *is that the abler, stronger people in our society must work a whole lot harder and that by doing so, they will have more fun.*

Robert K. Greenleaf

IN DECEMBER 1986, Dr. Joseph DiStefano, an old friend and colleague of Robert Greenleaf's, spent many hours talking with his mentor on a wide range of subjects: biographical details, professional experiences, the evolution of the servant theme, his years as director of management research at AT&T, his final years as a consultant, and other matters. During these remarkable sessions, Greenleaf shared many private thoughts and behind-the-scenes stories of his personal development. Following are excerpts from the transcript, in which Greenleaf speculates on the attraction of the servant theme, describes responses to his various essays, discusses people and events that have influenced him, and talks about his writing style. On the basis of these talks and other experiences with Greenleaf, DiStefano wrote an essay titled *Tracing the Vision and Impact of Robert K. Greenleaf,* published by the Robert K. Greenleaf Center in Indianapolis.

Joseph DiStefano is a professor in the School of Business Administration at the University of Western Ontario in London, Ontario. His special field of interest is international business, with special attention to management problems rooted in cultural differences. He has international experience as a teacher and consultant on management issues and is the coauthor of *International Management Behavior: From Policy to Practice* (Nelson, Canada) and *Effective Managerial Action* (Prentice Hall, Canada).

A CONVERSATION
WITH ROBERT K. GREENLEAF

DISTEFANO: I'd like to discuss the responsiveness of people to the first essay you did, *The Servant as Leader*.[1] The Orders of Sisters responded very positively, but in my experience, and particularly after looking through the list of repeat purchasers of the essay, the audience is quite a bit broader than that. Students and universities, professors, managers and business organizations, government leaders, executives, and many other kinds of institutions, from hospitals to elementary schools to foundations, have also resonated to these ideas. Do you have any sense of what longing, what need there is among such a diversity of people that has caused them to respond this way?

GREENLEAF: Well, it would be just speculation, but it would be my guess that in the population there are people who had a parent like I had, who set a servant model for them, in whom this model lay dormant, and this is what I had written. Although in that essay I didn't speak of my father particularly, apparently what I said touched something in the experience of quite a few people, though not large numbers. This is not a bandwagon idea; it is not a best-seller kind of thing; but nevertheless, these people do exist, and some of them have become very important to me. Now what the common basis of experience is, I am not sure.

In a way, I think I understand why the Catholic sisters responded, and that is because they, of all people, have probably made one of the largest servant commitments with their own lives, and they recognized an articulation of their principles of service that may have been new to them. But that's about the best answer I can give. I realize these people now are in all walks of life and they are, to some extent, lonely people; but they don't find themselves in environments that reinforce this disposition in their nature.

DISTEFANO: Picking up your last point, I would also suggest that people who have this notion lying dormant in their own lives, and who work in institutions that perhaps don't reinforce it, also recognize that these same institutions provide great opportunity for the release of this dormant idea and, in fact, have great need for that kind of leadership if they are going to be better institutions than they currently are. Perhaps the servant theme provides not only some hope that they can do something where they are but also a sense of inspiration and direction for how to do it. At least, that's been my experience with the people who have read the essay and responded to it with more than words, people who have tried to do something with the ideas in the organizations that they are in.

GREENLEAF: I suspect that it's quite common in our society that there are people with high levels of idealism who have had experiences that have shaken their hope that you can live productively with those ideals. Perhaps what I have written has given some people some encouragements that there are ways to deal with whatever situation one finds oneself in and to be more of a servant by trying than by not trying, granting that they may never achieve a perfect society or even a perfect institution, but that one should try. I suspect that's really what I've been doing in the past fifteen to twenty years. I've been free to do what I want to do, try to do some things that won't save the world but may leave a little bit of it a little better than if I hadn't tried. At least, that's what I learned from my father, and that's been pretty much my lifelong credo.

DISTEFANO: Bob, as we move from the topic of *The Servant as Leader* to *The Institution as Servant*,[2] the second of your essays that received wide distribution, I am interested in the transition from the first to the second, from the theme of servant-leadership, the kind and purpose of leadership, to the theme of organizing for effective leadership. Would you comment about how you got from one to the other?

GREENLEAF: It's a little hard to say. I hadn't gone very far with interacting with people as a result of that first essay before I realized that there were two interlocking phenomenon here. First, the one of people serving and, second, the one of institutions serving. As I reflected on that, I realized that with the exception of a very few people in our society, nearly everybody wielded their influence, such as they had, through some institutional involvement. Their ability to serve as people was conditioned considerably by what they were able to do through the institutions with which they were involved, and those might be very large or quite small, like a local church. I also realized that the two themes—individual and institution—are really inseparable. Our traditional roots, our biblical roots, are pretty much based on individuals functioning on their own. Institutions hardly existed in biblical times. As a matter of fact, they had very little existence in this country until this century. We had some institutions, of course, but it has been noted that when our Constitution was written, there were virtually no corporations. Corporations get their constitutional status due to the willingness of the courts to construe them as persons, which is all that is dealt with in the Constitution. So I realized that not much would be served by simply addressing people in their individual roles; that is adequately addressed in our culture.

The problem of individuals functioning through institutions and being both restrained and facilitated by institutions in their

345

personal serving is relatively unexplored. So after I had written that first essay, this kind of thinking led me to address ideas in the second essay, *The Institution as Servant*. This proved to be a very controversial writing. People who were intrigued by the first essay were intensely bothered by the second one, particularly people who were chief executives of *big things*.

I recall one very acrimonious session with the head of a large corporation who had been immensely impressed by the first essay and terribly bothered by the second one. He felt I shouldn't have written it and certainly shouldn't have distributed it. It was heresy. You couldn't manage the nation with that kind of idea. He was terribly upset. That reverberation was direct and personal, but there were quite a few I received indirectly.

Writing *The Institution as Servant* caused me to reflect on my own experience within a behemoth of an institution, AT&T. It was a terribly big and ponderous bureaucracy, yet one in which I felt quite comfortable. In other words, I learned to work with it. It took a lot of Machiavellian strategy to maneuver within it and to make any contribution to it, but I was comfortable in that relationship, and I realized that a lot of people were not. Many people were really ground down by it and were lesser people than they would have been had they been able to function purely as individuals.

Of course, as a consultant, I was involved with quite a range of institutions at that time. This gave me added insight into churches and universities, as well as other businesses, both large and small, that I really didn't have much knowledge of while I was still in my main career with AT&T.

DISTEFANO: I too have experienced a lot of resistance to the ideas in the second essay, *The Institution as Servant,* and I'm struck by the fact that most of the people who resist this are the same ones from your experience, significant people in their organizations. My understanding is that you have seen some very effective examples of the notion of *primus inter pares* (first among equals) that you put forward here, in which the designated chief shares decision making and leadership, and I wonder if it might be useful to have a few of those examples sketched, even in general form, perhaps to encourage some of those people who see this as a terribly idealistic formulation.

GREENLEAF: The three that come to mind are all in Europe: Philips in the Netherlands, Royal Dutch Shell, and Unilever, the latter two of which are both English and Dutch. In other words, they are sort of joint ventures between England and the Netherlands. Philips is the only place where I have encountered the term *primus inter pares*. All I can say is that these companies are, or were, organized in that way and are very successful, large, international companies.

I suspect there are institutions, including businesses in the United States, whose organization charts are drawn in hierarchical form with a single chief but who in effect operate as if the chief were a *primus* and not a chief.

I suspect that if you look closely at the European companies that are structured as a team, the head person, the *primus*, will, in an emergency, function like a chief and will be accepted. In other words, everybody will accept the conditions; it would require that. So they may not, in fact, be as different from an organization that has a straight hierarchical structure but in which the top group actually operates as a group. I think the idea of *collegiality* at that level is a larger idea than the idea of structure. My guess is that we have overemphasized the importance of formal structure, and maybe it really doesn't make too much difference how you draw the thing on paper. The difference between organizations is how the people relate and how they actually function, which may not bear a whole lot of relationship to how the thing is sketched out on paper.

DISTEFANO: I have the sense that the "sketching out on paper" is what threatens a lot of the senior people in organizations who have worked very hard and long to reach the top of that pyramid. Let me push that one a bit further with the observation that over the past decade or so, it's been a trend among larger organizations and the private sector to develop offices of the chairman or offices of the president. The idea behind this trend, I think, is that the complexity of the jobs and the burdens of the jobs are such that they do require that kind of collectivity of effort, and yet they still maintain the form of pretty clear structure, with the chief in it. This may reflect what you just said, that there's a tendency to acknowledge the operating style but not wanting to violate the structures that give power and status to people. Do you have any reaction to that as an idea?

GREENLEAF: You can't make a society run without recognizing the element of striving for power, for status. Again, I think it gets back to the central issue, the temperament of the top leader, whether he or she is called chief or *primus*. If the temperament of that person is to want and feel more comfortable with the collegial relationship with other top people, that's the way it's going to work. If that person's temperament is to be an authoritarian "I am the boss" leader, that's the way it will work, no matter how you sketch it out.

What we are dealing with here is basically a question of the values that are held by a society. How this society works is going to be very largely influenced by how the culture evolves, its leadership, and what values are stressed by the institutions that are most concerned about the quality of our society. The question of inculcating values ultimately led me to a concern for churches and seminaries.

DISTEFANO: It may not be by chance that the three large businesses that you mentioned are not based in the United States.

GREENLEAF: No.

DISTEFANO: The culture here stresses individualism to such an extent that it readily reinforces the individual's ambitions and power needs.

GREENLEAF: Yes, and the power strivings within the churches and the seminaries are just as acute as they are in the hot, competitive business world. In other words, competition is all through our society.

I suspect that if my essay has accomplished anything (I have no way of judging what it did accomplish), it has helped smoke out into the open an issue that I think we swept under the rug, and that issue is, What do we really value and what qualities are important to nurture in people who may evolve as strong people in leadership positions?

DISTEFANO: You have alluded to the fact that the concern with values is why you turned your attention to seminaries and churches. Before you did that, however, you also wrote another essay, *Trustees as Servants*.[3] What got you interested enough in trustees and the director role that you evolved another essay on the servant theme, directed toward the trustee person?

GREENLEAF: I have written about this elsewhere, but I guess it partly came from my discovery that the typical corporation law (these are state laws) says, "This corporation shall be managed by the board of directors or trustees, usually not less than three." I took that language seriously and wondered what the framers of those laws meant and what they do, in fact, mean. Then I went back over my own AT&T experience and my burrowings into the history of that company and realized that the great builder who is credited with having piloted it through its development into a modern corporation, in the years between 1907 and 1920, was really only able to do that because behind him stood a very powerful trustee, J. P. Morgan, the elder. He took control of the company in 1907, wrested it away from the Bostonians who had built it, moved it to New York, and installed Theodore N. Vail as the chief. Vail proceeded to become a distinguished institution builder. Morgan was the primary institution builder, and Vail could not have existed without Morgan and would not have became the statesman that he ultimately did in that position without the nurturing of this extraordinary owner-trustee.

So I've reflected a lot on that one particular relationship, and my guess is that when Vail, the great builder, died in 1920, there was not a powerful trustee like Morgan to determine his successor, and as a consequence, the institution evolved his successor. So from that point on, the business was managed by able managers who could carry on the tradition but who were not supported by able trustees who would nurture them as statesmen, and this happened to be a business that could survive only if its top leaders were statesmen, able to adapt the business to changing social conditions as Machiavelli defined it, seeing the problems that these institutions deal with far enough in advance that they could take the initiative and adapt the business to the conditions before events forced their hands. Of course, events ultimately did force their hands, and AT&T was broken up on January 1, 1984. I don't believe that would have happened had AT&T been able to produce trustees after Morgan died, trustees who were as able, bright, strong, and foreseeing as he was.

My guess is that managers are not apt to develop those qualities. These are not the qualities that bring a manager through a succession of steps to the top of an institution. These are qualities that are best developed, most likely to develop, in people who are intensely interested in the institution, who basically control it, but who stand outside its day-to-day operation and have a perspective on it that active managers are very unlikely to have. That kind of thinking brought me to do the writing of the essay *Trustees as Servants*. It seems to me that this is a very neglected role in our society, and being an institution-bound society, we're suffering because this role has not been generally recognized or accepted by the active managers of any institution or by chief executives of institutions of all kinds. Managers and executives of businesses, churches, universities, and foundations evolve a strategy to manage their trustees rather than the other way round.

DISTEFANO: And there might be an unwitting complicity in the sense that many of the trustees are themselves managers, who you just described as not being temperamentally suited to that role.

GREENLEAF: Yes, very unlikely that they would be.

DISTEFANO: That perhaps answers a subsequent question. My observation is that the essay *Trustees as Servants* has received more acclaim among nonprofit organizations than private sector institutions that have trustees who are not managers. I hadn't thought about that connection. Is that an observation that has held in your experience with the people who have corresponded with you about that essay, that it has been more widely discussed, more openly received by trustees of nonprofit organizations?

GREENLEAF: As a kind of intellectual discussion, yes. In the period since that essay came into circulation, I have gradually withdrawn from active participation. My knowledge on this is limited, but the most effective changes that I know about have been in business, where business boards have attempted to move into a very different relationship to the operation of the institution. They have not talked about this as such, but I had the uneasy feeling that most of the circulation of that pamphlet among nonprofit boards was in the category of what I will call "titillation" rather than serious engagement with the idea.

I am close to one Quaker institution in this area where the trustees threw the chairman out because he pushed that idea at them too hard. They just didn't want to be disturbed that much, so their reaction was to throw the chairman out and install a very compliant, easygoing kind of a chairman. I have mixed feelings about what has been accomplished as a result of that essay.

DISTEFANO: It is interesting, though, that you comment that the places where it seems to have made a difference have been business organizations.

GREENLEAF: I'm thinking of two businesses. I don't want to name them here, but they are large businesses that really made an effort to change the relationship between the board and the chief and put the board in a much stronger position.

DISTEFANO: I have seen some of that in other organizations, but those changes seem to have been forced more by the climate of litigation that makes the board members more responsible rather than a notion that the role itself should be more directly involved with leading the organization.

GREENLEAF: Yes, in this period, the liability factor has been operating—suing for malfeasance. The consciousness of that liability has risen, and there has been a tendency for institutions to take out liability insurance on their directors to protect them against personal suits. That's been a factor that has perked them up a bit, but the two businesses that I am thinking about did not do it for that reason. One learned from the other. One took the lead and took steps to develop the board, and a member of that board who was the head of an equally large company watched it operate and decided he would do the same with his own board, and he did.

DISTEFANO: It would be an example of interlocking directors' producing useful results.

GREENLEAF: Sure. Both of these chief executives have retired, and I am not sure that these relationships with the board have survived. It happened because first one and then the other really bought the idea that this was a better way to run a business. It would make for a stronger institution.

DISTEFANO: The irony is that it takes a chief executive officer who is self-confident and very secure to embrace that idea.

GREENLEAF: Yes, and both were chairmen of the directors. I

have very deep feelings on this. I think the root of this question is *theological* in the sense that directorship ought to come out of a sense of concern and of responsibility, motives that most directors, in my experience, simply do not feel and do not want to feel. In other words, the trustees of the Quaker institution who threw out their chairman just didn't want to accept the kind of personal responsibility that was being pushed on them by this kind of thinking. So they insisted on having a chairman who wouldn't disturb them with it, and they were happier with that arrangement.

This gets back to the question of how our society views the question of responsibility for our institutions. I suspect that far too many trustees and directors hold those positions for a combination of reasons: prestige, interest, titillation (just being involved superficially), and being in the know and that there is a very low feeling of responsibility for the institution—the kind of feeling that Morgan had back in the early part of the century. It seems to me that caring for the institutions one controls is what trusteeship is all about. Trustees are a group of people who not only legally control but also care very intensely about the quality of the institution and therefore devote their time and energy to take the risks that caring always entails, no matter what its context.

DISTEFANO: That gets me to business schools, institutions in our society that have, in the past twenty or thirty years, prepared more and more of the senior executives. To my knowledge, schools of business pay very little attention to the trustee role. The focus is on the functioning of the executive group, the functional heads in the business organization, and the general managers in the business organization. That training reinforces the notion that these are the people responsible. It is not too surprising that the people who emerge out of that kind of training don't pay much attention to the trustee role and assume that their job is to manage their trustees and manage their directors. Do you see the possibility that consciousness can be raised inside business schools, or is it your thinking that semi-naries really are the places where that can be best done?

GREENLEAF: I don't want to denigrate the role of management. It is a terribly important role; we need lots of people in that role, and I suspect that the development of managers is enough of a responsibility for the present business schools. Thinking about trusteeship in the sense that I've been viewing it is a very different kind of thinking. I've never wanted to manage, never in my AT&T experience. I had a strategy to avoid getting trapped into a managerial job because it's not in my tempera-ment to do that. I respect people who can do it, and I want them to be very good at doing it, but I am not one of them.

Now, trusteeship is a very different kind of role from that of a good manager. A trustee might not be any good as a manager, and I think someone else should develop the theory of that role and set up the facilities for training trustees, particularly the chairpersons of trustees. My guess is that it is not realistic to ex-pect the business schools to do that. I'd rather they did well what they are now doing.

DISTEFANO: Perhaps the role business schools might assume is one of conditioning the future managers to the differences that you are talking about so that at least they don't fight the trustee role that you envision.

GREENLEAF: Yes. If we have the facilities we ought to have for finding, nurturing, and developing trustees, it might be that we wouldn't make many managers trustees. Maybe some have the flexibility to put on another hat and look at this in quite an-other way, but the managers that I've seen in trustees' spots tended to continue to think like managers. They became as-sertive and insert managerial thinking where there ought to be trustee thinking.

We may not need as many trustees as we have. There's no reason for boards being as large as they are. Harvard University functions with a corporation of seven, which includes the president. The Quaker organization that I mentioned has a board of sixty, and obviously they can't involve those people in any depth. When they tried, the thing blew up on them. I've been very close to that. I know the chairman very well; he really took his lumps on that, and this is one of my best examples of how the effort to transform the thinking of a board will backfire when you have a situation that really can't be transformed. With a board of sixty, with people who are spread all over the country and can meet only once a year, if that often, people are just not going to take that kind of responsibility. It's not realistic to expect they would. So I think there's a lot more that needs to be thought on this subject. What I did was just try to open this can of worms so that more people will start to think about it.

DISTEFANO: It seems to me that you moved your own thinking to the next stage, contemplating which institutions might shape this notion of trusteeship and the values that define the roles of concern for the quality of institutions, and that's what I want to talk about next. In your earlier conversations about the connections between your essays *The Servant as Leader* and *The Institution as Servant,* you talked about the transition in modern society to large institutions mediating much of the caring in the society, and you said that there wasn't a tradition of helping people manage the leadership that comes in an institutional context, as opposed to individuals operating alone. It seems to me that what you are sketching is a challenge to seminaries to develop a notion of a theology of institutions—a phrase that I have heard you use before. Could you talk a little bit about what that means to you?

GREENLEAF: Yes, I mentioned earlier that when the Constitution of the United States was written, we were viewed as a nation of individuals. There were very few institutions and corporations. They practically didn't exist, and they're not mentioned in the Constitution, but the corporations get their legal status under the Constitution by the willingness of the courts to construe them as persons and bring them under the constitutional protections and obligations that are described for people. Our seminaries, largely based on events in biblical times, have a similar limitation in that these traditions are only concerned with individuals, relations of one individual to another. Seminaries have not yet accepted that the emergence of institutions in the past hundred years or so has created a different kind of society with concerns not addressed by a theology of individuals. Furthermore, seminaries are lacking in resources of information whereby they can enlarge theology to include not only individuals, who are still important, but also institutions, which have more to do with individual lives now. I suspect that the move into a theology of institutions, the move toward developing it into seminaries, will require of the seminaries that they create laboratories in which the basic knowledge that they need can emerge.

I have suggested that seminaries take the initiative to establish "institutes of chairing," institutes in which chairpersons of trustees and directors of all kinds of institutions will be prepared for a much more demanding, much more exacting role than most chairpersons now accept. It's a role that is clothed with much greater and more exciting opportunity than is within the awareness or acceptance of most chairpersons.

This will mean that the seminary will become quite a different place. It will become not only a place where scholars dig into books and from them learn what they want for developing their theology but also a place where scholars will be involved in the experience of preparing these key people, the trustee chairpersons, for a much more demanding and critical role. At least, that's my speculation how I see the role of seminaries evolving.

DISTEFANO: That kind of role provides a unique opportunity for seminaries, something that neither they nor other institutions are doing. At the same time, it seems to me that as you sketch out the demands for servant-leadership on the part of managers in large institutions, as distinct from trustees, there is an equally important role to develop a theology of institutions for the managers too, because they are also in positions that have the potential for greater service, but in a managerial role. Do you see it as possible for some leaders to take on both of these demands, and do you see a logic for starting with trustees or starting with how to help significant leaders in big institutions?

GREENLEAF: I have a theory that this might be accomplished. In other words, our present facility for training managers for the specific requirements of managerial jobs is probably as good as with any other professional group. But the raising of the level of caring of our institutions is not likely to emerge out of that preparation, and it's probably not realistic to expect that our present institutions, principally our business schools, that prepare managers for their tasks are likely to be able to take on the added burden of doing what theological schools can do best. My way of thinking about problems like this is not to try to think their implications all the way through but rather to find a place to start in the right direction and then learn as one's experience unfolds how to take the next steps.

My guess is that if a school of theology could start by setting up to train persons for the chairperson's role and if it did a good job with a given chairperson, that chairperson could then see to it that this dimension of caring was enlarged in the perceptions of the managers of the institution over which he or she were to preside. This view of life, of relationship, could be conveyed into the work of the world almost entirely through the leadership efforts of chairpersons. That may be an oversimplification, but I believe that if we started down the road of seminaries training chairpersons, we will see more clearly what next step we should take. When little or nothing is being done about this, we cannot see those further steps.

I realize how radical a move it would be for seminaries to take on this kind of role, and I suspect that it will be resisted stoutly. I have the feeling that maybe this is not an idea that can be expected to originate in the seminaries, and I am hopeful that some foundation will pick it up and take the initiative to go to a seminary and say, "Here is a role that we think you could play, one that we believe would enormously enrich your seminary if you took it on and played it well. And we will pay for it if you will take it on." Now that might get it done. But I doubt whether it will be possible to move this as an idea to seminaries as they are now, to expect that they will go to foundations with a grant request to do this.

DISTEFANO: You talked about seminaries as being the kinds of institutions that shape the churches, and the churches then shape individuals. Foundations also are tertiary institutions that shape universities, and now you are suggesting that they also shape seminaries. It strikes me that while you've turned your attention to writing about seminaries for the reasons that you've sketched in the past few minutes, you haven't published anything with respect to foundations having the potential for servant-leadership. What you are suggesting now is that they need to think about that role as well, because seminaries are unlikely to take this on on their own. Does that, then, beg the question a bit, saying that we now need to think about foundations, and ultimately the trustees of foundations, in the context of the servant theme?

GREENLEAF: It takes a lot more brainwork and a lot more risk taking for the foundation to make the decision, "This is what ought to be done, and this is the institution that ought to be doing it. We will go to them with the money and see if we can persuade them to do it." The problem of making that decision in foundations is that foundations, as I know them, generally do not have boards of trustees who will back up that kind of initiative. They would rather take the more comfortable, risk-free route of simply entertaining grant requests, of which they have plenty.

In other words, they don't have trouble giving away their money. There are legions of needy nonprofit institutions that are ready to come to foundations with requests for grants to do things that these grant applicants are accustomed to doing and are comfortable doing, and this is enough to keep the foundations busy and occupy their funds unless a trustee with a lot of stiffness in his or her backbone is willing to take the risk to go the other route.

DISTEFANO: There is a certain irony here, I think, because you use the expression of trustees of foundations backing this kind of shift in strategy of foundations. If one reads your *Trustee as Servant* essay with these thoughts in mind, one could imagine that it's more appropriate that *trustees* of foundations should demand these kinds of behavior from the foundation executives, as opposed to simply backing it from another idea coming from a source like your own. Foundations have underwritten your work and the publishing of your work, and perhaps some of them may want it back, but that may be unfair. Can you comment on that?

GREENLEAF: No, as I see it from the really detached "ivory tower" position that I now occupy, sitting here in the quiet of my study, thinking about and staying out of the hurly-burly of the world, the problem of our society is no different from what the problems of societies have generally been—not always, but generally. And that is that the abler, stronger people do not take enough responsibility. They have plenty of time for useless activity, and what I've been suggesting right from the start of writing *The Servant as Leader* is that the abler, stronger people in our society must work a whole lot harder and that by doing so, they will have more fun. They will get greater enjoyment out of life by doing that than by doing what most of them now do. Most now do some good works, sort of with their left hand, but they simply entertain themselves with most of their time, energy, and resources, which is what the populace in general does.

We've got to develop an ethic that says that the abler, stronger people must take a lot more responsibility. At the time of the founding of this country, we had it—an extraordinary group, a very strong and able people, who worked very hard to put this society together, at first instance. It has happened in other periods of history; it happened in ancient Greece under the influence of Solon, who put democracy together and gave the Greeks their initial charge of spirit. It hasn't happened very often, but when it does happen, great things ensue, and I think they could ensue now if somehow we could release the spirit of the abler and stronger people.

DISTEFANO: In a sense, that's what you are suggesting seminaries can help do, by addressing the special needs of the chairpersons.

GREENLEAF: Yes, it seems to me that it's fundamentally a theological issue that has to do with the human spirit and how it is nurtured, but it is a different way of acting responsibly with respect to that opportunity than seminaries are now accustomed to, and they may not have the people who have the starch in them to do this. It will take quite a push to make this change.

DISTEFANO: Bob, you've talked about seminaries, and earlier you referred to Catholic sisters as responding to your first essay, *The Servant as Leader*. Could you recount for us your first contact with people from Alverno College and tell us a bit about that part of your experience? It seems to have had the effect of crystallizing some of your thinking and propelling you these past few years to the topic of nurturing the human spirit, so it will be interesting to hear your perspectives on your early meetings at Alverno.

GREENLEAF: In my work at AT&T, during the later years, I took the initiative to get started in what has come to be known as assessment centers. These used a new novel way of making judgments about people that gives a better basis for avoiding the accusations of favoritism than almost any other process that involves subjective judgments.

A book had been published about assessment work that was dedicated by the authors to me. I had been long retired from AT&T when sisters from the Sisters of Saint Francis, based in Milwaukee, picked up this book and decided that they wanted their college to use this assessment approach. They had some problems as an order, as all institutions have, particularly Catholic institutions in this post–Vatican II period and most particularly Catholic women's religious orders. They thought I could address those problems. They called and asked if I would be willing to come and speak to them. "Well," I said, "the idea's intriguing, but I don't know anything about your problems." They said, "If you would be interested in doing it, we will come and tell you what they are." So I said, "Sure, come along." Several sisters came and spent three or four days in our area, and we had many conversations. I got a liberal education into the operation and problems of Catholic women's religious orders. It was a wholly new field to me, and I don't believe I'd ever known a Catholic sister so well before that time.

The sisters invited me to make a presentation the following summer to a meeting of their entire order, which convened only once every ten years. Fourteen hundred nuns were to meet in Milwaukee. I went out the next summer and made my talk. I was quite well received, and it was quite an experience to talk to fourteen hundred nuns in a big circus tent. I had never seen that many nuns together before.

During that visit, I met the president of the college, Sister Joel Read. We got well acquainted on this trip, and I became interested in what she was trying to do with Alverno College, which was at the time in the early throes of a shift to concern for what the faculty called competence-based education. In other words, they were trying to see to it that every woman who graduated from that place left with a marketable skill of some kind. They now have a number of channels of preparation, including some of the conventional ones like nursing. But they give a good liberal arts education in conjunction with that, and they've been very successful with it. Alverno is one of the few women's colleges that has in recent years had a constantly expanding enrollment. So it is attractive to students to get this kind of a start in life. Alverno has received a lot of notice for it. Faculty members are on conference programs all the time telling about how they do what they do and how they got to where they are. It's been a very rocky course, lots of bumps on the way to get this college converted from a rather conceptional, conservative women's Catholic college to a very modern and up-to-date institution.

I am very grateful for that contact. I hope some day to write up this story as an example of how a determined servant-leader, who commits herself or himself to an institution, can, by staying with it, turn the institution around and do something that is successful in contemporary terms. It is also what the leaders of many institutions would like to do to bring their institution prudently from where it is to a more viable contemporary form.

DISTEFANO: I would like to talk about how you prepared yourself for your work after retirement. You have written about the seminal idea of preparing for old age, which you got from Elmer Davis. What kinds of things did you do during your forties and fifties before you retired at AT&T, activities that were different from what you might have done if you hadn't read Davis?

GREENLEAF: When I was about forty, I read an article by Elmer Davis, who was a great radio commentator of that day. He had a heart attack in his sixties, which had slowed him down and made him quite reflective, as such things often do. One article of his that I read was titled "The Uses of Old People." In this article, Davis made the point that there are things that need to be done that are best done by old people—partly because they have the greater perspective of experience but also, or maybe largely, because some of these necessary things are too risky for people early or even in midcareer and are best done by old people who have already won all the chips they're going to win.

That suggested to me that I begin to prepare then, at about age forty, for a useful old age. This was a seminal idea. And over the next twenty years, I used all the spare moments that I could devote to that preparation. I was attentive to my family. I devoted plenty of time to relaxation. I devoted time to my job, and I think I was better on my job because of the effort, but I had no time for the usual time-using diversions. When I retired at age sixty, I was then free to do some of the things for which I had prepared myself.

During that period of twenty years, I did quite a bit of reading. I am a slow reader, and I am not a great reader. Most of what I read is what I will call serious reading. I don't go in for reading that just kills time.

But I think the greatest influence on me came from people. After the inspiration that Davis gave me, I made a more conscious effort to relate to people who might expand my horizons, and there were several very unusual relationships. I don't know if I can recall all of them, but I will name a few. They were people who I met in various relationships and decided, "Here's a person I really want to get to know, to learn what I can from this person."

Along the way, I met an unusual man by the name of John Lovejoy Elliott, who was then the senior leader of the Ethical Cultural Society in New York. He was quite old when I met him, and I knew him only a few years before he died. But John was a man with an extraordinary servant nature. Around 1940, I think, he walked into my office and introduced himself. He said that there was a problem of helping the refugees from Nazi Germany, particularly the professional people who were fleeing, and that there were not sufficient resources to give these people help. He was in the process of organizing a committee, the Good Neighbor Committee. Eleanor Roosevelt, the wife of the president, was its chairperson, and John was its president. He had come to me to ask me to be an incorporator and to serve as treasurer.

He had gone down to Philadelphia to talk to Clarence Pickett, who was the executive secretary of the American Friends Service Committee at that time. (Clarence was another extraordinary man, although I never developed a close relationship with him.) John went to Clarence and said that he was going to organize this committee and asked if there were, in New York, "a live Quaker who would work with me on it." John added, "I know plenty of dead Quakers who are alive in the flesh, but I don't want any of them." Clarence named me, probably partly because I was young and maybe a little more alive than some of the aged ones. Anyway, this was his introduction to me, and he sold me on the idea that I should join with him on this venture.

This was a very interesting occupation for a short number of years. It didn't last very long, and it didn't need to, because ultimately, all of the refugees had made whatever adjustment they were going to be able to make. But in the course of it, I got very well acquainted with John Elliott and his history and what had led him to be the kind of "cause man" that he was and the starter of useful work. This left a very deep impression on me, also because Eleanor Roosevelt was the chair of the committee. I got acquainted with her at a meeting at Hyde Park, where I served with her group, which met there.

The second person, whom I met at another meeting somewhere, was named Gerald Heard. Gerald was older than John. (All these people have since died.) Gerald was an Irishman, but he grew up in England. He had a tremendous mind and a photographic memory. To the extent that he had a profession, he was a historian. Although he really didn't have credentials, he wrote quite a bit; most of his writing was quite obtuse and hard to read. But he was a great man to know. I found him to be a lonely man, and I think he welcomed my interest in him. Gerald led me into reading widely in the field of religion. I'd never done that before. In fact, Gerald was the one who had the greatest influence on my reading.

A third person was a doctor by the name of William Wolfe in New York. Again, I met this man when he was quite old; I think he was seventy-five and semiretired. He was a man of small physical stature but a brilliant man with a wide-ranging mind and an extraordinary physician. He was one of the early endocrinologists. He wrote the first medical textbook on endocrinology and taught the subject in medical schools. Along the way, he had gone to Vienna and got himself analyzed by Freud. In his later years, he was more of a psychiatrist than he was an internist. We called him Uncle Bill; we visited him, and he visited in our home. We spent a lot of time with him.

These are examples of ways that I spent my time when I met a person like these three I've named: like John Elliott, Gerald Heard, and Uncle Bill Wolfe. I made it a point to relate to them as closely as they would find congenial, and all three of them found it congenial. I spent a great deal of time with them, and to the extent that I've stretched out my horizons, I think I did it more in the company of people like these than I did by reading. Although I also read, I think that what I was reading meant more to me because I could bounce around ideas with people like the three that I have named.

DISTEFANO: You also read poetry. You read biographies. Was that part of your earlier tradition, your earlier training?

GREENLEAF: I think I got my interest in poetry from my father. He read poetry and had a good memory; he quoted poetry often. I think that he had more influence on my poetry interest than on anything else I can recall. I've read some biographies, mostly when I encounter a biography of someone whose life was very significant, such as Justice Oliver Wendell Holmes.

DISTEFANO: What other kinds of activities did you engage in during this period of preparing for old age?

GREENLEAF: Well, I made an effort to engage in activities that were current at that time. I can recall two of those. One was the book of Alfred Korzybski in the field that he called general semantics. First, I attended a series of evening seminars in New York, and then I got acquainted with his institute up in Lakeville, Connecticut. I never really related to him personally. He was not my style of fellow. I think there's probably a residue from my having made a foray into that field, but it is not very clear what it is. I have a feeling that we don't do anything that doesn't leave a permanent residue, but we don't always know what that is.

In 1947, I got acquainted with the work of a refugee scholar by the name of Kurt Lewin. Lewin was an experimental psychologist who came over in the escape from Germany in the late 1930s. He was at the University of Iowa in the field of child psychology, and then he got picked up by one of the war agencies. At the close of the war, he decided to set up what he called the Research Center in Group Dynamics, which he established at MIT. Lewin was a very rigorous experimental psychologist, and shortly after the end of the war, he announced that he would hold the first training session to try to impart to people what he had collected on the subject of group leadership.

I got acquainted with this because of my work at AT&T. We were working with a consultant, a psychologist at Yale by the name of Carl Hovland. I guess he was chairman of the department at that time. Carl knew about this upcoming work of Lewin's and persuaded me to enroll in this first session, which was held in the summer of 1947 at a little academy up in Bethel, Maine. Lewin, unfortunately, died of sudden heart attack in the spring of 1947, so I never met him, although I read quite a bit of what he wrote.

The session was carried on by his students and associates. I've often felt that the world would be different if Lewin had lived and had headed that session himself, because his students took off into what was really a cultist movement that would have been anathema to Lewin, from all I know of him. The whole sensitivity activity really started there, in the summer of 1947, and I was deeply involved in it.

This was a three-week marathon, a very intensive thing. A young instructor from Columbia University's Teachers College, named Kenneth Harold, was in my small group. We got well acquainted and decided that when we got back to New York, we would see if we couldn't try leading one of these things ourselves. The following winter of 1947–1948, that's exactly what we did. I got the New York Adult Education Society to sponsor this, and the organizers put together a group that really was a group to end all groups! It was a very odd and interesting assortment of people. It contained a couple of psychiatrists, a couple of lawyers, and a little bit of everything in a series of eight long evening meetings (from about seven to ten P.M.). Ken and I jointly chaired this thing. At the end, I decided that this was enough for me. I would not have anything more to do with it. Ken went ahead and made a career in the sensitivity movement and made quite a name for himself.

We had one very interesting experience. We had a big round table. There were twenty-two of us around this big round table, and Ken sat on one side and I sat on the other side. Ostensibly we were co-leaders of this affair, but we had worked it out that at alternate meetings, one or the other of us would really be in charge in case something got out of hand. He drew the first meeting, and I drew the second.

At the second meeting, one of our psychiatrists had seen one too many patients that day. He walked in through the door talking wildly and sat down at the table. I looked across the table at Ken, and he was kind of grinning like the Cheshire cat, that this was mine, I ought to handle this one. So this was one of the most interesting evenings I've ever experienced. We devoted three hours to putting this fellow back together, and we succeeded. It was quite an undertaking, because I got everybody into the act without saying so. They accepted that this was the job we had to do, and we did it. For years afterward, when I would meet one of these people on the street, he would say, "Do you remember that night we put that fellow together?" And I would reply, "I sure do. I remember it vividly to this day." That was an experiment of sorts, and I think a valuable one, and I've had two occasions since to reassemble a psychiatrist who came unstuck.

Well, those are the kinds of things that happened.

DISTEFANO: Bob, I am reflecting on the forays into general semantics and sensitivity training and on where that led. The essence of these activities is the notion of increasing your awareness of what's going on. Certainly, through semantics, you understand a lot more about meanings and about symbols, and through the sensitivity training, you increase your ability to understand other people. From both of those elements, I can see quite easily moving to some of the core ideas in the servant-as-leader theme. I am also struck by the thought that much of your work at AT&T in developing other managers required similar kinds of forays, whether it was the active listening course that you organized or the use of literature to study decision making. All these experiences provided grist for this servant-as-leader mill. Were you conscious at the time of these elements' being linked together and giving you some unity that you might eventually write about?

GREENLEAF: No, not really. I've got a pretty good filing system in my head, and I mostly just file away important ideas. At the time, I had no notion that I would ever set out to be a synthesizer. I never had a master plan that said, here is where I'm going to wind up and these are the things I will do to get there. All I got from Elmer Davis was just "prepare yourself," and I just prepared myself the way you would keep your muscles in tone. You never know what you will use your muscles for, but you keep working on them so that they will be there when you need them, and that's really what I did.

DISTEFANO: That leads into a question about the degree of autobiographical influence in these essays. You've had a series of experiences that parallel the three major themes that you've addressed in your essays, and even though in those essays you used many rich examples of other people operating, I wonder if you are conscious of parallels that might exist in your own life, in your own experiences, and the themes that you then wrote about.

GREENLEAF: It's a little difficult to sort this all out, but yes, I think of my life as being pretty much of a piece that evolved. I didn't have a master plan as a young man, and I sort of took things as they came. At age sixty, when I retired from AT&T, I just took opportunities as they became available. I tried to remain open to things that were available on the outside of the business. I took advantage of opportunities within the business not only to develop myself but also to accomplish things that hadn't been accomplished before.

I took the advice of my old professor to get inside of a big institution and to be one who responded to the criticisms. I listened to the criticisms, and when I found an opportunity to do something about one of them, I did it. I was not seen within the business as a reformer. As a matter of fact, if I had announced my plan at the outset, I probably wouldn't have been hired, and if I had let it be known very early in my career, I probably would have been fired.

I piloted my life so as to be useful to the business, to develop myself, and to respond to its critics in a constructive way. So it's all autobiographical. Everything I've been into is autobiographical. I've never thought of myself as a writer. I have no aspiration to just let my imagination run and produce something that would sell. I don't think that I have the gift to do it or the inclination to cultivate that gift if I did have it. I don't think anything in my life has been detached from the idea of wanting to serve, which, as I said, I got from my father when I was very young.

DISTEFANO: Well, these conversations have been useful for me because in reading the essays, the links to your direct personal experience are not as clear. You tend to use examples from history that are removed from your direct personal experience in the writing, and that leaves many people curious about the nature of the man who has written these interesting, provocative ideas.

The other element that I wanted to mention has to do with the form of the essays. It seems to me that you write the essays in similar ways. In each essay, there are elements that might be freestanding, that might be discreet subthemes that get articulated and refined, but don't necessarily get fully integrated and synthesized until the reader brings his own perspective to the essays. Have you been conscious of that as part of your writing style and the form that these essays have taken?

GREENLEAF: Well, I have been conscious of the need for brevity. I think there are too many words in print, and so I've tried to package these things in few enough pages that people who must read on the run might make use of them. I am aware that someone who was of a different temperament could make a book out of either of these three pamphlets, each of which runs to less than forty pages.

I don't know that I consciously said, "I will stop here and let the reader supply the rest," but I did consciously *not* write for an uninformed audience. In all my experience with people, both in AT&T and other places where I would occasionally give talks, I was talking to experienced, seasoned people. This is the way I learned to communicate, so when I sat down to compose the essays, I simply wrote in a familiar style of communicating. I just didn't know any other way to write.

DISTEFANO: Bob, I'd like to thank you personally, and also for legions of students, businesspeople, and trustees that I know who have read your work and who have expressed that the work affected them in the very way you've been talking about here. Many people who've felt nurtured by your writing have not had the rare, privileged opportunity that I and others have had to experience this directly with you and to say, "Thank you!" So in closing this interview, I will take the opportunity to do that for them.

GREENLEAF: Thank you, Joe.

NOTES

INTRODUCTION

1 Robert K. Greenleaf, *The Servant as Leader* (Indianapolis, Ind.: Robert K. Greenleaf Center for Servant-Leadership, 1970), p. 7.

2 Robert K. Greenleaf, *Spirituality as Leadership* (Indianapolis, Ind.: Robert K. Greenleaf Center for Servant-Leadership, 1988), p. 1.

PART ONE

1 For a discussion of Erik Erikson's thinking on developmental crises available when Greenleaf wrote *The Ethic of Strength,* see Erik H. Erikson, *Young Man Luther: A Study in Psychoanalysis and History* (New York: Norton, 1962).

2 Gerald Heard was a personal friend of Robert and Esther Greenleaf. He wrote in the area of natural theology, including the essay *Is God Evident?* (New York: HarperCollins, 1948) and several books, including *Is God in History?* (New York: HarperCollins, 1950). Greenleaf credits Heard with sparking his interest in reading theology.

3 William Wordsworth, "The Happy Warrior," in *The Complete Poetical Works of William Wordsworth* (Boston: Houghton Mifflin, 1904), p. 341.

4 Ralph Waldo Emerson, "On Self-Reliance," in *The Essays of Ralph Waldo Emerson: The First Series and the Second Series* (Norwalk, Conn.: The Easton Press, 1841 and 1844), p. 65.

5 Herbert Spencer (1820–1903) was a wide-ranging thinker who wrote important works on sociology, ethics, psychology, and science.

6 Adelbert Ames, *Visual Perception and the Rotating Trapezoidal Window* (Washington, D.C.: American Psychological Association, 1951).

373

7   Walker Winslow, *The Menninger Story* (New York: Doubleday, 1956), p. 79.
8   Josh Billings [Henry Wheeler Shaw], "Proverb," in *The Complete Works of Josh Billings,* ed. Henry Wheeler Shaw (New York: Dillingham, 1874).
9   Emerson, "On Self-Reliance," p. 59.
10 Benjamin N. Cardozo, *Nature of the Judicial Process* (New Haven, Conn.: Yale University Press, 1921), pp. 167–170.
11 Vilhjalmur Stefansson, *Life with the Eskimo* (Norwood, Mass.: Norwood Press, 1913), pp. 75–79.
12 Winslow, *The Menninger Story,* p. 50.
13 Jean-Jacques Rousseau, *Emile or On Education,* Introduction, translation, and notes by Allan Bloom. (New York: Basic Books, 1963, originally published 1762), p. 167.
14 Ralph Waldo Emerson, "The Uses of Great Men," in *The Complete Works of Ralph Waldo Emerson,* vol. 4 (Boston: Houghton Mifflin, 1904), p. 35.
15 Karl Stern, *The Pillar of Fire* (Orlando, Fla.: Harcourt Brace Jovanovich, 1951), pp. 78–80.
16 Paul W. Pruyser, "The Idea of Destiny," *The Hibbert Journal,* 1954, 57, p. 381.
17 Luke 11:38–42 (Revised Standard Version).
18 Exod. 18:13–27 (Revised Standard Version).
19 Walt Whitman, "Song of the Open Road," in *Leaves of Grass with Autobiography* (Philadelphia: Sherman, 1900), p. 177.
20 Dean Inge, *The Things That Remain* (New York: HarperCollins, 1958), p. 104.
21 Whitman, "Song of the Open Road," p. 179.

PART TWO

1   Cardozo, *Nature of the Judicial Process,* p. 70.
2   Ralph Waldo Emerson, "Works and Days," in *The Complete Works of Ralph Waldo Emerson,* vol. 7 (Boston: Houghton Mifflin, 1904), p. 166.
3   Emerson, "Uses of Great Men," p. 35.
4   Jawaharlal Nehru, *An Autobiography* (London: John Lane the Bodley Head, 1936), p. 180.
5   Quoted in Robert K. Greenleaf, *Servant Leadership: A Journey*

into the Nature of Legitimate Power and Greatness (Mahwah, N.J.: Paulist Press, 1977), p. 133.

6 For a full discussion of Alfred Sloan's philosophy of employee incentives, see Alfred Sloan, *My Years with General Motors,* ed. John McDonald with Catherine Stevens (New York: Doubleday, 1964), pp. 407–428.

7 Lord Acton [John Emerich Edward Dalberg], letter to Bishop Mandell Creighton, April 5, 1887. Lord Acton's famous comment was often quoted by Greenleaf, including a reference in his book *Servant Leadership.*

8 Zech. 4:6 (Revised Standard Version).

9 Charles Beard's summary of history is related by former student George S. Counts in "Charles Beard: The Public Man," in *Charles A. Beard: An Appraisal,* ed. Howard K. Beals (Lexington: University of Kentucky Press, 1954), pp. 251–252.

10 Inge, *The Things That Remain.*

11 In 1979, Greenleaf published *The Teacher as Servant* (Mahwah, N.J.: Paulist Press), in which he told the story of a fictional college campus where young people who wished to nurture their servant tendencies committed themselves to a community of seekers and engaged in both practical and academic studies.

12 Irving Lee, *Language Habits in Human Affairs: An Introduction to General Semantics* (New York: Harper, 1941), p. 48.

13 Melvin Anshen, "Procedure for 'Coercing' Agreement," *Harvard Business Review,* 1954, 32(1), p. 91.

14 *Hamlet,* act 3, scene 1.

15 Abraham Lincoln made the remark in his "house divided" speech, given on June 18, 1858, at Springfield, Illinois, to the closing session of the Republican Convention. See *The Complete Works of Abraham Lincoln* (New York: Century, 1894), p. 240.

16 Committee on Research, Amos Tuck School of Administration and Finance, Dartmouth College, *Manual on Research and Reports* (New York: McGraw-Hill), 1937.

17 Rousseau, *Emile or On Education,* p. 167.

18 The actual quote is "If you are King, you are King." *The King and I,* book and lyrics by Oscar Hammerstein II (New York: Random House, 1951), p. 145.

19 Thomas Jefferson, "Autobiography," *The Complete Jefferson,* ed. Saul K. Papover (New York: Duell Sloan & Pearce, 1943), pp. 928, 1120, 1143–1144.

20 Robert K. Greenleaf, *Life's Choices and Markers* (Indianapolis, Ind.: Robert K. Greenleaf Center for Servant-Leadership, 1986).

21 Prov. 29:18 (Revised Standard Version).

22 John Brooks, *Telephone: The First Hundred Years* (New York: HarperCollins, 1975).

23 Brooks, *Telephone,* pp. 136–137.

24 Alvin Von Auw, *Heritage and Destiny: Reflections on the Bell System in Transition* (New York: Praeger, 1983).

25 This quote from Machiavelli's *Prince* (1640) is one of Greenleaf's favorite to illustrate the importance of foresight by a leader. The actual quote is "Even as falls it out in matters of state: for by knowing it aloofe off (which is given only to a wise man to do) the mischiefs that then spring up are quickly helped; but when, for not having been perceived, they are suffered to increase, so that every one sees them; there is then no cure for them." Niccolò Machiavelli, *The Prince* (Menston, England: Scholar Press, 1969), p. 45.

26 John Milton, Sonnet xix, "When I consider how my light is spent," in *The Complete Poetical Works of John Milton* (Boston: Houghton Mifflin, 1965), p. 189.

PART THREE

1 John W. Gardner, "The Antileadership Vaccine," *Annual Report of the Carnegie Corporation of New York* (New York: Carnegie Corporation), pp. 3, 12.

2 Inge, *The Things That Remain.*

3 John Woolman, *The Journal of John Woolman,* ed. Janet Whitney (Washington, D.C.: Regnery, 1950).

4 Daniel Burnham, attributed. This quote is now doubted. See Henry M. Saylor, "Make No Little Plans: Daniel Burnham Thought It But Did He Say It?" *Journal of the American Institute of Architects,* 1957, 27, p. 3.

5 Emerson, "On Self-Reliance," p. 66.

6 Alfred North Whitehead, *Process and Reality: An Essay in Cosmology* (New York: The Free Press, 1976), p. 13.

7 Percy Bridgman, *Science and the Mind,* ed. Gerald Holton

(Freeport, N.Y.: Books for the Libraries Press, 1971).

8 The complete quote is

> O Divine Master, grant that I may not so much seek
> To be consoled as to console;
> To be understood as to understand;
> To be loved as to love.

From Maria Stillo, *The Peace of St. Francis* (New York: Hawthorn Books, 1962), p. 285.

9 Edna St. Vincent Millay, "First Fig," in *A Few Figs from Thistles: Collected Lyrics of St. Vincent Millay* (New York: HarperCollins, 1939), p. 127.

10 Cardozo, *Nature of the Judicial Process,* pp. 169–170.

11 Wordsworth, "The Happy Warrior," p. 341.

12 Machiavelli, *The Prince,* p. 45.

13 Robert Browning, "Andrea del Sarto," in *The Poetry of Robert Browning,* ed. Stopford A. Brooke (New York: Crowell, 1902), p. 157.

14 William Blake, "The Marriage of Heaven and Hell," in *The Poems of William Blake,* ed. W. H. Stevenson (New York: Norton, 1971), p. 144.

15 Gardner, *On Leadership.*

16 Albert Camus, quoted by Robert Greenleaf in "On Being a Seeker in the late Twentieth Century," *Friends Journal,* 1975, 21(15), p. 53.

17 Robert K. Greenleaf, *Leadership in a Bureaucratic Society* (Indianapolis, Ind.: Robert K. Greenleaf Center for Servant-Leadership, 1966).

18 B. D. Napier, "Campus Reaction," *Stanford Daily,* Feb. 23, 1967, p. 1.

19 Exod. 18:13–27 (Revised Standard Version).

20 Daniel Burnham, see Part Three, note 4.

PART FOUR

1 Greenleaf, *The Servant as Leader.*

2 Robert K. Greenleaf, *The Institution as Servant* (Indianapolis, Ind.: Robert K. Greenleaf Center for Servant-Leadership, 1972).

3 Robert K. Greenleaf, *Trustees as Servants* (Indianapolis, Ind.: Robert K. Greenleaf Center for Servant-Leadership, 1974).

RECOMMENDED READING

Block, Peter. *Stewardship*. San Francisco: Berrett-Koehler, 1993.

Cheshire, Ashley. *A Partnership of the Spirit*. Dallas: TD Industries, 1987.

DePree, Max. *Leadership Is an Art*. New York: Doubleday, 1989.

DePree, Max. *Leadership Jazz*. New York: Dell, 1992.

Fraker, Anne T., and Spears, Larry C. (eds.). SEEKER AND SERVANT: REFLECTIONS ON RELIGIOUS LEADERSHIP. San Francisco, Jossey-Bass, 1996.

Greenleaf, Robert K. *Advices to Servants*. Indianapolis, Ind.: Robert K. Greenleaf Center for Servant-Leadership, 1991.

Greenleaf, Robert K. *Education and Maturity*. Indianapolis, Ind.: Robert K. Greenleaf Center for Servant-Leadership, 1988.

Greenleaf, Robert K. *Have You a Dream Deferred*. Indianapolis, Ind.: Robert K. Greenleaf Center for Servant-Leadership, 1988.

Greenleaf, Robert K. *The Institution as Servant*. Indianapolis. Ind.: Robert K. Greenleaf Center for Servant-Leadership, 1972.

Greenleaf, Robert K. *The Leadership Crisis*. Indianapolis, Ind.: Robert K. Greenleaf Center for Servant-Leadership, 1978.

Greenleaf, Robert K. *Life's Choices and Markers*. Indianapolis, Ind.: Robert K. Greenleaf Center for Servant-Leadership, 1986.

Greenleaf, Robert K. *My Debt to E. B. White*. Indianapolis, Ind.: Robert K. Greenleaf Center for Servant-Leadership, 1987.

Greenleaf, Robert K. *Old Age: The Ultimate Test of Spirit*. Indianapolis, Ind.: Robert K. Greenleaf Center for Servant-Leadership, 1987.

Greenleaf, Robert K. *Seminary as Servant*. Indianapolis, Ind.: Robert K. Greenleaf Center for Servant-Leadership, 1983.

Greenleaf, Robert K. *Servant: Retrospect and Prospect*. Indianapolis, Ind.: Robert K. Greenleaf Center for Servant-Leadership, 1980.

Greenleaf, Robert K. *The Servant as Leader*. Indianapolis, Ind.: Robert K. Greenleaf Center for Servant-Leadership, 1970, 1991.

Greenleaf, Robert K. *The Servant as Religious Leader.* Indianapolis, Ind.: Robert K. Greenleaf Center for Servant-Leadership, 1982.

Greenleaf, Robert K. *Servant Leadership: A Journey into the Nature of Legitimate Power and Greatness.* Mahwah, N.J.: Paulist Press, 1977.

Greenleaf, Robert K. *Spirituality as Leadership.* Indianapolis, Ind.: Robert K. Greenleaf Center for Servant-Leadership, 1988.

Greenleaf, Robert K. *The Teacher as Servant: A Parable.* Mahwah, N.J.: Paulist Press, 1976; Indianapolis, Ind.: Robert K. Greenleaf Center for Servant-Leadership, 1987.

Greenleaf, Robert K. *Trustees as Servants.* Indianapolis, Ind.: Robert K. Greenleaf Center for Servant-Leadership, 1974, 1990.

Hesse, Hermann. *The Journey to the East.* New York: Noonday Press, 1992.

Kelley, Robert. *The Power of Followership: How to Create Leaders People Want to Follow—and Followers Who Lead Themselves.* New York: Doubleday/Currency, 1992.

Kouzes, James M., and Posner, Barry Z. *Credibility: How Leaders Gain and Lose It, Why People Demand It.* San Francisco: Jossey-Bass, 1993.

Liebig, James E. *Business Ethics: Profiles in Civic Virtue.* Golden, Colo.: Fulcrum, 1991.

Renesch, John (ed.). *Leadership in a New Era.* San Francisco: New Leaders Press, 1994.

Rieser, Carl. *The Trusteed Corporation: A Case Study of the Townsend & Bottum Family of Companies.* Indianapolis, Ind.: Robert K. Greenleaf Center for Servant-Leadership, 1988.

Spears, Larry C. (ed.). *Reflections on Leadership: How Robert K. Greenleaf's Theory of Servant-Leadership Influenced Today's Top Management Thinkers.* New York: Wiley, 1995.

THE EDITORS

Don M. Frick works with the Robert K. Greenleaf Center for Servant-Leadership as an associate on the Greenleaf Archives project. He is also an independent consultant, writer, and producer of print, television, and radio projects. He received his B.S. degree in education in 1968 from Eastern Illinois University and his M.Div. degree from Christian Theological Seminary, Indianapolis, in 1972. His work life has included major positions at radio and television broadcast facilities, the Indianapolis Museum of Art, Indiana Central University (now the University of Indianapolis), and media production companies.

Frick has written and produced hundreds of television programs, articles, and corporate training programs. He is the author of *Target Ethics* (1994), a book about ethical practices for insurance professionals. He was first introduced to Robert Greenleaf's work in 1986 and has since sought to understand and apply the principles of servant-leadership, always remembering Greenleaf's insight that wisdom begins with taking responsibility for oneself first.

Larry C. Spears was named executive director of the Robert K. Greenleaf Center for Servant-Leadership in February 1990. He grew up in Michigan and Indiana and later graduated from De Pauw University with a B.A. degree in English. Spears then lived in the Philadelphia region for fourteen years before returning to Indiana. He has previously served as either director or staff member with the Greater Philadelphia Philosophy Consortium, the Great Lakes Colleges Association's Philadelphia Center, and *Friends Journal,* a Quaker magazine. He is also a writer, editor, and publications designer who has published more than two hundred articles, essays, and book reviews over the past two decades and has written numerous successful funding proposals. Spears is the editor of *Reflections on Leadership: How Robert K. Greenleaf's Theory of Servant-Leadership Influenced Today's Top Management Thinkers* (1995), coeditor of *Seeker and Servant* (Jossey-Bass, 1996), and a contributing author to an anthology of essays on leadership, *Leadership in a New Era* (1994).

INDEX

A

Abortion, 130–131
Acceptance, as leadership strategy, 309–310
Acquaintances: of Greenleaf, 363–365; for openness, 71–72
Acton, Lord J., 154, 277
Administrators, 247
Affirmative action, 166
Alcoholics Anonymous, 62, 329
Alverno College, 360–362
American Foundation for Management Research, 4
American Institute of Certified Public Accountants, statesmanship of, 256–258
American Telephone and Telegraph Company (AT&T): breakup of, 241–242, 350; Greenleaf's career at, 235–238, 239–241, 245, 346; history of, 238–240, 241–243, 250–252; J. P. Morgan's influence on, 239, 349–350; sense of history in, 243–245, 252; statesmanship in, 252–256; Vail's influence on, 114, 300–301, 349–350
Ames, A., 35
Anshen, M., 194–195

Anti-intellectualism, 61, 76
Antitrust laws, 164–165
Assessment centers, 360–361
Attitudes: causing knowledge loss, 201; of young people, 109–111
Awareness, 35–39, 74–76, 322–323

B

Bakke case, 166
Beard, C. A., on lessons of history, 158–161
Beekeeping, 31–32
Beethoven, L., 44
Behavioral research, 202–204; concept of, 189–190; definition, 190; management and, 202–204, 213–216; practical view of, 205–206; status of, 191–195; team approach to, 206–209, 214–215
Bell, A. G., 238
Biases, restrictive, 61–62
Billings, J., 53
Blake, W., 323
Block, P., 3
Bridgman, P., 304

383

"Lessons on Power" is excerpted from four unpublished manuscripts by Robert K. Greenleaf as contained in the Greenleaf Archives: "Persuasion as Power," "India: Persuasion as Power," "Note on the Dynamics of Power," and "Meditation on Power." It is used with the permission of the Franklin Trask Library, Andover Newton Theological School.

"Building the Ethic of Strength in Business" is edited from "The Ethic of Strength," an unpublished manuscript by Robert K. Greenleaf as contained in the Greenleaf Archives. It is used with the permission of the Franklin Trask Library, Andover Newton Theological School.

"Industry's Means for Personality Adjustment" is edited from an unpublished manuscript by Robert K. Greenleaf as contained in the Greenleaf Archives. It is used with the permission of the Franklin Trask Library, Andover Newton Theological School.

"Behavioral Research: A Factor in Tomorrow's Better Management" is edited from an unpublished manuscript by Robert K. Greenleaf as contained in the Greenleaf Archives. It is used with the permission of the Franklin Trask Library, Andover Newton Theological School.

"The Operator Versus the Conceptualizer: An Issue of Management Talents" is edited from an unpublished manuscript by Robert K. Greenleaf as contained in the Greenleaf Archives. It is used with the permission of the Franklin Trask Library, Andover Newton Theological School.

"The Managerial Mind" is edited from an unpublished manuscript by Robert K. Greenleaf as contained in the Greenleaf Archives. It is used with the permission of the Franklin Trask Library, Andover Newton Theological School.

"Growing Greatness in Managers" is edited from an unpublished manuscript by Robert K. Greenleaf as contained in the Greenleaf Archives. It is used with the permission of the Franklin Trask Library, Andover Newton Theological School.

"My Work at AT&T: An Adventure in Spirit" is edited from an unpublished manuscript by Robert K. Greenleaf as contained in the Greenleaf Archives. It is used with the permission of the Franklin Trask Library, Andover Newton Theological School.

"Manager, Administrator, Statesman" is edited from an unpublished manuscript by Robert K. Greenleaf as contained in the Greenleaf Archives. It is used with the permission of the Franklin Trask Library, Andover Newton Theological School.

"The Making of a Distinguished Institution" is edited from an unpublished manuscript by Robert K. Greenleaf as contained in the Greenleaf Archives. It is used with the permission of the Franklin Trask Library, Andover Newton Theological School.

"Retirement Communities" is edited from an unpublished manuscript by Robert K. Greenleaf as contained in the Greenleaf Archives. It is used with the permission of the Franklin Trask Library, Andover Newton Theological School.

"Leadership and the Individual" is edited from an unpublished manuscript by Robert K. Greenleaf as contained in the Greenleaf Archives. It is used with the permission of the Franklin Trask Library, Andover Newton Theological School.

"A Conversation with Robert K. Greenleaf" is excerpted from an unpublished transcript of a conversation with Robert K. Greenleaf by Dr. Joseph DiStefano. It is used with the permission of the Greenleaf Center.